Frankie Welch's Americana

Frankie Welch's Americana

Fashion, Scarves, and Politics

Ashley Callahan

Published in
association with
Georgia Humanities

The University
of Georgia Press
Athens

a Friends Fund publication

Publication of this work was made possible, in part, by a generous gift from the University of Georgia Press Friends Fund.

IMAGE CREDITS: ii–iii, iv, collection of Frankie Welch, Peggy Welch Williams, and Genie Welch Leisure; v, Frankie Welch Collection, Rome Area History Center; vi, Frankie Welch Textile Collection, Hargrett Rare Book and Manuscript Library, University of Georgia Libraries; viii, Frankie Welch Collection, Rome Area History Center

Designed by Erin Kirk
Set in Miller Text with Kansas New display
Printed and bound by Friesens
The paper in this book meets the guidelines for permanence and durability of the Committee on Production Guidelines for Book Longevity of the Council on Library Resources.

Most University of Georgia Press titles are available from popular e-book vendors.

Printed in Canada
25 24 23 22 21 C 5 4 3 2 1

Library of Congress Cataloging-in-Publication Data
Names: Callahan, Ashley, author.
Title: Frankie Welch's Americana : fashion, scarves, and politics / Ashley Callahan.
Description: Athens : Published in association with Georgia Humanities, The University of Georgia Press, 2022. | Includes bibliographical references and index.
Identifiers: LCCN 2021031549 | ISBN 9780820360485 (hardback)
Subjects: LCSH: Welch, Frankie, 1924– | Women fashion designers—United States—Biography. | Fashion—United States—History—20th century. | Scarves—United States—History—20th century.
Classification: LCC TT505.W45 C35 2022 | DDC 746.9/2092 [B]—dc23
LC record available at https://lccn.loc.gov/2021031549

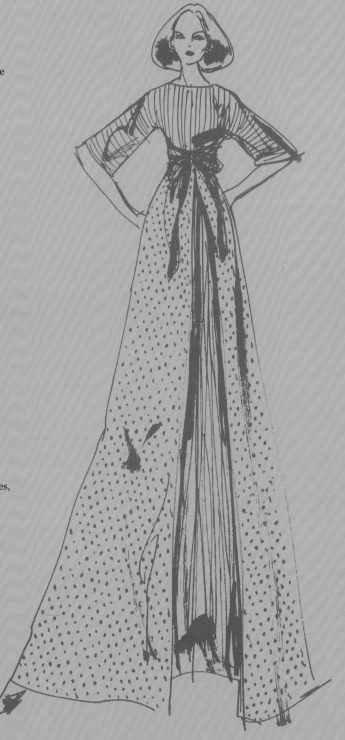

"Scarves are forever."

—FRANKIE WELCH, 2010

Contents

Foreword

Frankie Welch and I became good friends in the mid-1960s. I was new to Washington, D.C., and I was just starting AIO (Americans for Indian Opportunity), a national Indigenous advocacy organization. We had met before, but we really grew closer when she asked me to find a copy of the Cherokee alphabet. At a time when most people in the fashion industry were misappropriating Native designs, if they were not ignoring them altogether, Frankie was interested in taking real history and celebrating the creation of the first alphabet in what is now the United States. As an enrolled citizen of the Comanche Nation, I applauded her efforts to showcase Native history.

She also made a significant impact because at the time Native Americans were struggling to get into the fashion industry. The attention Frankie's work garnered in D.C., in New York, and among stores that were her outlets, elevated the interest in Native designs. This in turn opened up more opportunities for Native American designers.

I have always found women who make a difference the most enjoyable to be around. If you did not live through the 1950s and 1960s it is difficult to appreciate what an accomplishment it was for Frankie to make such great strides in an industry that was even more male-dominated then. She was not only able to make a living with her designs of dresses and accessories, she was able to create a successful store in the prestigious location of Alexandria, Virginia.

Frankie was very charming. I used to delight in going to her store. It was always a lovely experience. I even brought my oldest daughter along.

In addition to making such an impact on fashion, Frankie had a strong marriage and raised two wonderful girls. It is very challenging for anyone to have an active and successful career and a fulfilling home life. Frankie was a role model in that regard.

Later when I was honored as a Woman of the Year at the Kennedy Center, Frankie designed my evening dress. I was able to showcase her design in front of the press as I stood next to Cicely Tyson. Perhaps the most response I received was when I was interviewed by Dick Cavett on his show wearing one of Frankie's creations. I wore her Cherokee Alphabet pantsuit and scarf.

Frankie's charm extended into the political world. It is a unique cross-confluence between politics and fashion. Many fashion designers work with celebrities. Frankie worked with women in the political world from both sides of the aisle.

She even created designs for both sides of contentious partisan campaigns. I wore her designs for a dress and scarf for the Hubert Humphrey campaign for president. At the same time she had designed a pinafore for the Republican convention and a Nixon scarf for the inauguration.

The amazing feat wasn't that she designed for them all. It was that she did so without anyone getting angry at her. She balanced an exquisite line between the camps.

Everyone was proud to wear her designs. Frankie designed for congressional wives and wives of senators. She designed for the wives of ambassadors from various countries. She spent time in the White House. She designed for at least three first ladies: Lady Bird Johnson, Betty Ford, and Pat Nixon.

I am so pleased that this book will finally celebrate Frankie Welch's proper place in fashion history. She was a unique and remarkable woman. Her impact supporting Native Americans is important. Her ability to open up the world of politics to fashion was unusual and timely. I am proud to have been Frankie's friend.

This book is important. It is time to let the world know about an exceptional woman with an impressive talent for design and the ability to actualize those talents. Frankie's story is an engaging and wonderful story. I hope you enjoy it as much as I have.

LaDonna Harris

Acknowledgments

First and foremost, a warm thank-you to Frankie Welch's daughters, Peggy Welch Williams and Genie Welch Leisure, for trusting me with this project. I appreciate the support, guidance, and answers to my many, many questions that they generously provided throughout the process of preparing this text. Their mother is precious to them, and I am honored to have a part in preserving her legacy.

Like Welch, I grew up in northwestern Georgia, and it is a pleasure to work with the University of Georgia Press to help tout the accomplishments of one of our own stars. Welch's initial association with the University of Georgia was brief—just a couple of summers in the 1940s to meet her teacher certification requirements—but over time she developed a strong connection to UGA that has blossomed into a contemporary network of admirers on campus.

Welch donated a large collection of her work to UGA in 1982, and it was through these materials that I first encountered her designs shortly after moving to Athens in 2000. Thank you to my friend José Blanco, former head of the Historic Clothing and Textile Collection in the College of Family and Consumer Sciences (which holds part of the collection Welch donated) for helping me access the materials under his purview for my early research, and to the late Carolyn Benesh at *Ornament* magazine for publishing my first article on Welch in 2011. Thank you to Dale Couch at the Georgia Museum of Art for inviting me to speak about Welch at the Seventh Henry D. Green Symposium of the Decorative Arts in 2014—and to all of the symposium attendees who were on eBay even before my talk was over to buy their own Welch scarves. I have enjoyed hearing about their acquisitions at subsequent symposia and am pleased that the Georgia Museum of Art has added a few Welch scarves to its collection as well.

Thank you also to the wonderful staff in the Special Collections Libraries at UGA, especially to Kat Stein and Jan Levinson with the Hargrett Rare Book and Manuscript Library (where the bulk of Welch's donation is housed) for their willingness to work with me as a guest curator to organize an exhibition on Welch for 2022 and for going above and beyond to help me with this text, even during a pandemic. Everyone at Special Collections makes me feel welcome each time I enter their building, and it is always a pleasure to be there. Jim StipeMaas, Jason Hasty, Mazie Bowen, Anne Meyers DeVine, Margie Compton, Ruta Abolins, and everyone who helps me in the reading room and with my various queries: thank you for your professionalism and friendliness. And thank you to Mary Linnemann for all of the photography assistance and patience.

At the University of Georgia Press, thanks particularly to acquisitions editor Pat Allen for his enthusiasm for this project—and for keeping me updated on his own Frankie Welch purchases, and to Erin New for her lovely design work. Thanks also to director Lisa Bayer, intern Garrett Alan Fetner for his helpful notes, Jon Davies and freelancer Lori Rider for their careful editing, and Nathaniel Holly for advising me on the correct words to use when writing about Native American issues.

Thanks also to the wonderful women in Welch's hometown of Rome who have helped make the important archival materials she donated to the Rome Area History Center available to me: Bambi Berry, Janet Byington, Susan Harvey, Debbie Galloway, Lisa Smith, and Heather Shores at the Chieftains Museum.

Also, thanks to the many folks who have answered questions big and small and regularly pointed me in the right direction: Lucy Allen; Peggy Galis; Elizabeth Avett; Marsha Welch; Sumru Belger Krody at the Textile Museum; Jade Papa at the Textile and Costume Collection at Thomas Jefferson University–East Falls; Nicole R. Johnston at the Missouri Historic Costume and Textile Collection at the University of Missouri; Susan J. Jerome at the Historic Textile and Costume Collection at the University of Rhode Island; Gail Chovan at the Historical Textile and Apparel Collection at the University of Texas at Austin; Melissa Montgomery, who is special assistant to Rosalynn Carter; Pamela V. Ulrich at Auburn University; Rachel McLucas at Oak Hill and the Martha Berry Museum; Peter Chabot; Wick and Prissy Parcells; Tom Camden at Special Collections and University Archives at Washington and Lee University; Mary Beth Newbill in the Southern History Department at Birmingham Public Library; Marshall Akers with the *To Tell the Truth* website; Jeffrey Schlosberg at the National Press Club; Gilbert Klein; Julian Tomchin; Kimberly Chrisman-Campbell; Krista Oldham at the Special Collections and Archives at Clemson University; Ryan S. Flahive with the Institute of American Indian Arts; America Meredith with *First American Art* magazine; Karen King at the Special Collections Research Center in the Earl Gregg Swern Library at William and Mary; Gina Price

White at the Louise Pettus Archives at Winthrop University; Cherokee genealogist Kathy White; Demetrius Curington at the D.C. Public Library; Susan Clay; Tricia Miller; Michael McKelvey; Russell McClanahan; Muhammad Hamzah Toraby; Lindsey Reynolds; Rhonda Bowles; Chris Tucker Haggerty; Arrow Callahan; Copper Callahan; the diligent staff in the Interlibrary Loan Office at UGA; Ginger Howard, who worked at Frankie Welch of Virginia in the late 1980s; Jamie Waldrop, whose mother, Opal Beverly, worked as a fashion coordinator and model for Welch; and Jeannette M. Black, whose mother, Mariko Marshall Edwards, was head seamstress in the Alterations Department of Frankie Welch of Virginia.

Thank you to Welch's charming friends, Dorothea Johnson, Susan Thompson, and LaDonna Harris, who shared stories with me and gave me a much richer understanding of Welch earlier in her life and what it was like to shop at Frankie Welch of Virginia. And I offer additional gratitude to Harris for adding her own words to this book by writing the foreword and to her daughters Kathryn Harris Tijerina and Laura Harris for their help; it was an honor to have her involved.

And thanks to my proofreaders! Madelyn Shaw, my mentor and friend whom I met as a graduate student at the Smithsonian in Washington, D.C., and whose expansive knowledge never fails to amaze me, gave me sound, honest advice early on about what chapters worked and what chapters needed rethinking. Susan Brown at the Cooper Hewitt, Smithsonian Design Museum, offered clear and thoughtful editorial notes later in the process that were immeasurably helpful. My parents, Priscilla and Mike Brown, caught errors and provided encouragement. And Mark, my husband, asked me the hard questions so I could improve my writing—I may not always seem like I appreciate the critiques, but I do. We make a good team.

Frankie Welch died on September 2, 2021, late in the process of making this book. I wish she could have seen it. She was a remarkable person, and I am thankful to have had the opportunity to research her career. I look forward to continuing to wear her scarves and share the stories behind them.

Frankie Welch's Americana

Introduction
Let Frankie Welch Design a Scarf for You

Warm and ebullient, tremendously upbeat and ambitious, Frankie Welch captivated the Washington, D.C., social scene for more than three decades. Her bipartisanship in business was widely admired. A native Georgian, she was unmistakably southern—one reporter even noted her "syrup and hot biscuits voice." Another suggested that she could be the original "Designing Woman," referring to the popular sitcom starring Delta Burke and Dixie Carter, while her friend Eleni Epstein, a fashion editor, deemed her a true Steel Magnolia—both of them acknowledging Welch's mix of charm and determination. Dorothea Johnson, who founded the Protocol School of Washington, described her as "a delight to be around and just so full of life, always, always." And LaDonna Harris, Native American rights advocate and former wife of Oklahoma senator Fred Harris, remembers Welch as smart and inquisitive, as someone people wanted to know and who could easily draw information from others so that she could learn about them.[1] When I met Welch, in January 2019, even though dementia had taken much of her memory, she was smiling and gracious and radiated positivity.

Welch's long career in Alexandria, Virginia, as a dress shop owner, scarf designer, and fashion adviser was well chronicled by the media. The mostly female reporters who covered her activities did so primarily through the fashion and society pages, and their widely read work records valuable details about her. Collectively, their articles are the core written histories of her life. But Welch carefully cultivated her media image—just as she advised her customers to do. She was discreet and kept the private parts of her life private. For example, when her friend Betty Ford became first lady in 1974 and Welch came under the media spotlight as Ford's frequent fashion adviser, few people were aware that the wedding of Welch's daughter Peggy took place the day after Gerald Ford's swearing in as president or that at home Welch was helping care for her husband, Bill, who was sick with lung cancer. Welch had a life beyond the newspapers.

OPPOSITE: Frankie Welch in front of her shop, ca. 1968; collection of Frankie Welch, Peggy Welch Williams, and Genie Welch Leisure.

RIGHT: From the Frankie Welch Textile Collection, Hargrett Rare Book and Manuscript Library, University of Georgia Libraries.

Frankie Welch at a luncheon for wives of delegates to the Virginia Municipal League Convention (models, *left to right*: Marge Beatley, wife of the mayor of Alexandria; Edna Clarke, member of the Falls Church City Council; Ruth Russell, wife of the mayor of Fairfax; Elissa Spriggs, wife of the mayor of Vienna; Libby Bennett, wife of the mayor of Herndon). The convention was in Arlington and the luncheon and fashion show were at Gadsby's Tavern in Alexandria, Virginia, 1970, photo by Warren Mattox; Frankie Welch Collection, Rome Area History Center.

Frankie Welch at a fashion show at the Congressional Club, Washington, D.C., with Martha Mitchell modeling a scarf, 1972; Frankie Welch Collection, Rome Area History Center.

Bill Welch, who worked in the federal government, was a crucial support for Frankie as she pursued her professional career. They shared an interest in the historical sources that informed many of her designs, and both enjoyed the success she achieved. His embrace of her work during their thirty-year marriage also helped her balance a busy job with time for her family. Her daughter Peggy remembers, "Genie and I did not have a traditional stay-at-home mother, but one who was always there for us when it mattered. She was a Brownie leader, made Georgia pralines for every bake sale, and eagerly planned and attended our birthday parties while building her business," adding, "In an era when many women did not have full-time careers, Frankie did but also loved being a mother and grandmother."[2]

Bill Welch and Frankie Barnett,
ca. 1944; collection of Frankie Welch,
Peggy Welch Williams, and Genie
Welch Leisure.

Bill and Frankie Welch, 1964; collection of Frankie Welch,
Peggy Welch Williams, and Genie Welch Leisure.

Frankie and Bill Welch at their
daughter Peggy's rehearsal dinner,
1974; collection of Frankie Welch,
Peggy Welch Williams, and
Genie Welch Leisure.

Frankie Welch and Al Neher,
2013; collection of Frankie Welch,
Peggy Welch Williams, and
Genie Welch Leisure.

Rod Rodriguez and Frankie Welch,
2002; collection of Frankie Welch,
Peggy Welch Williams, and
Genie Welch Leisure.

Frankie Welch and her family at a family wedding in Charlottesville, Virginia
(*left to right*: David Leisure, Genie Welch Leisure, Ramsey Ratcliffe, Chris Reynolds,
Peggy Welch Williams, Page Williams, Dana Chandler Williams, Kevin Williams,
Frankie Welch, Al Neher, Lindsay Williams Dota, Bryan Dota), 2013; collection
of Frankie Welch, Peggy Welch Williams, and Genie Welch Leisure.

With her usual determination, Welch refocused on her shop and her design business after Bill's death in 1975; she reconnected with her friends, established new contacts in Washington, and traveled widely, mixing business and pleasure. Though she was widowed in her early fifties and missed her husband, she did not languish in loneliness, instead enjoying flirtations later in her life. Her daughter Genie describes how, even in Welch's nineties, "her eyes lit up and she turned on the charm whenever a man entered the room."[3] In particular, Welch delighted in the company of Al Neher and Rod Rodriguez. Neher worked as a business consultant to Welch, so their relationship began as a professional one and developed into a close and devoted lifelong friendship.[4] Rodriguez, the son of a Cuban mother and Spanish father, graduated from the University of Georgia, then worked for the Commerce Department in Washington.

INTRODUCTION

According to her daughters and his family, the two shared many wonderful times.[5]

Welch was surprisingly sentimental, sometimes taking a jar of red dirt back to Virginia after a visit to Rome to remind her of her Georgia home.[6] For the ceremony marking the donation of the dress she designed for Betty Ford to the Smithsonian Institution's First Ladies Collection, Welch sewed pennies into her hem to have as mementoes to mark the occasion.[7] Though she lived in the Alexandria area for most of her life, Georgia remained dear to her and is where she placed two large archives of her work—at the University of Georgia's Hargrett Rare Book and Manuscript Library in Athens and in her hometown at the Rome Area History Museum (now the Rome Area History Center).

Welch adored her adopted town of Alexandria as well. She moved there in the early 1950s, shortly after Old Town was designated as the country's third historic district but well before the area developed into a popular tourist destination. Her shop, less than a block from Gadsby's Tavern, was one of the early businesses to find success there.[8] She actively engaged in the community—volunteering with the Twig hospital auxiliary from the 1950s, participating in the Red Hills Garden Club, and becoming one of the first women to join the Rotary Club of Alexandria. Peggy recalls that Welch attended the Old Town Farmers' Market in front of City Hall on Market Square—where almost two centuries earlier George Washington had sent produce from nearby Mount Vernon to be sold—every Saturday morning and believes that her mother "enjoyed bringing recognition to her historic and vibrant city."[9]

Genie, when interviewed in 1989, described her mother's passion for beauty, design, and fashion: "Mom has the most keen eye for beauty. It's one of the most important things in her life. . . . When she's reading, it's fashion publications, it's house decorating magazines, it's books on fashion, design, creativity, and it's something she's always thinking about. That's one of the reasons I think she's so successful."[10] Indeed, Welch was remarkably successful, critically and financially, in a profession that she loved.

Frankie Welch was not, however, a linear thinker or a details person. Peggy explained this to me as we went through piles of cardboard boxes with multiple generations of photocopies of the same few images and articles over and over, interspersed with gems like an envelope of original snapshots of her trip to Europe in 1960, a swatch of fabric from Betty Ford's green dress, and a rare hand-painted scarf from a fashion show at the White House. Welch kept a lot of material, but not always in a discernable order. There are not chronological account books, or diaries, or tidy folders on individual scarf designs. Certainly this creates challenges in researching her career, and many fascinating details probably are still buried in dusty files (for example, are there photographs of the "ladylike outfits for streetwear" that she designed for Hugh Hefner's Bunnies in 1968?),

Frankie Welch, 1977; collection of Frankie Welch, Peggy Welch Williams, and Genie Welch Leisure.

but the volume of accessible information that survives is satisfying.[11] It tells her story.

In addition to the paper archives, key audio and video recordings exist as well. Welch participated in interviews earlier in her life, while her memory was stronger—in particular with South Carolina's Winthrop University in 1984 and the Gerald R. Ford Presidential Foundation in 2010—that add to what the media reported. Another important resource is a talk she gave at the Smithsonian Institution's National Museum of American History in 1991, saved by her family on a VHS cassette and recently digitized by the University of Georgia's Walter J. Brown Media Archives. In this talk she shared many anecdotes from her childhood, tales about her scarves, and thoughts about her point system in fashion; the grainy video also reveals her sense of humor and luminous charisma.

Like today's social media mavens, Welch was aware of the importance of her own persona in popularizing her designs and presented a whole lifestyle approach. Her customers could not only buy dresses and scarves but also learn practical tricks (like the best way to hold a purse when being photographed) and attend an endless series of lively events at her shop. Later in her career she applied her fashion knowledge to interiors and corporate consulting, advising clients on a wide array of items such as wall treatments, holiday gifts, and attire for receptionists. Her legacy is in how she combined fashion, business acumen, social connections, nonpartisanship, and a multitude of scarves to define her own career and fill it with constant change and creativity.

OPPOSITE: Frankie Welch, 1974, Craig Photography; Frankie Welch Collection, Rome Area History Center.

Shortly before finishing this manuscript, I finally had the pleasure of watching Frankie Welch tie a scarf—on another old VHS cassette—and as I had imagined, it was magic—a colorful piece of flat fabric gaining dimension and style with a quick, confident flourish and smile. When I spoke with Dorothea Johnson, she had marveled at how Welch could add a scarf to a simple black outfit and make it sparkle; the video made Johnson's words come to life.[12] Welch's scarves have an almost biographical quality to them now—celebrating the places, people, events, and institutions that were part of her world. The communicative power of her scarves has remained strong over time, and even now I find myself wanting the Daughters of the American Revolution's Love Administration scarf on Valentine's Day, the Christmas trees scarf during the winter holidays, and the Cherry Blossom scarf for the first day of spring. The expressive possibilities are abundant and attest to a timeless element in her designs.

The following chapters expand Welch's narrative beyond the standard, streamlined newspaper account. They record the many remarkable accomplishments of a young woman from Rome, Georgia, who built a prosperous business, designed for first ladies, and gave confidence-building fashion advice to innumerable women involved in society and politics in Washington, D.C. They also present a visual timeline of Welch's life through scarves and fashion. She designed thousands of scarves, many more than could be included here. In addition to surviving in the carefully preserved collections of museums and archives, Welch's scarves exist in the real world—in antiques shops, in online auctions, in our grandmothers' chifforobes—waiting to be rediscovered and treasured anew.

Frankie Welch, 1987; collection of
Frankie Welch, Peggy Welch Williams,
and Genie Welch Leisure.

Chapter 1
From Mary Frances Barnett of Georgia to Frankie Welch of Virginia

Mary Frances "Frankie" Barnett was born in Rome, Georgia, on March 29, 1924, to Eugenia "Genie" Morton and James "Jamie" Wyatt Barnett. She was much younger than her siblings—Lawrence was sixteen years older, Horace thirteen, and Katherine eleven. In a characteristically touching and humorous way, she later recounted how her mother revealed to her when she was thirteen that even though her parents were older (both around forty) when she was born, she was a planned baby; their doctor had suggested to Genie that Jamie needed either a baby or a puppy dog, and they opted for a baby. She had a happy childhood (despite the Great Depression) and relished being with her wonderful brothers, who both studied at Martha Berry's Boys Industrial School near Rome, and going everywhere with them, even on their dates.[1]

Evidence of Welch's self-assuredness arose at an early age, and she asserts that she took charge of her life when she was six years old. That year she visited Santa Claus at the local Sears Roebuck with her mother the day before Christmas, and she announced to him that she wanted a huge box of paints she had seen. Instead she received a huge Bible and cried all day long. She refers to this episode as her first "creative fit." The next day her mother took her to the store and purchased the paints (on sale), and her father subsequently bought her all of the fabrics and art supplies she desired. Her aunt (Fannie Adams) taught her to sew when she was six years old, and she designed clothes for her dolls by age eight.[2]

Her family recognized her style acumen when she was young as well. Around age ten, she began joining her mother and her mother's friends on trips to Atlanta, which was about a two-hour drive away, to look at clothes, fabrics, or furniture, so that she could offer advice. Welch began to gain confidence in her abilities and got upset if her mother's friends did not follow her suggestions, sometimes even refusing to join particular outings.[3]

At age fifteen, she "defied [her] parents and went to work in one of the *three* shops in Rome," J. Kuttner Company, the beginning of a lifelong

OPPOSITE: Frankie Barnett wearing her May Day dress at Furman University, 1943; Frankie Welch Collection, Rome Area History Center.

RIGHT: From the Frankie Welch Textile Collection, Hargrett Rare Book and Manuscript Library, University of Georgia Libraries.

Frankie Barnett, 1935; collection of Frankie Welch, Peggy Welch Williams, and Genie Welch Leisure.

Frankie Barnett with her sister Katherine, 1928; collection of Frankie Welch, Peggy Welch Williams, and Genie Welch Leisure.

career as a working woman.[4] She approached the owner and proposed that if he let her work for him, she would make him money. She went to Atlanta with him and told him what to buy for her friends, and she was correct—her friends happily purchased what she had selected, and he enjoyed the profits. The owner even offered to open a store for her when she was sixteen if she would stay in Rome rather than go to college; she declined but continued working for him on holidays. In 1941 she graduated from Rome High School, where she played piccolo and was in the glee club, a literary club, and Tri-Hi-Y (a girls' club related to the YMCA).[5]

In fall 1941 Welch enrolled at Furman University in Greenville, South Carolina, where she studied clothing and design.[6] Her activities there reveal the budding professional ambition, social prowess, and authoritative taste that would prove essential to her future career. Her father, who worked for Southern Bell Telephone Company, had saved money for her college tuition, but not for books and clothes, so she started her own small business to cover those expenses. She opened a little studio in her dormitory and helped "the rich girls" with their ball dresses—selecting appropriate patterns and fabrics, doing the fittings (in their rooms "so they didn't have to walk three blocks down the street"), and having a trio of local

The Barnett family, ca. 1940 (front row, *left to right*: Horace Elias Barnett, Lawrence Frederick Barnett; back row, *left to right*: Katherine Barnett, Eugenia Morton Barnett, Mary Frances "Frankie" Barnett, James Wyatt Barnett); collection of Frankie Welch, Peggy Welch Williams, and Genie Welch Leisure.

Frankie Barnett, 1941; collection of Frankie Welch, Peggy Welch Williams, and Genie Welch Leisure.

seamstresses sew the dresses.[7] She made enough money to pay the seamstresses to make a ball gown for her to wear to parties as well.[8]

While at Furman she also was secretary of her sophomore class and worked with the student newspaper, the *Hornet*, and the yearbook, the *Bonhomie*, in various positions.[9] She wrote an article for the paper, titled "For Men Only," advising her male peers on what colors and items would help with "the beautification of [their] physiques."[10] She gained modeling experience at Meyers-Arnold, a local department store—likely highlighting American fashion and how to tastefully adhere to the restrictions of wartime design.[11] She served several times on the May Queen's court (part of the school's annual May Day festivities), and in 1944 she was selected as one of eight "beauties" for the *Bonhomie*.[12] A column in the *Hornet* provided the following description of her in 1943, further indicating her popularity, as well as reflecting the sexism typical of the era: "One of the two nicest girls we've ever known. . . . The usual amusing and stupid feminine vanities are strongly missing in her. . . . As good looking as she's nice, Frankie would remind a writer of emeralds against black velvet. . . . One of the few times this year that we have written up a girl without our tongue in our cheek."[13]

Bill and Frankie, ca. 1944; collection of
Frankie Welch, Peggy Welch Williams,
and Genie Welch Leisure.

Frankie and Bill on their wedding day,
Rome, Georgia, 1944; collection of Frankie
Welch, Peggy Welch Williams, and Genie
Welch Leisure.

Bill and Frankie Welch at Furman University, ca. 1948 (this image ran in the 1948 *Bonhomie*); collection of Frankie Welch, Peggy Welch Williams, and Genie Welch Leisure.

The *Hornet* reported her engagement to William Calvin Welch in spring 1944: "No, it wasn't a fire that caused all that excitement in West [Hall] Monday night—Frankie Barnett brought forth a diamond from Bill. Looks like they did all right this week-end."[14] On June 3, 1944, after her junior year of college, she married Bill Welch—wearing the first gift he ever gave her, a cameo lavalier.[15] They were childhood sweethearts, and Bill had joined the Marines shortly after the bombing of Pearl Harbor, serving in Cuba and the Pacific during World War II, while she was at Furman.[16] After they married, they first lived in Pensacola, Florida, where he was stationed until January 1946 (he had hitchhiked from Pensacola to Rome for the wedding), and Frankie, taking time off from Furman, taught nursery school.[17] She then taught fifth grade for a few months in 1946 near Rome and taught home economics at Rome High School for the 1946–47 school year, completing summer courses in 1946 and 1947 at the University of Georgia in Athens to meet her teacher certification requirements.[18]

The couple returned to Furman in fall 1947 and Frankie finished her senior year, graduating in 1948 with a bachelor of arts degree in clothing and design.[19] Bill, who had worked for an insurance company in Rome between his high school graduation in 1938 and joining the war effort, attended Furman on the G.I. Bill and graduated in 1950.[20] Indicating

Frankie's early interest in interior design, the *Hornet* described how the couple decorated their apartment: "dark green floors, green walls, one wall is green-white striped, bath is green plaid along with kitchen, she is dying the curtains chartreuse, and has a wine floor lamp and rose chair."[21] She considered focusing on furnishings as her profession and "hung up a shingle as a decorator for a year," but she decided instead to concentrate on fashion.[22]

While Bill completed his studies, Frankie modeled and then was a salesclerk in ladies' ready-to-wear for the Patton-Tillman-Bruce store in Greenville.[23] In summer 1948 she got a job teaching distributive education (a vocational program), focusing on clothing and personality, for the South Carolina State Department of Education. This involved helping organize and conduct business institutes, as well as teaching classes on merchandising and salesmanship for department stores and students in towns within a ten-county area around Furman.[24]

The young couple next moved to Madison, Wisconsin, in 1950 for Bill to pursue his master's degree in history at the University of Wisconsin, supported by a scholarship from the General Education Board of New York.[25] Frankie took courses on the Bishop Method of Sewing—a new approach that helped home sewers create garments with a professional look—and then taught adult education classes in sewing at the Madison Vocational and Adult School (now the Madison Area Technical College) to help

Peggy, Frankie, and Genie Welch, 1960; collection of Frankie Welch, Peggy Welch Williams, and Genie Welch Leisure.

The Welch family, 1956; collection of Frankie Welch, Peggy Welch Williams, and Genie Welch Leisure.

CHAPTER ONE

support the couple.[26] The first of their two daughters, Peggy, was born in Madison in 1951.

Welch later expressed that she had hoped to study with Frank Lloyd Wright while she was in Wisconsin, but, according to her, "he wouldn't take women students."[27] (Welch once even described herself as a frustrated architect.)[28] She attended lectures by Wright, though, purchased some of his fabrics (and used them to make things for around her house, like shower curtains), and observed him walking on the street, offering this description in the early 1980s: "His clothes were wonderful—a gray herringbone suit, a beige and chocolate brown cape. He dressed perfectly for his size and image."[29] She knew when he regularly went to the bank, so she would sit in her car at a nearby corner and sketch what he was wearing. She later joked about her behavior but added, "I just loved him. He was arrogant, but I thought he deserved to be arrogant." Welch regarded Wright as a great influence on her life.[30]

The family moved to Alexandria, Virginia (near Washington, D.C.), in 1952 for Bill's work, first with the Central Intelligence Agency, then as a congressional aide from 1954 to 1961 (for Henderson Lanham, Erwin Mitchell, and John Davis of Georgia), and lastly directing the Veterans

The Welch family, ca. 1961; collection of Frankie Welch, Peggy Welch Williams, and Genie Welch Leisure.

Administration Congressional Liaison Service.[31] Their second daughter, Genie, was born in Alexandria in 1955. Welch began teaching "fashion know-how" in various formats and to a variety of audiences by about 1953, the year she won third place in the McCall National Sewing Contest.[32] In particular, she taught the Bishop Method of Sewing at the YWCA in Washington, from 1954 to 1960, and at the YWCA in Alexandria. She joined the Fashion Group of Washington and met with other instructors of the Bishop Method in the area.[33]

By 1960, Welch taught home economics at Washington-Lee High School in Arlington, Virginia. For one class project she advised students (both girls and boys) studying French as they planned what clothing to pack for a trip to Paris.[34] She submitted designs related to the class to a contest for home economics teachers sponsored by the teen magazine *Ingenue* and won a twelve-day trip to Paris and Rome to visit fashion houses, including Christian Dior, Pierre Cardin, and Germana Marucelli, as well as tourist sites.[35] According to the *Paris-Jour*, she also planned to visit interior decorators and fabric manufacturers.[36] She limited the colors

Frankie Welch designs for *Ingenue*, 1960; Frankie Welch Collection, Rome Area History Center.

CHAPTER ONE

Frankie Welch at a market in Paris, 1960, photo by
guide Christian Beatrix; collection of Frankie Welch,
Peggy Welch Williams, and Genie Welch Leisure.

Frankie Welch in Paris, 1960, photo by guide
Christian Beatrix; collection of Frankie Welch,
Peggy Welch Williams, and Genie Welch Leisure.

Frankie Welch sightseeing in Paris with French
hostess, 1960, photo by guide Christian Beatrix;
collection of Frankie Welch, Peggy Welch
Williams, and Genie Welch Leisure.

of her traveling wardrobe to black and white with a little tan so that items could be mixed and matched, included multifunctional and reversible elements, and kept the volume and weight low.[37] In Rome she photographed women on the street for hours and described "a well-dressed Italian woman" as "a walking lesson in good taste."[38] She wrote that the trip "made [her] all the more determined that someday [she] would try [her] hand at designing," but that most of all it made her want her own clothing specialty shop.[39]

One reporter noted a change in Welch following the trip abroad, a shift from the "'amateur status' of consultant to friends and relatives . . . to 'professionalism.'"[40] She continued teaching—including offering a figure analysis course at the Congressional Club (a social group for congressional spouses as well as congressional mothers and daughters) in spring 1961, a two-day seminar for the NASA Wives Club at Cape Canaveral, Florida, in November 1961, and an adult course in fashion coordination at Wakefield High School in Arlington in fall 1961—while offering private consultation in styling and coordination as well.[41]

Welch maintained confidentiality in her relationships with her clients, stating, "My clients know that my service is like the doctor's. . . . I do not disclose their names."[42] Consulting with Welch involved evaluating what was in the individual's closet, considering what was current, what needed repairs, what could be remodeled, and what best complemented the individual's personality. She typically advised: "Buy fewer things of better quality, spend money on classics rather than high fashion fads . . . [and] buy season-spanning items as much as possible."[43] In 1963 she charged ten to fifteen dollars an hour for wardrobe counseling.[44] Her clients were "capital VIPs," and through her individual consulting and courses for prominent groups, she was establishing connections with influential women in the Washington area.[45]

Welch advocated for the following five standard principles of fashion composition: *proportion* ("The size of any one part of your body is really not important, but its size in relation to other parts and the whole effect is important"), *balance* ("Balance gives a dress a sense of restfulness"), *rhythm* ("We achieve rhythm in our costume by the way we use color, texture, line, and shape"), *center of interest* ("The emphasized detail should be flattering to the individual, suitable to the other parts of the garment, and to the occasion"), and *harmony* ("Harmony is the result of unity; it is a oneness that recognizes an appropriate degree of variation, variety, and contrast").[46] She once expressed that coordinating a costume could be "as technical and creative as a painting."[47]

Welch devised a point system, inspired by the Duchess of Windsor (the famously understated fashion icon Wallis Simpson), to help women avoid overdressing.[48] She recommended that women allow ten points for daytime wear and twelve for evening wear if they were small, and twelve points for daytime and fifteen for evening if they were tall. She assigned

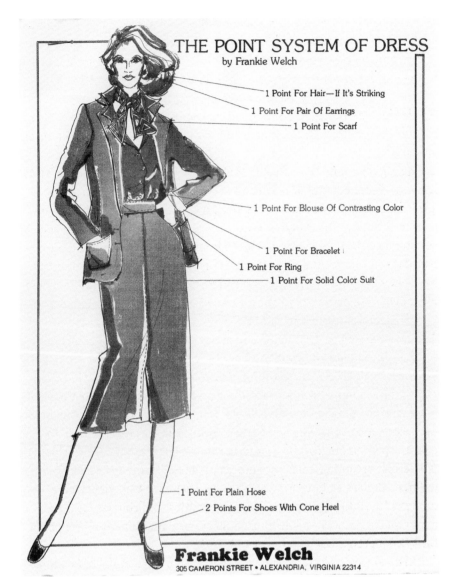

THE POINT SYSTEM OF DRESS
by Frankie Welch

1 Point For Hair—If It's Striking
1 Point For Pair Of Earrings
1 Point For Scarf

1 Point For Blouse Of Contrasting Color

1 Point For Bracelet
1 Point For Ring
1 Point For Solid Color Suit

1 Point For Plain Hose
2 Points For Shoes With Cone Heel

Frankie Welch
305 CAMERON STREET • ALEXANDRIA, VIRGINIA 22314

frankie welch
styling consultant
fashion seminars

king 8-9809

3723 holmes lane
alexandria, virginia

Frankie Welch business card, n.d.;
collection of Frankie Welch, Peggy Welch
Williams, and Genie Welch Leisure.

The Point System of Dress by Frankie
Welch flyer, ca. 1970s; collection of
Frankie Welch, Peggy Welch Williams,
and Genie Welch Leisure.

each element of dress one point if it was simple, or more if it was fancy; for example, a monochromatic dress equaled one point, a patterned dress two, and a two-piece simple suit two, and she added an additional point for each item like a belt, gloves, a bracelet, plain flat shoes, or hose, and two points for more elaborate accessories such as shoes with heels, shoes with buckles, or colored hose.[49] She emphasized the importance of having coordinated wardrobes and versatile dresses that could serve a woman throughout a day that might move from a tour of the city with visitors, to a tea at the White House, to an evening dinner party, without time to fully change clothes.[50]

In a community obsessed with protocol because of the complexities of political life and international interactions, Welch's clear fashion guidance

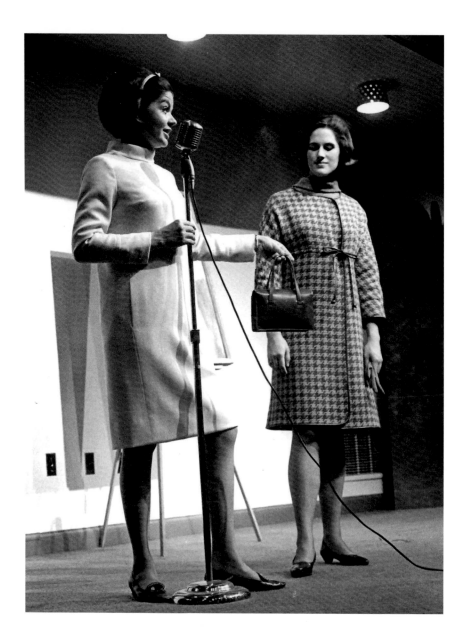

Frankie Welch speaking about fashion, ca. 1966, photo by Joe F. Jordan, Greenville, South Carolina; collection of Frankie Welch, Peggy Welch Williams, and Genie Welch Leisure.

and refined style found an eager audience.[51] Even though Washington, D.C., may seem an unlikely style center, the prominent women there— mostly wives of politicians, diplomats, and military leaders rather than elected or appointed officials themselves when Welch began her career— attended an endless calendar of formal events often covered by the media, elevating the importance and influence of their fashion choices.[52] Of course, Jacqueline Kennedy, during her time as first lady (January 1961– November 1963), drew international fashion attention with her iconic style. Welch once described her as "the greatest thing fashion ever had" in the White House.[53]

Interest in Welch's advice continued to grow, and by February 1963 she established Frankie Welch Fashion Services, through which she employed three dressmakers, three "alterers" (who wore "matching beige A-line sheaths"), a speech therapist, a makeup specialist, and a bridal consultant.[54] Helen Colson, women's editor at the *Washington Daily News*, outlined Welch's activities at that time: "She teaches good grooming for businesses who want their lady employees to look just right. She gives fashion seminars or entire fashion courses to ladies clubs. She handles brides and debutantes. And she supervises her dressmaking and alterations department."[55] That fall Welch continued to teach, including two classes in design at the University of Maryland and various seminars.[56] But the frequent travel required to help her clients compose coordinated wardrobes was creating a schedule that she viewed as incompatible with her young family. She explained, "It was then I began to think of a shop where everything I needed would be under one roof—coordinated in advance."[57]

In September 1963 Welch took the monumental step of opening her own store, Frankie Welch of Virginia.[58] She and her husband, with a loan she was to repay through her business, purchased a mid-eighteenth-century, three-story brick home, known as Duvall House, in Old Town Alexandria at 305 Cameron Street. Initially, the shop occupied the ground floor while the family lived on the upper two levels, which allowed her to be near her young daughters while having a professional career.[59] In the early years of the shop, Bill often worked in the basement in the evenings, doing the paperwork for the shop that, as her daughter Peggy explains, Frankie preferred to avoid.[60]

Welch filled Duvall House with antiques and a few splashes of modern design, including fabrics by Jack Lenor Larsen. She emphasized the building's history, which included visits by George Washington in the 1780s (when it was a tavern) and 1790s (when it was a bank). The shop even had a fireplace that was a replica of one at nearby Mount Vernon. For the opening she decorated with Colonial-style dried flower arrangements by the official flower arranger for Mount Vernon, Jane Glazener Hearn.[61] Patricia Mann, the wife of Alexandria's mayor, stood at the top of the steps with Welch, in front of a "Cherokee

Invitation to Frankie Welch of Virginia opening, 1963; collection of Frankie Welch, Peggy Welch Williams, and Genie Welch Leisure.

Duvall House, Alexandria, Virginia, ca. 1960s, photo by City News Bureau, Washington, D.C.; collection of Frankie Welch, Peggy Welch Williams, and Genie Welch Leisure.

Early Frankie Welch of Virginia label, n.d.;
collection of Frankie Welch, Peggy Welch
Williams, and Genie Welch Leisure.

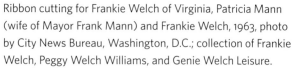

Ribbon cutting for Frankie Welch of Virginia, Patricia Mann
(wife of Mayor Frank Mann) and Frankie Welch, 1963, photo
by City News Bureau, Washington, D.C.; collection of Frankie
Welch, Peggy Welch Williams, and Genie Welch Leisure.

red" door (a nod to Frank Lloyd Wright), and cut the ceremonial ribbon, and the neighboring businesses welcomed her with a block party.[62]

Frankie Welch of Virginia was an "instant success."[63] In preparation for the opening, Welch purchased as many clothes as she could afford—American clothes in a medium price range—and filled three rooms, almost selling out after two days; she traveled to New York on the third to restock.[64] Her first customers included congressional wives, Virginia Rusk (wife of Secretary of State Dean Rusk), and friends in Alexandria. Ruth Wagner of the *Washington Post and Times Herald* described the shop as having "a kind of warm, friendly, intensely personal character" like Welch herself, adding, "Most of her customers are friends who earnestly ask her, 'Do you think this dress is right on me?' and give her notes about the kind of costume they'd like her to find just for them in New York."[65] A business card from when the shop opened reads, "Frankie Welch of Virginia, Clothes for the Individualist," emphasizing the idea of personal attention and consideration of individual style.[66] She focused on providing honest, customized advice, and she delighted in helping women look their best and feel good about their clothes. After a year, with the business growing, she converted two rooms on the second floor from residence to shop space.[67]

Welch described her business as "an American shop, with American clothes, for American women."[68] When it opened she featured couture designs by Patricia D'Arascu, a French-born designer in Georgetown, and furs by Michael Mouratidis, a Greek-born New Yorker with a salon in Georgetown. One of her earliest trunk shows, in fall 1964, highlighted the work of "a bright young creator of very 'swinging' fashions" named Vi Feigin.[69] By 1965 she carried designs by Tina Leser, best known for her earlier sportswear designs, and she showed Leser's new designs inspired by India in February 1966 during a morning event for which Shobha Nehru (wife of the ambassador from India, Braj Kumar Nehru) served as patroness.[70] She offered a selection of classic, practical, and relatively affordable garments by designers including Oscar de la Renta, Geoffrey Beene, Halston, Adele Simpson, and Mollie Parnis.

Welch worked with designer Vera Maxwell to coordinate a fashion show for Princess Grace in Monte Carlo in July 1966 as part of Monaco's Centennial Year Celebration.[71] That September Welch and Maxwell recreated the show on the sidewalk in front of Duvall House, "[competing] with the roar of airplanes from National Airport," as an event titled "Indian Summer Fashion Festival."[72] Maxwell's garments were Native American–inspired and featured many fabrics designed by Lloyd Kiva New of Santa Fe, New Mexico, whose mother was Cherokee.[73] The models included several wives of congressmen, notably LaDonna (Mrs. Fred) Harris of Oklahoma, a Comanche activist. Ermalee Udall, wife of Secretary of the Interior Stewart Udall, served as honorary chairperson.[74]

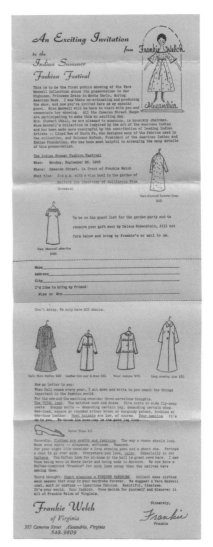

Invitation to the Indian Summer Fashion Festival, 1966; collection of Frankie Welch, Peggy Welch Williams, and Genie Welch Leisure.

Shortly after opening her shop, Welch introduced what became her signature dress design, the "Frankie." The versatile dress followed a simple, paper-doll-like pattern that Welch first created for a class she taught at the University of Maryland in order to demonstrate various historic waistlines. The Frankie design with its wide side sections and long ties could be worn multiple ways: tied in the front or in the back, with a high waist or natural waist, crossed over the chest or not, with the zippered side in back or front.[75] Welch cited Claire McCardell's "Popover dress" and Japanese kimonos as sources of inspiration. Both Eleni, fashion editor of the *Washington Star*, and Nancy Ross, writing for the rival *Washington Post and Times Herald*, likened the Frankie in the Washington area to Lilly Pulitzer's "Lilly" dress in Florida's Palm Beach—the printed shift trendy with the "international Jet Set." Ross believed that, like the Lilly, the Frankie was "also designed for maximum comfort and adaptability." Eleni quoted one woman on why the Frankie was popular, saying, "It's sensible, comfortable, different, attractive, feminine, completely individual, and real smashing to wear at home." Eleni also described the Frankie as chameleon-like because of how it changed character depending on the fabric, color, texture, trim, and method of tying.[76]

While Frankies fit into the casually elegant tradition of the hostess gown, popular from the 1930s to the 1970s for home entertaining and defined in the *New York Times* as "a billowing, brightly colored maxi-dress, often with a forgiving waistline, or no waistline—sort of a cross between an evening formal and a bathrobe," their realm extended beyond the domestic setting.[77] In fact, one woman requested a Frankie in gray flannel to wear to a ball at Versailles, noting, "That place is so old and drafty, it'll be perfect." A "top Washington secretary," though, wore it more casually as a robe when traveling on "the private plane of her very VIP boss." While most Frankies are long, Welch made short versions when she heard that students at Sarah Lawrence College had started wearing long ones to class, which she did not consider advisable.[78]

Eleni reported in spring 1964 that there were around four dozen Frankies "being worn by quite a cross-section of young fashionables."[79] By April 1965 *Women's Wear Daily* informed readers that the shop had sold 905 Frankies, in prices ranging from $15 to $100, depending on the fabric.[80] (In 1969 she sold them in cotton for $18 or silk for $85.)[81] By 1968, Welch stated that more than four thousand had sold, and she continued making the popular design well into the 1980s.[82]

Welch's prominence rose steadily after she opened her shop. She even appeared on the television game show *To Tell the Truth* in late 1964 or early 1965.[83] Through her work as a fashion coordinator and consultant and the welcoming and lively atmosphere of her shop, which generated devoted customers, Welch built a network among Washington's political elite that poised her for skyrocketing renown when she added the next element to her repertoire: scarves.

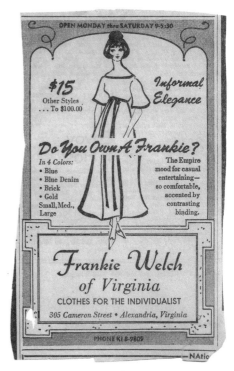

Frankie newspaper advertisement from the *Washington Star*, 1964; collection of Frankie Welch, Peggy Welch Williams, and Genie Welch Leisure.

OPPOSITE: Frankie Welch and Vera Maxwell with models in Monaco, 1966, photo by René Maestri; collection of Frankie Welch, Peggy Welch Williams, and Genie Welch Leisure.

Josefina Tejera París, wife of the ambassador of Venezuela, wearing a black velvet Frankie in the Venezuelan embassy, 1964, Star Staff photo by Tom Hoy, reprinted with permission of the D.C. Public Library, Star Collection © *Washington Post*; Frankie Welch Collection, Rome Area History Center.

Frankie Welch wearing a Frankie, ca. 1964; Frankie Welch Collection, Rome Area History Center.

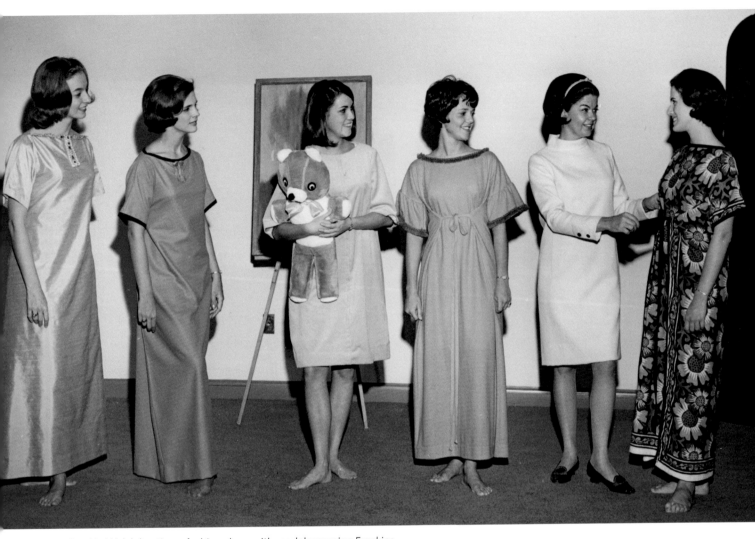

Frankie Welch hosting a fashion show with models wearing Frankies,
ca. 1966, photo by Joe F. Jordan, Greenville, South Carolina;
Frankie Welch Collection, Rome Area History Center.

Chapter 2
Political Fashion Specialist

Though not expressly political in subject, Frankie Welch's first scarf came to be and came to prominence through political connections. Virginia Rusk, wife of Secretary of State Dean Rusk (who, like Welch, was from Georgia), asked Welch to design something "truly American" for the White House and State Department to use as gifts.[1] Rusk raised the issue during one of her regular Friday visits to Welch's shop for a friendly meal of vegetable soup and cornbread in the kitchen, joking that Steuben glass, a frequent presidential gift, was getting heavy.[2] Inspired by the popularity of Yves Saint Laurent's recent scarves, which caused "a stampede for the scarf table" at his 1966 spring opening in Paris, and by a family trip to her hometown in northwestern Georgia, where she had seen an image of the Cherokee syllabary in a book, she conceived her Cherokee Alphabet scarf and introduced it in 1967.[3] She explained at the time, "When I was in Rome, I saw this book called 'History of Rome and Floyd County.' My father showed it to me. And I thought what a good idea a signature scarf would be, made from the Cherokee alphabet."[4]

The syllabary comprises eighty-four to eighty-six characters that represent syllables in the Cherokee language (rather than phonemes as in an alphabet). Sequoyah, an influential Cherokee born in Tennessee, created it around 1820, and he is recognized as the only member of a nonliterate group to independently devise a successful system of writing. In particular, the syllabary was used along with the Roman alphabet in the *Cherokee Phoenix* newspaper, which was published from 1828 to 1834 at New Echota.[5] For Welch, Cherokee was "really the original American language," offered a connection to Georgia, and met Rusk's desire for something truly American.[6] Though there were, of course, hundreds of Indigenous languages, Cherokee is recognized as one of the earliest to have a system of writing.

Welch worked on the scarf with prominent textile designer Julian Tomchin, a Brooklyn-born New Yorker who first gained widespread media attention in 1965 when he adapted op art paintings, with their abstract,

OPPOSITE: Hubert H. Humphrey supporters, 1968, Star Staff photo by Joseph Silverman, reprinted with permission of the D.C. Public Library, Star Collection © *Washington Post*; Frankie Welch Collection, Rome Area History Center.

RIGHT: Photo by Mary Linnemann, Hargrett Rare Book and Manuscript Library; private collection.

Frankie Welch wearing a Cherokee Alphabet scarf, ca. 1967; collection of Frankie Welch, Peggy Welch Williams, and Genie Welch Leisure.

Cherokee Alphabet scarf, 1967, silk, photo by Mary Linnemann, Hargrett Rare Book and Manuscript Library; Frankie Welch Textile Collection, Hargrett Rare Book and Manuscript Library, University of Georgia Libraries.

vibrating patterns, as printed fabrics.[7] Welch showed him the syllabary when he visited Washington to give a talk on fashion, and, according to Welch, he thought her plan to make it into a scarf "was a great idea."[8] When asked in 2011 about his involvement with Welch's scarf, Tomchin replied: "Yes, I helped Frankie get her idea realized. She gave me a well-used sheet of paper with the alphabet printed on it including the hand lettered title. . . . Other than the layout, my contribution was cleaning up the graphic to make it more suitable for silk-screen printing."[9]

The first scarves were screen-printed on silk in a square format (soon followed by long rectangular scarves) with borders in a choice of three bright colors Welch called Cherokee red, Sequoyah green, and Sabra brown.[10] (According to Welch, Sabra was the daughter of the only Native American general in the Confederate Army.)[11] Of the oblong version, Tomchin explained, "I used the alphabet twice as you can see, so that no matter how it was worn, the Title and the alphabet would be viewable."[12] The early scarves were produced by Tomchin's Chardon Marché, a division

Betty Ford, Frankie Welch, and Hote' Casella at the debut of the Cherokee Alphabet scarf, 1967, photo by Don. Mac Afee; collection of Frankie Welch, Peggy Welch Williams, and Genie Welch Leisure.

of Maxwell Industries in New York, of which he was vice president.[13] Nina Hyde in the *Washington Post* described Chardon Marché as "the prestige fabric house" and noted that it made designs for "the top names on Seventh Avenue," including Donald Brooks and Chester Weinberg, indicating a strong start for Welch's entrée into scarf design.[14]

Wauhillau La Hay, a reporter of Cherokee descent working for the Scripps Howard News Service, described for the *Washington Daily News* the scarf's debut on October 23, 1967, at Alexandria's Athenaeum (home of the Northern Virginia Fine Arts Association), an event attended by Washington "notables" including Virginia Rusk, Aida Gardner, Trudye Fowler, and Lady Patricia Dean—the wives of the secretary of state; secretary of health, education, and welfare; secretary of the treasury; and British ambassador.[15] The mayor of Alexandria, Charles Beatley (whose daughter later wore a white batiste Frankie for her wedding dress), welcomed the guests and remarked that "he wished that politicians might be as successful in predicting results two years hence as Frankie is in her fashion predictions."[16] Hote' Casella, a mezzo-soprano whose father was Cherokee, played drums and chanted as models demonstrated various

Long Cherokee Alphabet scarf, ca. 1967, silk, photo by Mary Linnemann, Hargrett Rare Book and Manuscript Library; Frankie Welch Textile Collection, Hargrett Rare Book and Manuscript Library, University of Georgia Libraries.

OPPOSITE: Frankie Welch wearing a Cherokee Alphabet dress in front of Duvall House, 1968; collection of Frankie Welch, Peggy Welch Williams, and Genie Welch Leisure.

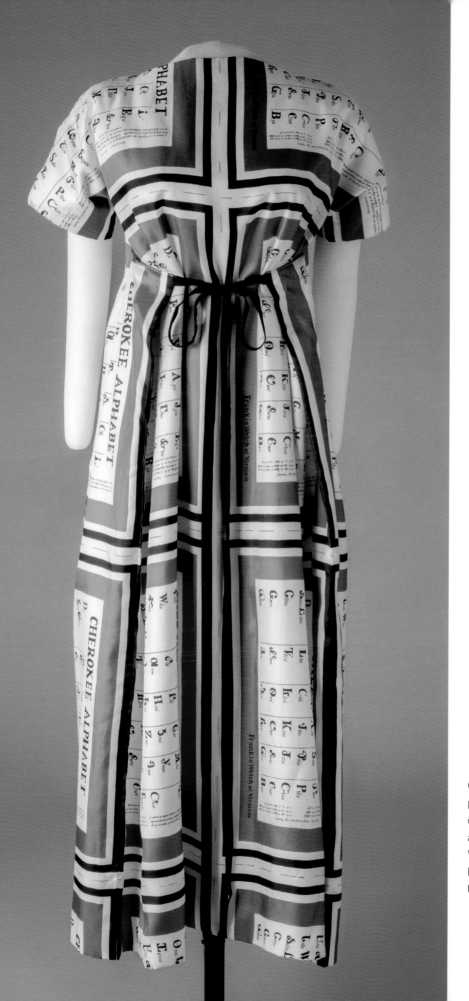

Cherokee Alphabet Frankie, n.d., photo by Michael McKelvey, courtesy of the Hargrett Rare Book and Manuscript Library; Frankie Welch Textile Collection, Hargrett Rare Book and Manuscript Library, University of Georgia Libraries.

Frankie Welch wearing a coat lined with Cherokee Alphabet, 1968, *Baltimore Sun* photo by William L. Klender; Permission from Baltimore Sun Media, All Rights Reserved; collection of Frankie Welch, Peggy Welch Williams, and Genie Welch Leisure.

ways to wear the scarves.[17] Among the models were two wives of presidential aides, Libby Cater and Shirley Pierson; the wife of the Venezuelan ambassador, Josefina Tejera París; the wife of a Democratic congressman from Florida, Rebecca Rogers; and the wife of the House minority leader from Michigan, Welch's friend, Betty Ford. That Welch's event attracted such a renowned audience and that so many prominent women agreed to model for her indicate how well connected she was politically by this time.

Welch hoped that her design would spark interest in, or at least awareness of, the Cherokees and donated a dollar from each sale to a scholarship fund she established for the higher education of the Eastern Band of Cherokee Indians.[18] She stated, "I hope that every time a woman ties this scarf around her neck she thinks something nice about Indians."[19] On the day of the scarf's debut, Chief Walter S. Jackson of the Eastern Band of Cherokee Indians sent Welch a congratulatory telegram, which she was pleased to receive.[20] Years later, in 1998, White House reporter Helen Thomas indicated that Welch's efforts were successful and long-lasting by crediting her as being the one person in the Washington area to raise "our threshold of understanding about the Native Americans, especially the Cherokees."[21]

Welch self-identified as ¹⁄₃₂nd Cherokee, an enticing detail that journalists frequently mentioned beginning with the introduction of her

Cherokee Alphabet scarf. She enjoyed hearing stories growing up and as an adult about her Cherokee heritage—which her family traced by oral history through her great-great-grandparents, Nellie Morton and Samuel Martin—and happily incorporated them into her image as a designer.[22] Though current genealogical research does not support the existence of a clear Cherokee connection in her family, she and her family and peers accepted the stories as fact and never saw a reason to question them.[23] Such claims to Cherokee familial connections were, and are, popular among white Americans, especially in the Southeast, and reflect, in part, a desire to establish ties to the early inhabitants of the land where they lived.[24]

Welch, like many others, romanticized the idea of being part Cherokee, and rather than focusing on the extreme maltreatment of the Cherokee by the United States, idealized the identity as enchanting and American.[25] For example, she wrote of a particularly delightful spring afternoon as a child with her friend Mary Earle, when they splashed in a creek, admired tiny flowers, then found Native American arrowheads outside of a small cave. She reflected on the significance of this experience, writing: "Maybe it's because this day has been such a happy memory for me. Maybe it's because of my own Indian heritage. But that day was the beginning of my life-long fascination with Indians, their jewelry, baskets, pottery and history."[26] Though also claiming English and German ancestry, Welch was especially proud to consider herself a small part Cherokee, which proved to be a helpful marketing point for her designs.[27]

As planned, Secretary Rusk and Lady Bird Johnson, the first lady at the time, both used the Cherokee Alphabet scarf for official gifts, and Nancy Kefauver (widow of Democratic Tennessee senator Estes Kefauver), through the State Department's Art in Embassies program, selected two of the scarves to be framed and hung in embassies abroad.[28] In addition to serving its political purpose, the scarf achieved fashion success, receiving a nod of approval from fashion designer Norman Norell when he made a flowing silk skirt of yardage of the red-bordered scarves, worn with a trim black jersey top and wide patent leather belt.[29] A fashion writer in California described the design as "an intriguing blend of chic and Americana."[30] Welch soon used it to create her own garments as well, including her eponymous Frankie.

The following year, in February 1968, Lady Bird Johnson, wearing a white wool dress from Welch's shop, hosted the first, and only, fashion show at the White House.[31] It was attended by the wives of the governors (the only female governor, Lurleen Wallace of Alabama, was ill at the time) as well as prominent fashion designers including Rudi Gernreich, John Moore, Sydney Wragge, and Mollie Parnis.[32] The emphatically patriotic event promoted the American fashion industry as it sought to emerge from the shadow of Paris's long dominance, and, through its theme "How to Discover America in Style," connected to Mrs. Johnson's interests in roadside and urban beautification and President Lyndon B. Johnson's

Model Harriet Simmel wearing the Norman Norell Cherokee Alphabet skirt, 1967; collection of Frankie Welch, Peggy Welch Williams, and Genie Welch Leisure.

efforts to encourage domestic vacation travel as a counter to the increasing foreign travel made possible by the growing commercial jet business.[33] Models walked a U-shaped runway in the State Dining Room against a projection of slides of popular tourist spots like the Grand Canyon and Mount Rushmore while the U.S. Marine Band performed.[34]

One notable element of the event was a scarf designed by Welch, her second.[35] This large red, white, and blue silk square with an abstract depiction of the continental United States boldly features the words "Discover America." Welch described the scarf to Frances Cawthon, fashion editor for the *Atlanta Journal*, saying, "It has a sort of poster quality. . . . You can actually see the outline of the United States, but it's free form. It also looks like mountains and lakes. And when you have it tied, it looks like a signature scarf, too."[36] The scarf appeared as flags held on poles by models at the beginning of the fashion show, as the first of the background slides, sewn into a wide-brimmed hat, as an umbrella, and, of course, worn in a traditional manner around the neck (including by Mrs. Johnson).[37] Welch recalled that she sat next to Happy Rockefeller, first lady of New York, and wept "when the scarves came out on those fancy New York models."[38]

The fashion show was planned quickly, the *New York Times* estimating in fewer than three weeks, with the scarf production having even less time.[39] A press release from the White House noted that volunteers, some recruited through a television advertisement put out by the White House, worked with Welch to hand paint and screen-print the scarves at Duvall House.[40] Fashion columnist Eugenia Sheppard commented that some of the freshly prepared scarves "were scarcely dry," and, in fact, the photographs of Welch and others working on the scarves are date-stamped February 26, just three days before the event.[41] Cawthon added, "Right up until the time of the historic White House show, Mrs. Welch and coworkers were hemming, hemming, and hemming scarves at a frantic pace."[42] A short verse on a card enclosed with the scarves, which were given in custom envelopes as gifts to the governors' wives, addressed this detail:

> Please wear your hand screened scarf today
> Tomorrow, frame it or pack it away.
> Within a month we'll send to you
> A color fast one to wear in lieu.[43]

Welch described the colors of the initial scarves as true red and cobalt blue, explaining "these colors are much more stylish than the flag colors . . . and besides, they go with more things," though she had the scarves professionally manufactured later using a darker blue.[44] Welch may have worked again with Julian Tomchin and Chardon Marché, but by early 1969 Baccara in Lyon, France, was printing this design for her.[45]

With two scarves connected to the White House and innumerable links through her shop to Washington's political elite, Welch was a natural pick in 1968 for politicians seeking fashion components for their campaigns.

OPPOSITE: Lady Bird Johnson with models (*left to right*: Toni Bailey, Lady Bird Johnson, Helen Hite, and Harriet Simmel), 1968, official White House photo by Robert L. Knudsen; collection of Frankie Welch, Peggy Welch Williams, and Genie Welch Leisure.

Hand-painted Discover America scarf, 1968, silk, photo by
Mary Linnemann, Hargrett Rare Book and Manuscript Library; collection
of Frankie Welch, Peggy Welch Williams, and Genie Welch Leisure.

Genie and Frankie Welch at the White House with framed Discover America scarf, 1968, photo by John and Ann Reisman; collection of Frankie Welch, Peggy Welch Williams, and Genie Welch Leisure.

Frankie Welch working on
Discover America scarves,
1968, official White House
photo by Robert L. Knudsen;
collection of Frankie Welch,
Peggy Welch Williams,
and Genie Welch Leisure.

Marlee Inman and Frankie Welch working on Discover America scarves, 1968, official White House photo
by Robert L. Knudsen; collection of Frankie Welch, Peggy Welch Williams, and Genie Welch Leisure.

Frankie Welch and assistants working on Discover America scarves, 1968, official White House photo by Robert L. Knudsen; collection of Frankie Welch, Peggy Welch Williams, and Genie Welch Leisure.

Caroline Sydnor ironing Discover America scarves, 1968, official White House photo by Robert L. Knudsen; collection of Frankie Welch, Peggy Welch Williams, and Genie Welch Leisure.

Discover America scarf, ca. 1968, unidentified fabric, photo by Mary Linnemann,
Hargrett Rare Book and Manuscript Library; Frankie Welch Textile Collection,
Hargrett Rare Book and Manuscript Library, University of Georgia Libraries.

Despite 1968's political season being fraught with turmoil and tragedy—President Johnson surprised the nation by not running for reelection, popular Democratic candidate Robert F. Kennedy was assassinated, anti–Vietnam War protests marred the Democratic National Convention in Chicago, and George Wallace of Alabama ran as an Independent advocating for racial segregation—it was a successful campaign season for Welch from the standpoint of fashion. She even, from the kitchen in Duvall House, offered a fashion consulting service called the Campaign Flying Boutique, originally with Toni Peabody, wife of the former governor of Massachusetts. Welch explained, "If Mrs. Rockefeller wants to find the right wardrobe, we would fly to her with ideas. Perhaps a committee woman from Milwaukee would want thousands of baskets or umbrellas. We can have them to her in 48 hours."[46] She excelled in providing designs on short notice during the 1968 political season.

Women's Wear Daily reported that Welch felt "there is a new style of campaigning that calls for interesting, fashionable women who are uniquely and tastefully dressed," adding that Welch intended to help set the campaign fashion trends and create designs that would last beyond the election season.[47] She considered practical details of the modern age as they related to fashion, thinking about how the designs and colors would appear in photographs and on television.[48] Joann Harris in the *Baltimore Sun* acknowledged the importance of Welch's experience consulting prominent women who were often photographed in public.[49] Welch stated, "After all . . . they're merchandising themselves in a very big way. And it's important. So I just try to help out."[50]

Jean Sprain Wilson, fashion editor for the Associated Press, described how campaign fashion had shifted dramatically from the previous presidential campaign, four years earlier, when simple buttons or paper hats sufficed, to 1968, when women advertised "their political allegiances from the bands of their hats to the bows on their toes."[51] The craze for political fashion in 1968 is reflected in the existence of dedicated shops for presidential candidates—Sen. Eugene J. McCarthy's campaign had a boutique in New York called McCarthy's Mart that offered, among other items, a $100 campaign button studded with precious stones, while Vice President Hubert H. Humphrey's campaign had the Pharmacy in Georgetown, opened by Toni Peabody, that offered bows, shorts, scarves, dresses, skirts, and hats as well as lunch, making it a social destination for shoppers.[52] Headlines proclaimed "Women Have Become Walking Political Billboards" and "Politics Steps Out in Fashion," and highlighted "Campaign Couture" and "Campaign Baubles, Bangles, Beads."[53] In the midst of this fashion phenomenon, Judith Axler, in New York's *Daily News*, described Welch as "the hottest thing in politics this year," "as far as the ladies are concerned."[54]

Betty Ford and Pat Nixon with daisy fabric, 1968; Courtesy: The Richard Nixon Presidential Library and Museum (National Archives and Records Administration).

Asked by Betty Ford—the day after the White House fashion show—to design "something fresh, a new approach" for the Republicans, Welch settled on the theme of "fresh as a daisy" and created a printed fabric patterned with red, white, and blue flowers with bright yellow centers and small green leaves, subtly incorporating the text "Republican National Convention" (RNC), "Miami, Florida," and "August 5, 1968."[55] *Women's Wear Daily* described the material as a "pretty design, neither too corny nor too flag waving."[56] Welch referred to it as a "documentary fabric," and it joined a long tradition in the United States of commemorative textiles, through which Americans have displayed their patriotism, announced their political allegiances, and participated in and recorded historical events.[57]

Textile showing the first seven American presidents, ca. 1830, roller-printed cotton made in England and distributed in the United States of America, bequest of Elinor Merrell, Cooper Hewitt, Smithsonian Design Museum, 1995-50-270-a,b.

Windsor Print Works (North Adams, Mass., 1829–1956), textile square commemorating the World's Columbian Exposition in Chicago, 1893, Cooper Hewitt, Smithsonian Design Museum, 1934-7-1.

LEFT: B. B. Tilt and Son (New York and Paterson, N.J.), commemorative bookmark, 1876, woven silk, gift of Mrs. Edward C. Moën, Cooper Hewitt, Smithsonian Design Museum, 1962-111-1.

RIGHT: Thomas Stevens (English, 1828–1888), bookmark memorializing Abraham Lincoln, 1865–1869, American Textile History Museum Collection, gift of Henry Semonds, Cooper Hewitt, Smithsonian Design Museum, 2016-35-69.

Loraine Percy (wife of Senator Charles H. Percy from Illinois) wearing a Republican National Convention Frankie, 1968, Star Staff photo by Ken Heinen, reprinted with permission of the D.C. Public Library, Star Collection © *Washington Post*; Frankie Welch Collection, Rome Area History Center.

The RNC material debuted at a fashion show for a Republican luncheon on May 1 at the Mayflower Hotel in Washington, appearing as tablecloths and several dress designs including a pinafore, a shirtdress or skimmer, and a floor-length Frankie, with Betty Ford again serving as a model.[58] Pablo of Elizabeth Arden (Pablo Manzoni), who spoke at the luncheon, wore a necktie of the fabric.[59] Welch described the event as "a show of reality," explaining beforehand that she would not make fashion predictions but would "show what the woman will actually wear for campaigning and to conventions," adding, "I'll give tips on how to dress for press or TV appearances."[60]

The following month Betty Ford (while wearing a daisy-print dress) presented Happy Rockefeller with a scarf of the RNC material at a luncheon in Rockefeller's honor given by the Republican Congressional Wives Club. The *Washington Post and Times Herald* reported that Ford was not playing favorites, though, and would send a kerchief and yardage for a dress of the material to Pat Nixon as well, since both of their husbands, Nelson Rockefeller and Richard Nixon, were vying for the Republican nomination for president.[61] By early August, Nixon's campaign had ordered some of the fabric, in the form of kerchiefs, reflecting the textile's widespread acceptance (among Republicans) despite its lack of the traditional elephant imagery.[62]

Fifty hostesses wore dresses of the fabric to the opening luncheon for the Republican National Convention in Miami Beach, Florida, on August 5, and Welch also sold the dresses to individuals for twenty-eight dollars each and retailed the fabric by the yard so that Republicans could make their own garments.[63] Nancy Reagan wore a dress of the fabric to the convention, and Ronald Reagan, another presidential candidate that year, received a Western shirt made of it.[64]

Welch provided custom hostess dresses—with two days' notice—for Hubert Humphrey's luncheon on April 27 announcing his candidacy for president, and the design remained popular throughout the election.[65] When first contacted, Welch learned that the Humphrey campaign had not yet chosen the shades of green and blue that it would use and requested that she be allowed to do so.[66] She selected emerald green for the short "H-Line" dresses with sapphire blue Hs (one in front and one in back) outlined in white rickrack, and they sold for twelve dollars (less than the RNC dresses because they were not made of a custom fabric or lined).[67] The large Hs created a clever play on, and a slightly straighter skirt than, the popular A-line dress silhouette. Welch recommended wearing them with white stockings and navy shoes with low or medium heels.[68] Society columnist Betty Beale described the H-Line dresses as "the best looking campaign dresses" she'd ever seen, while Joann Harris in the *Baltimore Sun* praised Welch's consideration of "the 'H' symbol's visibility in TV camera closeups and long shots."[69] The *New York Times* reported in June that the enthusiastic campaign was having 1,150 made.[70] Welch's older daughter Peggy attended the Democratic National Convention with her mother, and she recalls that the scarves and dresses were highly visible and generated a lot of interest.[71] For custom orders, including from

Humphrey's sister Frances Humphrey Howard, Welch created the dress in a long version, "in blue crepe with a blue and green sequined H on the front."[72] One Humphrey supporter, Mrs. Francis H. Blum, even donned a long H-Line dress for a lavish ball given by São and Pierre Schlumberger near Estoril, Portugal.[73]

That the H-Line dress design succeeded as fashion beyond its political statement is reflected in stories of customers admiring and trying on the dress without realizing it was for Humphrey, including one woman who "took it off and said in horror, 'Humphrey? I'm for McCarthy,'" and Betty Ford who liked it but politely said, "I don't think I'll take it after all," when she was selecting clothes to wear to the Republican National Convention.[74] Welch told Judith Axler of New York's *Daily News*, "Two girls walked out of here one day in H-Line dresses with big Rockefeller pins on the front," unintentionally sending a mixed political message.[75] For both the Republican and the Humphrey designs, Welch offered coordinated parasols and handbags/lunchboxes (thermos equipped)—helpful items for door-to-door campaigners.[76]

Welch soon designed a Humphrey scarf as well (for United Democrats for Humphrey), a large white square in cotton or silk featuring blue Hs in a checkerboard pattern with a green-and-blue border and the candidate's signature in one corner.[77] Many designers and individuals used the large scarves and yardage of the design to create shirts, minidresses, and other garments.[78] Virginia Guest, who worked for Humphrey and was the daughter of the recent U.S. ambassador to Ireland, even had a dinner dress made of the design, a custom order through Washington's high-end shop Erlebacher's, for $200.[79] Welch later described the Humphrey scarves as what really made her business tick (meaning it provided the money to focus on her design work) and as the largest political order she ever had.[80] She also recounted how once, well after the campaign, she was on an airplane with Humphrey and he exclaimed to her, "You know, Frankie, if we'd had [that scarf] one more week, I would have won!"[81]

Welch additionally created, again on short notice, outfits for a youth group supporting Gov. Nelson Rockefeller's bid for the Republican presidential nomination, royal blue and chrome yellow high-necked jumpsuits called "Happy Jams" (after Nelson's wife Happy) worn with rock pendant necklaces.[82] The suggested guidelines to Welch from the young campaigners were to make the design "way out, but in good taste."[83] She created the Happy Jams for the opening of the Washington branch of the Rock, a discotheque for Rockefeller supporters.[84]

Numerous reporters remarked on the ease with which Welch moved between customers of opposing political parties, with the *New York Times* describing her as "the nonpartisan fashion spokesman for both Republicans and Democrats."[85] And when asked which presidential candidate she wanted to win, she generally replied, "I'm really bipartisan," and throughout her career she declined to publicly announce her political

OPPOSITE: Republican National Convention Frankie and pinafore, 1968, photo by Michael McKelvey, courtesy of the Hargrett Rare Book and Manuscript Library; (*left*) Frankie Welch Collection, Rome Area History Center and (*right*) Frankie Welch Textile Collection, Hargrett Rare Book and Manuscript Library, University of Georgia Libraries.

Frankie Welch and Mildred Pepper (wife of Florida congressman Claude Pepper) with Hubert H. Humphrey supporters at the campaign headquarters in Washington, D.C., for the announcement of Humphrey's candidacy for president, 1968; Frankie Welch Collection, Rome Area History Center.

OPPOSITE: H-Line dress for Hubert H. Humphrey campaign, 1968, photo by Michael McKelvey, courtesy of the Hargrett Rare Book and Manuscript Library; private collection.

Janet Dempsey Steiger (wife of
Representative William Steiger of
Wisconsin) wearing a Republican
National Convention pinafore and
Joan Mondale (wife of Senator Walter
Mondale of Minnesota) wearing an
H-Line dress in the Duvall House
garden, 1968, *Milwaukee Sentinel*
photo; collection of Frankie Welch,
Peggy Welch Williams, and
Genie Welch Leisure.

OPPOSITE: Frankie Welch in her shop, 1968, *Baltimore Sun* photo by William L. Klender;
Permission from Baltimore Sun Media, All Rights Reserved.

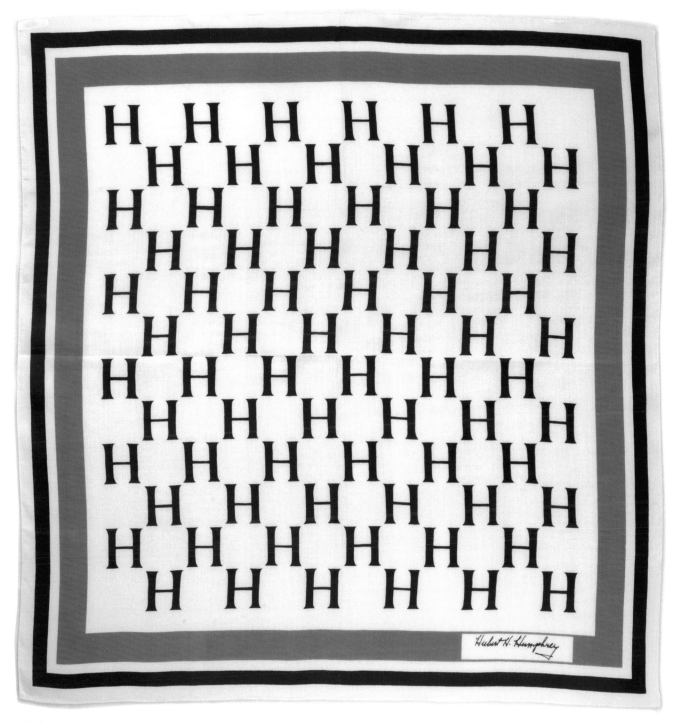

Hubert H. Humphrey scarf, 1968, silk, photo by Mary Linnemann, Hargrett Rare Book
and Manuscript Library; Frankie Welch Textile Collection, Hargrett Rare Book and Manuscript
Library, University of Georgia Libraries.

Models wearing Frankie Welch's political fashion designs, *left to right*: Republican National Convention pinafore, Hubert H. Humphrey dress made from two scarves, long H-Line dress for eveningwear, and Happy Jams with a rock pendant necklace, 1968, photo by Thomas DeFeo, from the *National Observer*, August 5, 1968.

affiliations.[86] She took pride in being able to state, "The Democrats and the Republicans shop side by side in my shop."[87] She admitted to *Women's Wear Daily*, though, that she did have a favorite candidate in 1968, stating, "There would be something wrong with me if I didn't," but she added, "In the line of merchandising, I just do my best for each client."[88] Axler noted that while Welch had custom designs for Republicans and supporters of Humphrey and Rockefeller that year, voters who still wanted Johnson could wear the Discover America scarf.[89]

Concluding the election season, Welch designed hostess outfits—short, metallic sequined dresses accompanied by silver shoes and sheer silver stockings worn by Nixonaires (airline stewardesses who supported the campaign)—and a commemorative scarf for Nixon's presidential inauguration.[90] The red, white, and blue square silk scarf features a large N in the middle, Nixon's signature in a reserve in one corner, "by Frankie Welch" in another, and the repeated words "Forward Together," which Welch later noted was not the first theme for the inaugural—Nixon changed his mind partway through the design process and she had to redo the design.[91] Pat Nixon received the first scarf at the Pierre in New York City on January 11, 1969, during her debut news conference.[92] Inaugural ball guests sitting in the $1,000 boxes received twenty-one-inch-scarves, and larger scarves were printed for cabinet members, governors, and Supreme Court justices.[93] Welch had gold-filled bracelets with a large, square charm featuring the scarf design on one side and the presidential seal on the other and round cuff links with the presidential seal manufactured for inaugural mementoes as well. Reflecting Welch's enterprising attitude, the chair of the inaugural committee noted that they selected her to design for the event "because 'she got to us first.'"[94]

Following this quick succession of high-profile fashion accomplishments, Welch formalized her scarf business and expanded beyond political designs, though campaign scarves and scarves with political connections remained an important part of her output, even earning her the label "political fashion specialist."[95] In March 1969 *Women's Wear Daily* announced that she had "decided to go national as a scarf designer," and, through appealing to businesses, institutions, schools, clubs, and individuals, her scarf production grew exponentially.[96]

Frankie Welch with women modeling her 1968 political fashions, *left to right*: Jocelyn Monroney
(daughter-in-law of Senator A. S. Mike Monroney of Oklahoma) wearing an H-Line dress; Libby
Cater (wife of Douglass Cater, special assistant to President Lyndon B. Johnson) wearing a Discover
America Frankie; Frankie Welch; and Susan MacGregor (daughter of Representative Clark MacGregor
of Minnesota) wearing a Republican National Convention pinafore, 1968, photo by George Tames,
Copyright *The New York Times*; Frankie Welch Collection, Rome Area History Center.

Richard Nixon inaugural scarf, 1969, silk, photo by Mary Linnemann,
Hargrett Rare Book and Manuscript Library; collection of Frankie Welch,
Peggy Welch Williams, and Genie Welch Leisure.

Flyer showing how to tie the Richard Nixon inaugural scarf, 1969;
collection of Frankie Welch, Peggy Welch Williams, and
Genie Welch Leisure.

Chapter 3
Frankie Welch Signature Scarves

Frankie Welch entered the world of scarf design at a vibrant point in its history. Scarves had increased in popularity during the middle of the twentieth century, thriving as the advertising industry grew and used them to promote entertainment, travel, and a never-ending range of products. Consumers were familiar with the use of logos on scarves, and also, in part through the designs of Vera Neumann, had grown accustomed to seeing designers' names on scarves. Neumann, who established her influential home textiles brand Vera Industries in 1942, introduced her first scarf in 1947 and by the 1950s copyrighted all of her designs.[1] Neumann was prolific and worked with a large support staff to design thousands of bright and colorful scarves that emphasized her artistic abilities. She presented an array of subject matter, "no matter how quotidian . . . from eyeglasses to musical instruments to chestnuts," that helped pave the way for the variety of imagery Welch used on her scarves.[2]

By the time Welch designed her Cherokee Alphabet scarf in 1967, the presence of a designer's name on a scarf was expected and desired, to the point that the signature scarf had become its own category of fashion accessory. While some scholars credit Neumann with starting the trend, period reporters often attributed it to luxury designers, especially in Europe, including Cristóbal Balenciaga.[3] In 1966 noted fashion columnist Eugenia Sheppard praised signature scarves as "the best new things that have happened to fashion in a long time," and both Peg Zwecker for the Chicago Daily News Service in 1968 and Dee Dee Bower for the *Shreveport Times* in 1969 described the signature scarf as the number one fashion accessory.[4] Many European and American designers, including Donald Brooks, Geoffrey Beene, Adele Simpson, Rudi Gernreich, Christian Dior, and Patrick de Barentzen, indulged in this fad and added signature scarves to their collections.

One reason for the popularity of signature scarves was that they provided an affordable and obvious—if tied so that the name was visible—way

OPPOSITE: Frankie Welch with the See Georgia First Scarf, 1969; Frankie Welch Collection, Rome Area History Center.

RIGHT: From the Frankie Welch Textile Collection, Hargrett Rare Book and Manuscript Library, University of Georgia Libraries.

Frankie Welch holding a long Cherokee Alphabet scarf, 1974, photo probably by Walker Montgomery, Athens, Georgia; collection of Frankie Welch, Peggy Welch Williams, and Genie Welch Leisure.

to acquire and show off ownership of a designer item.[5] They were appealing for women of all ages to collect, easy to give as gifts, and practical to ship since they were lightweight and not breakable.[6] Prices for signature scarves in the mid-1960s ranged from Vera's affordable scarves at $2–$10, to $20–$50 for higher-end labels.[7] Welch sold her early silk scarves based on their size, with 22-inch squares selling for $9 and 32-inch squares for $22, placing her in a low-middle price range.[8]

While most of the signature scarves at this time were silk squares, there was also a vogue for long rectangular silk scarves. Yves Saint Laurent introduced his "six-footer" with his monogram on one end in Paris in 1967, while Bill Blass offered a five-foot scarf called "The Lanky" in 1968.[9] The movie *Bonnie and Clyde* (1967), in which Faye Dunaway wore "long, lean scarves," and the general revival of interest in 1930s fashion that the movie amplified, contributed to the popularity of this style.[10] Yves Saint Laurent sold his six-footer for $45, while Welch sold her long Cherokee Alphabet scarves, some with fringed ends, for $22.[11]

Interest in the signature scarf began to wane by late 1969.[12] However, the designer scarf, which might indicate the designer or retailer through means other than a signature (such as logos or initials), remained a standard high-end fashion product through the 1980s.[13] Also, the mania for branded fashion items of many kinds, such as buttons and handbags, continued to grow.[14] Welch capitalized on this awareness of brand identity and cultivated her own as her business evolved.

After establishing a reputation in scarf design through her Cherokee Alphabet, Discover America, Humphrey, and Nixon scarves, Welch in 1969 decided to expand this part of her business. She sent brochures about her work to five thousand large companies and institutions inviting them to commission her to design custom scarves with the company's logo or motto and the executives' signatures.[15] In the brochure she acknowledged that including typography, calligraphy, or handwriting would make a scarf fashionable and that having her name associated with it would be meaningful to the women who purchased or received a custom scarf.[16] And, in fact, *Newsweek* stated that hers was "perhaps the most newsworthy trademark" on scarves at that time.[17]

Welch broadened the scope of the signature scarf from just promoting the designer's name to expressing the specific interests of the wearer. In 1969 she explained, "Ten years ago . . . people tried to cover up their affiliations. They wore their labels on the inside. Now they're wearing them on the outside."[18] Embracing this element of advertising in her fashion, she stated, "The message is the thing. . . . We're in a period of honesty, identification and communication."[19] Welch's approach met an

Frankie Welch at a trade show, ca. 1977; collection of Frankie Welch,
Peggy Welch Williams, and Genie Welch Leisure.

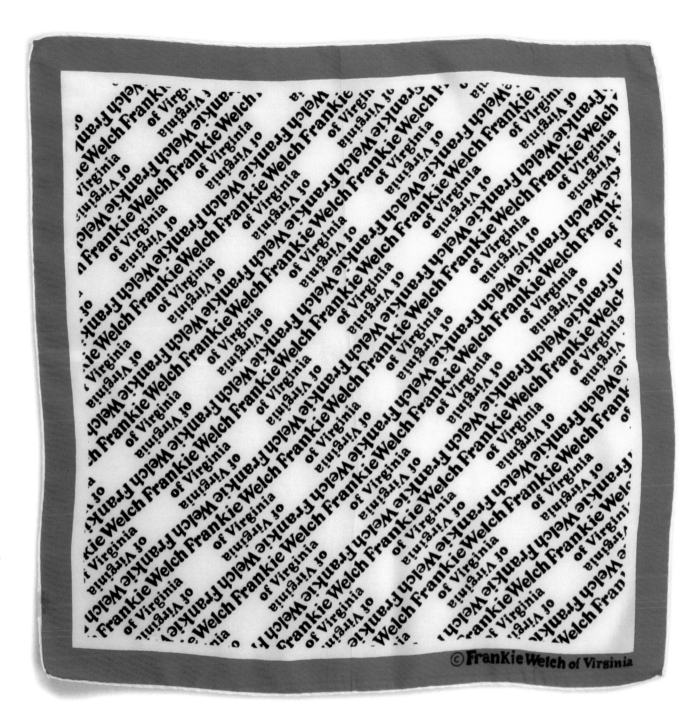

Frankie Welch of Virginia scarf, 1969, silk, photo by Mary Linnemann,
Hargrett Rare Book and Manuscript Library; Frankie Welch Textile Collection,
Hargrett Rare Book and Manuscript Library, University of Georgia Libraries.

enthusiastic audience, and Marian Christy of the *Boston Globe* reported that the "specially-designed, highly-personalized scarfs" were "making Frankie a millionaire."[20] As her scarf trade increased, she expanded the title of her business to Frankie Welch of America, though the shop in Alexandria retained its original name.[21]

Subjects for Welch's early scarves (and many later ones as well) often related to events and places near or important to her, such as the federal government, her alma mater, and her hometown. When she visited Furman in 1969 for alumni weekend, she received a Distinguished Alumni Award and unveiled a Furman scarf.[22] She also returned to Rome, Georgia, that year, where she was honored by the Rome Area Chamber of Commerce with a Frankie Welch Day and debuted her See Georgia First scarf, a variation of her Discover America design produced in both red, white, and blue as well as brown, orange, and white.[23] Another popular early design came from her younger daughter Genie in 1969, an abstract painting of bright blocks of color presented as a twenty-fifth wedding anniversary gift to her parents that Welch then turned into a scarf.[24] Her early designs also included clients from farther afield, such as the Algonquin Hotel and Princeton Club in New York, the National Tuberculosis and Respiratory Disease Association (now the American Lung Association), and a theatrical production in South Africa.

In the early 1970s Welch introduced a new design approach that governed the production of the majority of her scarves through the 1970s and the first half of the 1980s. For this approach—inspired by Frank Lloyd Wright—she employed an eight-by-eight-inch module, typically using a column of four modules with a little space between each to make a scarf measuring eight by approximately thirty-four inches.[25] (A few transitional scarves, and a handful of later scarves, adhere to this smaller oblong size, but do not use the modules.) The repeated module gave her scarves a look that was clean and modern as well as recognizably hers.

One of Welch's earliest module-based scarves was for the Georgia Libraries Association (GLA), and it features a module with a border of books and a center filled with scattered Library of Congress and Dewey Decimal call numbers. When a longtime friend of Welch's, Emily Payne, director of the Tri-County Regional Library (now the Sara Hightower Regional Library) in Rome, visited Washington to advocate for libraries, she decided that having a scarf by her popular friend would help bring attention to her less popular cause. Payne convinced the GLA to commission a scarf from Welch, who was "most excited" about the project. Payne requested that the state of Georgia be acknowledged very subtly, which Welch did by including the Dewey Decimal and Library of Congress call numbers that designate books on Georgia (975.8 and F281). The scarf debuted during a social hour at a GLA conference on Jekyll Island in Georgia in 1971.[26]

Frankie Welch wearing the National Tuberculosis and Respiratory Disease Association (now the American Lung Association) scarf, 1969; Frankie Welch Collection, Rome Area History Center.

Member of Congress scarf, 1969, silk, photo by Mary Linnemann, Hargrett Rare Book and Manuscript Library; Frankie Welch Collection, Historic Clothing and Textile Collection, College of Family and Consumer Sciences, University of Georgia.

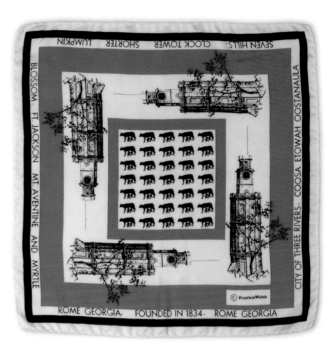

Rome, Georgia, scarf, 1969, silk, photo by Mary Linnemann, Hargrett Rare Book and Manuscript Library; Frankie Welch Collection, Rome Area History Center.

Furman University scarf, ca. 1969, silk, photo by Mary Linnemann, Hargrett Rare Book and Manuscript Library; collection of Frankie Welch, Peggy Welch Williams, and Genie Welch Leisure.

See Georgia First scarf, 1969, cotton, photo by Mary Linnemann, Hargrett Rare Book and Manuscript Library; collection of Frankie Welch, Peggy Welch Williams, and Genie Welch Leisure.

Princeton Club of New York scarf, 1969, silk, photo by Mary Linnemann, Hargrett Rare Book and Manuscript Library; collection of Frankie Welch, Peggy Welch Williams, and Genie Welch Leisure.

Cabaret scarf (for show opening in Johannesburg, South Africa, with signature of Taubie Kushlick), 1969, unidentified fabric, photo by Mary Linnemann, Hargrett Rare Book and Manuscript Library; Frankie Welch Collection, Rome Area History Center.

International Azalea Festival, Norfolk, Virginia, scarf (with signature of Tricia Nixon, that year's festival princess), 1969, cotton, photo by Mary Linnemann, Hargrett Rare Book and Manuscript Library; collection of Frankie Welch, Peggy Welch Williams, and Genie Welch Leisure.

June Fete scarf (Abington Memorial Hospital, Abington, Pennsylvania), ca. 1969, silk, photo by Mary Linnemann, Hargrett Rare Book and Manuscript Library; collection of Frankie Welch, Peggy Welch Williams, and Genie Welch Leisure.

Washington, D.C., scarf design, ca. 1978; collection of Frankie Welch, Peggy Welch Williams, and Genie Welch Leisure.

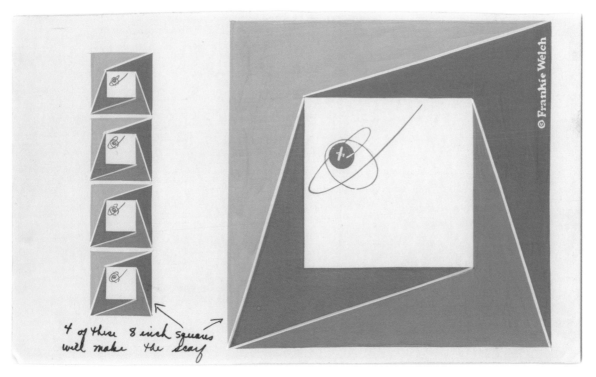

4 of these 8 inch squares will make the scarf

Scarf design for the National Air and Space Museum, Smithsonian Institution, 1976; Frankie Welch Textile Collection, Hargrett Rare Book and Manuscript Library, University of Georgia Libraries.

Scarf design for the Women's Auxiliary to the Texas Dental Association, 1978; Frankie Welch Textile Collection, Hargrett Rare Book and Manuscript Library, University of Georgia Libraries.

Scarf design for the Textile Museum in Washington, D.C., 1980; Frankie Welch Textile Collection, Hargrett Rare Book and Manuscript Library, University of Georgia Libraries.

In addition to facilitating design and production, the use of a standard, repeated unit inspired creative variations. Occasionally Welch produced scarves in other formats, such as 1 x 5, 3 x 3, or 6 x 6 modules, and she used yardage of the modules to make Frankies. Some scarves alternated units with reverse color schemes, and occasionally the four modules showed different related designs. Often Welch had the fabric hemmed as single modules that she called "napachiefs," a combination of "napkin" (cocktail napkin) and "handkerchief." She suggested that these napachiefs could be tied as bows on bouquets of flowers, wrapped around gift boxes or wine bottles, sewn into pillows or as quilt squares, tucked into blazers as pocket squares, or used as cocktail napkins to provide conversation pieces at parties.[27]

The various approaches to tying scarves allowed for expression and interpretation as well. Welch suggested a multitude of options for the early large square scarves, including tied as a knapsack, used as a pair stitched together to make a top to wear with white pants, knotted as a halter, or, with five strategically arranged, as a swimsuit. Raymonde Alexander, fashion editor for the *Atlanta Constitution*, described how, starting with three basic folds—triangle, bias, and oblong—Welch could "create almost anything," including "the usual neck scarf; the men's necktie look with variations of your own imagination; a bib; a pussy-cat bow, high or low; a poof; a stock tie; a bow for your hair; a scarf for your arm, waist, head; or a turban."[28] The smaller one-by-four module scarves also could be worn numerous ways around the neck or tied on a ponytail, wrist, or purse. One reporter quipped that some people believed that Welch knew "one hundred ways to tie a scarf."[29]

Welch promoted her scarf business in a charming but relentless way. She even proposed ideas during media interviews, and in one sixteen-minute segment for a Rome television program, she suggested seven unsolicited ideas for scarves.[30] Her daughter Peggy believes that Welch, because she was such a people person, enjoyed selling her scarves as much as designing them.[31] Once, while Welch was having her hair done, the woman sitting under an adjoining dryer asked about the scarf Welch was wearing and expressed interest in having one for her husband's company; about an hour later Welch "was standing at the couple's door with sketch in hand."[32] Her friend Susan Thompson, who worked with Clyde's, a fashionable saloon-style restaurant in Georgetown that commissioned two designs from Welch, recalls Welch describing how she pursued a commission from the Republican National Committee: aware that time to create and print the design (probably in advance of the 1984 convention) was limited, she sat in the RNC office for three consecutive days, "'dressed to the nines' with a new outfit, and a different hat [each day] . . . with a big smile," waiting for a check so that she could begin.[33] *Southern Living* described her approach in terms of *Gone with the Wind*, crediting Welch with "the determined get-up-and-go of Scarlett and the gentleness of Melanie."[34]

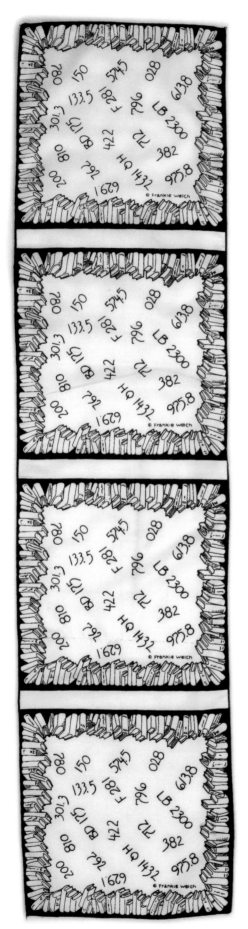

Genie Welch wearing a Georgia
Libraries Association scarf, 1977;
collection of Frankie Welch,
Peggy Welch Williams, and
Genie Welch Leisure.

Georgia Libraries Association scarf, 1971, Qiana,
photo by Mary Linnemann, Hargrett Rare Book
and Manuscript Library; Frankie Welch Textile
Collection, Hargrett Rare Book and Manuscript
Library, University of Georgia Libraries.

Napachief being used as a cocktail napkin, n.d.; collection of Frankie Welch, Peggy Welch Williams, and Genie Welch Leisure.

Flyer showing how to use napachiefs, ca. 1981; Frankie Welch Textile Collection, Hargrett Rare Book and Manuscript Library, University of Georgia Libraries.

OPPOSITE: (left to right) United States Senate Frankie, ca. 1983; Member of Congress Frankie, ca. 1983; Thirteen Original States Frankie, ca. 1976, collection of Frankie Welch, Peggy Welch Williams, and Genie Welch Leisure; United States Senate scarf, ca. 1983, Frankie Welch Collection, Historic Clothing and Textile Collection, College of Family and Consumer Sciences, University of Georgia; Thirteen Original States scarf, ca. 1976, private collection, photo by Michael McKelvey, courtesy of the Hargrett Rare Book and Manuscript Library.

Frankie Welch tying a halter scarf top on Cathy Douglas (wife of Supreme Court justice William O. Douglas), 1969, photo possibly by James Pickerell; Frankie Welch Collection, Rome Area History Center.

OPPOSITE: Cherry Blossom scarf skirt and blouse, n.d., photo by Michael McKelvey, courtesy of the Hargrett Rare Book and Manuscript Library; Frankie Welch Textile Collection, Hargrett Rare Book and Manuscript Library, University of Georgia Libraries.

Scarves were integral to the experience of shopping at Frankie Welch of Virginia. She had an employee tie a scarf to the brass knocker on the shop's front door every morning, so that every visitor was greeted with a scarf. When customers went to the dressing rooms to try on garments, the employees assisting them would bring scarves to go with each outfit. An undated handbook for employees directed them to "be on the alert for potential clients for a scarf design—such as a gentleman waiting for his wife."[35]

Welch's customers themselves proved to be good at selling, often persuading their husbands to commission scarves for their businesses.[36] Sometimes, especially later on, women with their own businesses and careers commissioned designs from Welch, including sewing instructor Kitty Rotruck, philanthropist Holly Coors, vintner Felicia Rogan, and political strategist Sandy Liddy Bourne. Welch also created a scarf and tote bag for her friend Moya Lear, president of LearAvia Corporation, for the Lear Fan 2100 business plane.[37]

To begin a scarf, Welch typically created an eight-by-eight-inch preliminary sketch with markers.[38] She explained, "I often met someone and in

Frankie Welch of Virginia scarf flyer, ca. 1969;
collection of Frankie Welch, Peggy Welch Williams,
and Genie Welch Leisure.

Frankie Welch of Virginia scarf flyer, early 1970s;
collection of Frankie Welch, Peggy Welch Williams,
and Genie Welch Leisure.

Frankie Welch of Virginia scarf flyer, ca. 1976;
Frankie Welch Collection, Rome Area History Center.

Frankie Welch of Virginia scarf flyer, ca. 1977; private collection.

Peggy Welch Williams wearing a
Nautical Flags scarf, 1977; collection of
Frankie Welch, Peggy Welch Williams,
and Genie Welch Leisure.

Genie Welch wearing a Georgetown
University Hoya scarf, 1977; collection of
Frankie Welch, Peggy Welch Williams,
and Genie Welch Leisure.

Genie Welch wearing a Tennis scarf,
1977; collection of Frankie Welch,
Peggy Welch Williams, and
Genie Welch Leisure.

Genie Welch wearing a Basket Weave
scarf, 1980; collection of Frankie Welch,
Peggy Welch Williams, and Genie
Welch Leisure.

Genie Welch wearing a Harlequin
scarf, 1980; collection of Frankie Welch,
Peggy Welch Williams, and
Genie Welch Leisure.

Genie Welch wearing a Time Life scarf,
1980; collection of Frankie Welch,
Peggy Welch Williams, and
Genie Welch Leisure.

Shoppers at Frankie Welch of
Virginia, ca. 1973; collection of
Frankie Welch, Peggy Welch
Williams, and Genie Welch Leisure.

Frankie Welch at a drawing table, ca. 1975; collection of Frankie Welch,
Peggy Welch Williams, and Genie Welch Leisure.

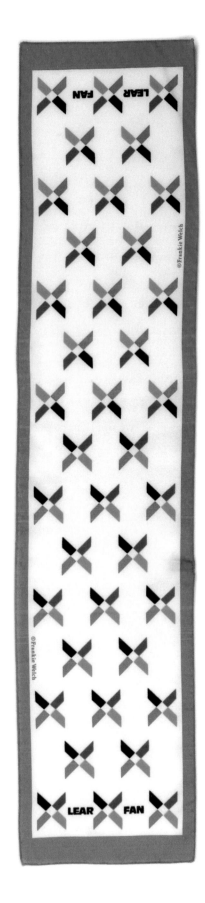

LEFT: Lear Fan scarf, 1981, polyester, photo by Mary Linnemann, Hargrett Rare Book and Manuscript Library; Frankie Welch Textile Collection, Hargrett Rare Book and Manuscript Library, University of Georgia Libraries.

RIGHT: Burke & Herbert Bank scarf, 1979, polyester, photo by Mary Linnemann, Hargrett Rare Book and Manuscript Library; Frankie Welch Textile Collection, Hargrett Rare Book and Manuscript Library, University of Georgia Libraries.

a conversation would ask about them, their logo, and as we talked I would begin sketching. I would grab a cocktail napkin from the airplane, a note-card from the person, a scrap of paper and we went over the design right then."[39] She also stated, "You have to study the organization and find out what makes it tick to come up with a design that really signifies them."[40] For example, for the Burke and Herbert Bank in Alexandria, Welch combined a subtle background of dollar signs with an unexpected and charmingly appropriate element—a parrot inspired by Taylor Burke Jr.'s pet and bank mascot, Runyon.[41] For a commission from Cortes Randell, a businessman in McLean, Virginia, who wanted a scarf for his wife, Welch included the names of their house, boat, plane, and child, as well as when and where they met, using the wife's favorite colors.[42] Some designs she developed exclusively through correspondence, though she also conducted extensive business by telephone and utilized fax machines when they became popular.[43]

Welch encouraged her assistants to suggest to clients "graphically simple custom designs which can be designed, presented quickly, approved, and produced by our plants as effortlessly as possible," and she emphasized dropping new logos or themes into "proven designs."[44] Indeed, some compositions appear repeatedly in her scarves, and many rely heavily on logos for their designs, though sometimes with a clever twist, such as with her design for McDonald's where the iconic golden arches overlap the outer border to suggest the company's global dominance.[45] She hired artists, including Laura Maxine Bell and, for a longer period, Richard W. Severance, to prepare the final designs for transfer to the screen-printing process.[46] Generally she charged clients half of the fee on signing a contract, with the second half due when they received the scarves, to ensure that her production costs would be covered in advance—an approach that demonstrates how she supported her designs with a strategic business model.[47]

Welch worked with a complex and ever-shifting network of fabric manufacturers, screen printers, and hemmers to have her scarves produced. Many of her early silk scarves and some later synthetics were printed by Baccara in Lyon, France, which she worked with from 1969 until around 1976.[48] Bellotti in Italy also produced some of her early scarves, as did the Chardon Marché Division of Maxwell Industries in New York.[49] She worked extensively with the high-end manufacturer Onondaga Silk Company in New York for much of the 1970s, as well as Fisher & Gentile Ltd. in New York.[50] She used multiple hemming techniques, including hand rolled and machine rolled, and she sometimes engaged a separate company to hem the scarves, such as Sabana Grande Embroidery Company in Puerto Rico.[51] By the late 1970s reporters noted that she owned—though her daughters believe that she more likely owned a partial interest in—a screen-printing factory, which allowed her to consolidate and better oversee the production of her scarves.[52]

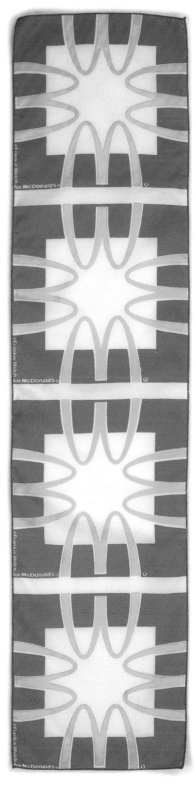

McDonald's scarf, 1976, Qiana, photo by Mary Linnemann, Hargrett Rare Book and Manuscript Library; private collection.

Frankie Welch on the telephone in Duvall House,
ca. 1972, photo by Joan Larson; Frankie Welch
Collection, Rome Area History Center.

Frankie Welch on the telephone in Frankie Welch of Virginia, ca. 1980; collection of Frankie Welch, Peggy Welch Williams, and Genie Welch Leisure.

Frankie Welch on the telephone in her office/studio, ca. 1995; Frankie Welch Collection, Rome Area History Center.

For the typical production of the scarves with the eight-by-eight-inch modules, the manufacturer unrolled fifty to a hundred yards of 44–45-inch-wide fabric on long tables, smoothed it and checked for wrinkles and distortions, laid a silk screen the same width as the yardage (with four modules aligned with the length of the fabric and five with the width) on top, and used a squeegee to apply the ink through the screen.[53] The workers printed one panel, skipped a panel's width, then printed another panel, repeating the process as necessary.[54] Next the printed yardage was cut into five scarf widths—"like long streamers or spaghetti"—with the long length running parallel to the selvage, and hemmed on the long sides first.[55] Welch charged clients an extra fee for each color after the initial one to cover the costs of additional screens and labor.

While Welch's first scarves primarily were silk or cotton, she soon transitioned in the early 1970s to synthetics, particularly favoring Qiana, a silky nylon introduced by DuPont in June 1968.[56] In 1973 Welch wrote to one client, Bruce Sundlun of Executive Jet Aviation, about Qiana: "We are really so thrilled with the fabric; it is softer than silk, has such marvelous drapability and still has washing ability."[57] Several years later, when corresponding with a business associate, Welch described herself as "practically 'Miss Qiana,'" because she used so much of it and touted it so enthusiastically.[58] Qiana's popularity peaked around 1977 (especially in double-knit garments), and DuPont ceased production of it in the early 1980s.[59] Welch also made module scarves in other popular synthetics of the era including nylon, polyester, and triacetate, and she occasionally returned to cotton or silk.

In keeping with fashion trends, Welch decreased the emphasis on logos and typography—while keeping her name on the scarves—and began including more small floral elements and architectural details toward the late 1970s. For example, though close in date, her two designs for McCormick, the spice company, reflect this shift. The first, from 1977, is a bold three-by-three checkerboard of the "Mc" trademark alternating with individual spices labeled in a heavy font, printed in "black pepper, sage green, [or] cinnamon." The other design, from 1978, features a floral pattern of delicately drawn lines depicting various spices, each identified in cursive. Records in Welch's papers describe this second scarf as demonstrating the "new

Genie Welch and Peggy Welch Williams wearing
McCormick scarves, 1977; collection of Frankie Welch,
Peggy Welch Williams, and Genie Welch Leisure.

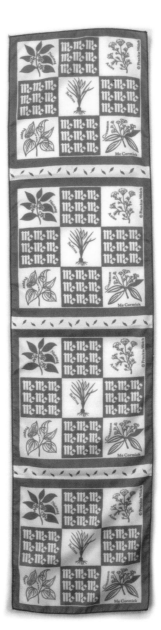

McCormick necktie, 1978, photo by
Mary Linnemann, Hargrett Rare Book
and Manuscript Library; Frankie Welch
Collection, Rome Area History Center.

LEFT: McCormick scarf, 1977, Qiana, photo by
Mary Linnemann, Hargrett Rare Book and
Manuscript Library; Frankie Welch Textile Collection,
Hargrett Rare Book and Manuscript Library,
University of Georgia Libraries.

RIGHT: McCormick scarf, 1978, polyester, photo
by Mary Linnemann, Hargrett Rare Book and
Manuscript Library; Frankie Welch Textile Collection,
Hargrett Rare Book and Manuscript Library,
University of Georgia Libraries.

Red Cross napachief, 1981, polyester,
photo by Mary Linnemann, Hargrett
Rare Book and Manuscript Library;
Frankie Welch Textile Collection, Hargrett
Rare Book and Manuscript Library,
University of Georgia Libraries.

Interior architectural detail, American
Red Cross National Headquarters,
Washington, D.C.; Frankie Welch
Textile Collection, Hargrett Rare Book
and Manuscript Library, University of
Georgia Libraries.

concept" in her design work: "small scale interrelated elements forming a subtle feeling."[60] Her scarf for the Red Cross, for its centennial in 1981, has a similarly small-scale design and shows her interest in historic architecture; this scarf draws from elements of the Red Cross's early twentieth-century classical revival headquarters building in Washington.

Welch's scarves worked well with the "power dressing" business style of the late 1970s and 1980s, in which women wore conservative dress suits in the workplace. Welch's friend Dorothea Johnson, who founded the Protocol School of Washington in 1988 after advising government officials on issues of protocol for many years, dressed conservatively, in Armani suits with minimal jewelry, but she easily and regularly incorporated Welch's designs as pocket squares.[61] John T. Molloy, in his best-selling guide *The Woman's Dress for Success* of 1977, strongly recommended that women wear slightly below-the-knee skirts and white "man-tailored" blouses with contrasting scarves—worn ascot, necktie, or scout style.[62]

Starting with her first scarf, the Cherokee Alphabet, Welch recognized the benefits of making the unveiling of each new design an event. These special occasions, whether a reception at her store, a dedicated press briefing, an element of a fashion show luncheon, the start of a fundraiser, or part of a conference schedule, helped garner media attention for the design and heightened the excitement for those receiving the scarves. Her daughter Peggy believes that many people commissioned scarves in part simply to have Welch be present at their event for the unveiling. Peggy explains that her mother was a "coveted and popular speaker," and that the talk she developed about how to tie a scarf and how to be fashionable "went beyond the fashion shows of the past."[63] Welch offered clients the option of packaging their scarves in individual Frankie Welch envelopes, which could also hold promotional material for the client as well as information about Welch herself, so that opening the scarf even after an event would involve a hint of ceremony.

Welch produced some scarves in large quantities and regularly reprinted them to have on hand in her shop (like her Washington, D.C., design that depicts a view of the district from the Veterans Administration building) and for other select retailers (including department stores Hecht's and Woodward & Lothrop).[64] However, most were limited runs for individual clients. Unlike Vera Neumann, who wanted her scarves to be available to everyone, Welch cultivated exclusivity around many of her designs.[65] This increased their value as keepsakes and their ability to convey the particular interests, affiliations, and experiences of their owners.[66] Mary Mathews, wife of the president of the University of Alabama, deemed Welch's scarves for UA "treasured items," and she told Welch that after she gave the first scarf to Betty Ford, who visited the campus in 1978, other scarves were "used for special gifts for national alumni officers, [the] wife of the Ambassador from Singapore and assorted guests like that."[67]

General Louis H. Wilson Jr., commandant of the Marine Corps, presenting a Marine Corps scarf to an unidentified woman, ca. 1980; Frankie Welch Textile Collection, Hargrett Rare Book and Manuscript Library, University of Georgia Libraries.

Some of Welch's scarves served as mementos of specific events, like her daughter Peggy's marriage to Page Williams in 1974, the Virginia Women's Meeting in June 1977 about women's rights, or the meeting of the Women's Auxiliary to the Texas Dental Association in 1978 in Austin. Many of her designs allowed women to proclaim through fashion their involvement in business, academia, and politics, like the scarves for Zonta International, the Delta Sigma Theta sorority founded at Howard University, and the American Association of University Women. Others show allegiances to schools, and she created at least five for the University of Georgia. All of the scarves attested to their wearers' experiences and interests.

One design in particular that reflects the changing role for women in America in the early 1970s is Welch's first scarf for the National Press Club (NPC). The group, founded in Washington in 1908, began presenting speakers with NPC neckties in 1966, several years before opening its membership to women in 1971. When U.S. representative Bella Abzug from New York received a tie after speaking at an NPC luncheon, she said, "I'll give it to my husband and tell him it came from a chauvinistic organization."[68] And when Gloria Steinem received a tie after speaking, she sardonically responded, "Well, I suppose I could put it on and get a jacket and confirm everybody's worst suspicions. Right?"[69] Clearly the group needed an appropriate gift for women, so it turned to Welch for a scarf in

Napachief from the wedding of Peggy Glynn Welch and James Page Williams,
Alexandria, Virginia, 1974, cotton, photo by Mary Linnemann, Hargrett Rare
Book and Manuscript Library; collection of Frankie Welch,
Peggy Welch Williams, and Genie Welch Leisure.

Washington, D.C., scarf, ca. 1978,
polyester, photo by Mary Linnemann,
Hargrett Rare Book and Manuscript
Library; collection of Frankie Welch,
Peggy Welch Williams, and
Genie Welch Leisure.

Frankie Welch scarf envelope, n.d.; private collection.

1973.[70] Her design featured the NPC seal in gold and blue on white. She created a second NPC scarf in 1977 in the line-drawing style with a small NPC seal and pattern of leafy branches. Before settling on the gender-neutral gift of an NPC mug in the 1980s, the National Press Club with Welch's help was able to present its female speakers with a token they appreciated—not only replacing a man's necktie with a woman's scarf, but signaling its acceptance of their involvement by giving them an exclusive memento that they could easily wear to announce their association with a prestigious organization.[71]

Collectively Welch's module scarves provide a unique chronicle of American life, especially in the Washington area, in the 1970s and the first half of the 1980s as she and her peers experienced it. The scarves document the causes they supported, the places they banked, where they studied and worked, the politicians they admired, the businesses they owned. Welch's designs embody the national pride she and her friends and clients felt as they participated in and shaped the culture of the United States. While these associations place almost all of her work within the category of Americana, Welch created several individual designs and series of designs that specifically and intentionally embraced the theme of Americana and came to be career-defining successes.

Zonta International scarf, 1980, polyester, photo by Mary Linnemann, Hargrett Rare Book and Manuscript Library; Frankie Welch Textile Collection, Hargrett Rare Book and Manuscript Library, University of Georgia Libraries.

American Association of University Women scarf, 1981, polyester, photo by Mary Linnemann, Hargrett Rare Book and Manuscript Library; Frankie Welch Textile Collection, Hargrett Rare Book and Manuscript Library, University of Georgia Libraries.

American Association of University Women scarf advertisement, from *Graduate Woman*, March/April 1981; collection of Frankie Welch, Peggy Welch Williams, and Genie Welch Leisure.

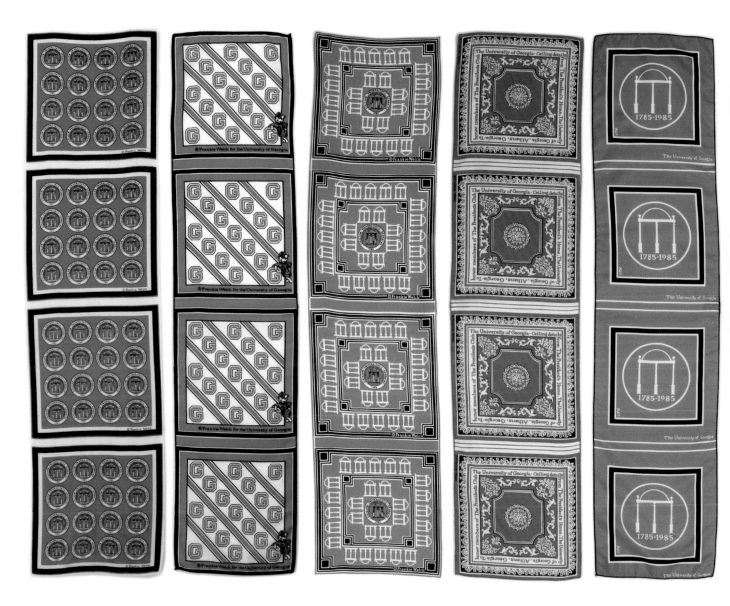

LEFT TO RIGHT:

University of Georgia scarf, ca. 1975, cotton, photo by Mary Linnemann,
Hargrett Rare Book and Manuscript Library; private collection.

University of Georgia scarf, ca. 1977, polyester, photo by Mary Linnemann,
Hargrett Rare Book and Manuscript Library; private collection.

University of Georgia scarf, ca. 1978, polyester, photo by Mary Linnemann,
Hargrett Rare Book and Manuscript Library; private collection.

University of Georgia scarf for the Presidents Club, 1982, polyester, photo by
Mary Linnemann, Hargrett Rare Book and Manuscript Library; private collection.

University of Georgia Bicentennial scarf, 1984, polyester, photo by Mary Linnemann,
Hargrett Rare Book and Manuscript Library; Frankie Welch Collection, Rome Area
History Center.

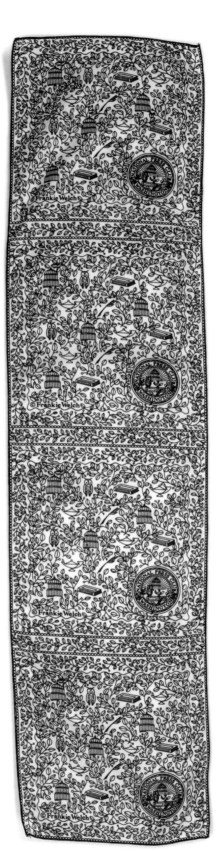

LEFT: National Press Club scarf, 1973, unidentified fabric, photo by Mary Linnemann, Hargrett Rare Book and Manuscript Library; collection of Frankie Welch, Peggy Welch Williams, and Genie Welch Leisure.

RIGHT: National Press Club scarf, 1977, Qiana, photo by Mary Linnemann, Hargrett Rare Book and Manuscript Library; Frankie Welch Textile Collection, Hargrett Rare Book and Manuscript Library, University of Georgia Libraries.

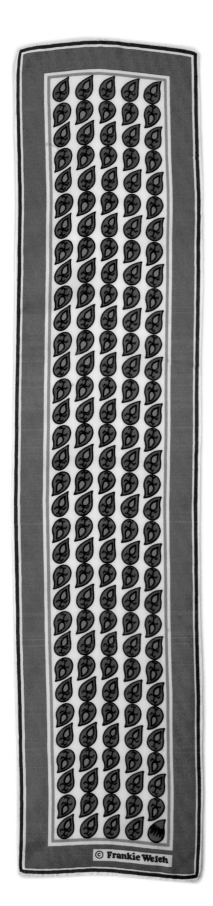

American Water Works Association event, ca. 1970, photo by I. or J. Hugh Campbell, LaGrange, Georgia; Frankie Welch Collection, Rome Area History Center.

American Water Works Association scarf, ca. 1970, unidentified fabric, photo by Mary Linnemann, Hargrett Rare Book and Manuscript Library; Frankie Welch Textile Collection, Hargrett Rare Book and Manuscript Library, University of Georgia Libraries.

LEFT: Virginia Home Economics Association scarf, 1971, silk, photo by Mary Linnemann, Hargrett Rare Book and Manuscript Library; Frankie Welch Collection, Historic Clothing and Textile Collection, College of Family and Consumer Sciences, University of Georgia.

RIGHT: Auto-Train scarf, early 1970s, cotton, photo by Mary Linnemann, Hargrett Rare Book and Manuscript Library; collection of Frankie Welch, Peggy Welch Williams, and Genie Welch Leisure.

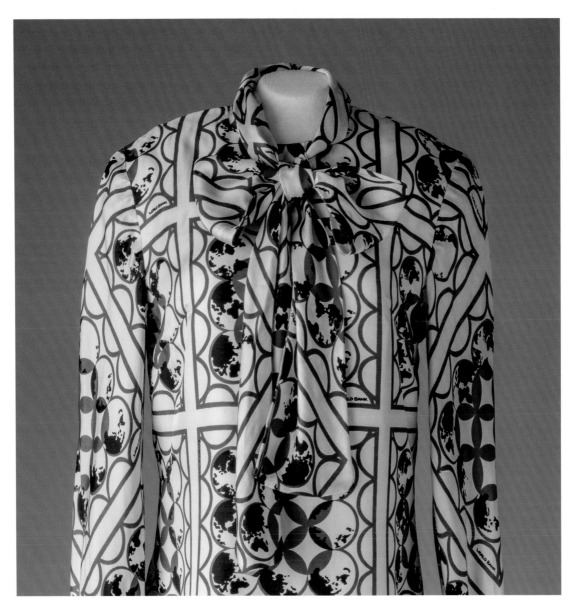

World Bank dress (commissioned, along with scarves, by Margaret McNamara, whose husband Robert was the president of the World Bank Group after serving as secretary of defense), 1971, photo by Michael McKelvey, courtesy of the Hargrett Rare Book and Manuscript Library; Frankie Welch Collection, Rome Area History Center.

LEFT: Nautical Flags scarf (for a marina in Maryland, flags spell out West River, later used as shop stock), designed 1972, polyester, photo by Mary Linnemann, Hargrett Rare Book and Manuscript Library; Frankie Welch Textile Collection, Hargrett Rare Book and Manuscript Library, University of Georgia Libraries.

RIGHT: Bert Lance for Governor of Georgia scarf, 1974, Qiana, photo by Mary Linnemann, Hargrett Rare Book and Manuscript Library; Frankie Welch Textile Collection, Hargrett Rare Book and Manuscript Library, University of Georgia Libraries.

Clyde's (a restaurant in Georgetown) scarf, ca. 1973, Qiana, photo by Mary Linnemann, Hargrett Rare Book and Manuscript Library; Frankie Welch Textile Collection, Hargrett Rare Book and Manuscript Library, University of Georgia Libraries.

Marymount College (Arlington, Va.) napachief, ca. 1974, cotton, photo by Mary Linnemann, Hargrett Rare Book and Manuscript Library; Frankie Welch Textile Collection, Hargrett Rare Book and Manuscript Library, University of Georgia Libraries.

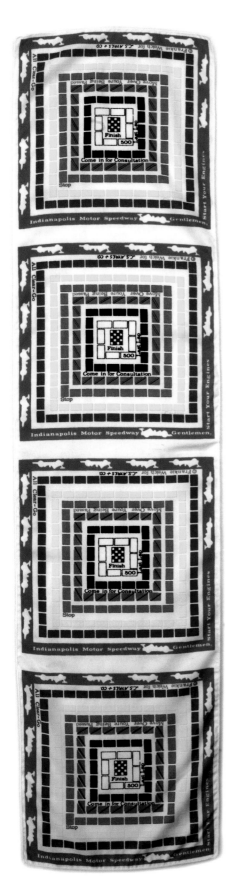
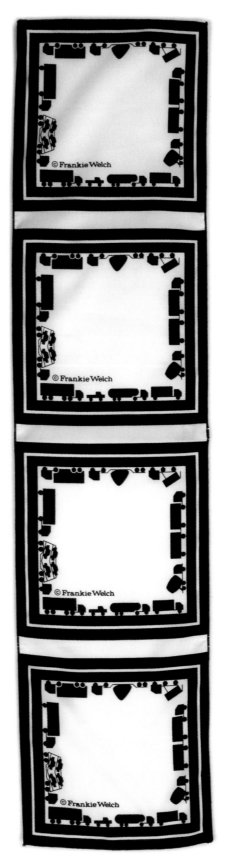

LEFT: Indianapolis Motor Speedway, L. S. Ayres & Co., scarf, 1974, unidentified fabric, photo by Mary Linnemann, Hargrett Rare Book and Manuscript Library; collection of Frankie Welch, Peggy Welch Williams, and Genie Welch Leisure.

RIGHT: American Trucking Associations scarf, ca. 1975, Qiana, photo by Mary Linnemann, Hargrett Rare Book and Manuscript Library; Frankie Welch Textile Collection, Hargrett Rare Book and Manuscript Library, University of Georgia Libraries.

LEFT TO RIGHT:

Christmas Trees scarf, designed early 1970s, polyester, photo by Mary Linnemann, Hargrett Rare Book and Manuscript Library; Frankie Welch Textile Collection, Hargrett Rare Book and Manuscript Library, University of Georgia Libraries.

Country Curtains for Jack and Jane Fitzpatrick scarf, 1976, Qiana, photo by Mary Linnemann, Hargrett Rare Book and Manuscript Library; Frankie Welch Textile Collection, Hargrett Rare Book and Manuscript Library, University of Georgia Libraries.

Gum Drop Square scarf, ca. 1976, Qiana, photo by Mary Linnemann, Hargrett Rare Book and Manuscript Library; Frankie Welch Textile Collection, Hargrett Rare Book and Manuscript Library, University of Georgia Libraries.

Duvall House American Ironwork scarf (used as gifts by the State Department), 1976, polyester, photo by Mary Linnemann, Hargrett Rare Book and Manuscript Library; private collection.

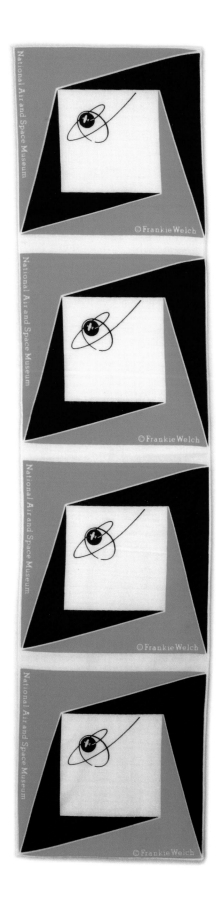

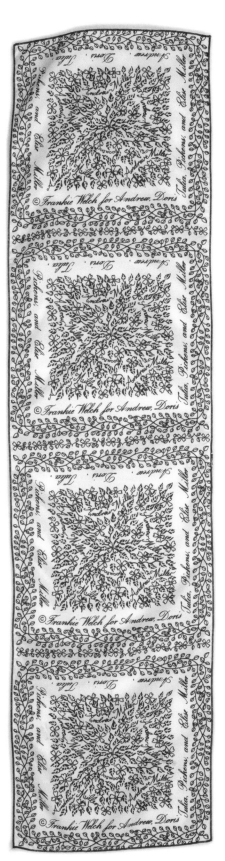

LEFT: National Air and Space Museum, Smithsonian Institution, scarf, 1976, cotton, photo by Mary Linnemann, Hargrett Rare Book and Manuscript Library; Frankie Welch Textile Collection, Hargrett Rare Book and Manuscript Library, University of Georgia Libraries.

RIGHT: Andrew Miller campaign for governor of Virginia scarf, 1976, Qiana, photo by Mary Linnemann, Hargrett Rare Book and Manuscript Library; Frankie Welch Textile Collection, Hargrett Rare Book and Manuscript Library, University of Georgia Libraries.

Models wearing Clyde's scarf and neck tie, ca. 1976; collection of Frankie Welch, Peggy Welch Williams, and Genie Welch Leisure.

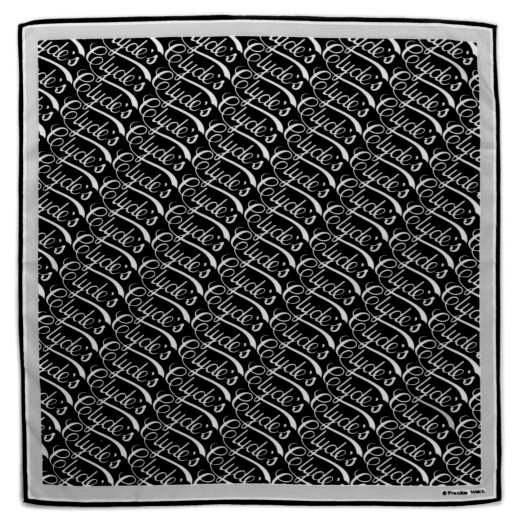

Clyde's (a restaurant in Georgetown) scarf, ca. 1976, Qiana, photo by Mary Linnemann, Hargrett Rare Book and Manuscript Library; Frankie Welch Textile Collection, Hargrett Rare Book and Manuscript Library, University of Georgia Libraries.

Alexandria Junior Woman's Club Embassy Tour flyer, 1977; Frankie Welch Collection, Rome Area History Center.

Alexandria Junior Woman's Club Embassy Tour scarf, 1977, Qiana, photo by Mary Linnemann, Hargrett Rare Book and Manuscript Library; collection of Frankie Welch, Peggy Welch Williams, and Genie Welch Leisure.

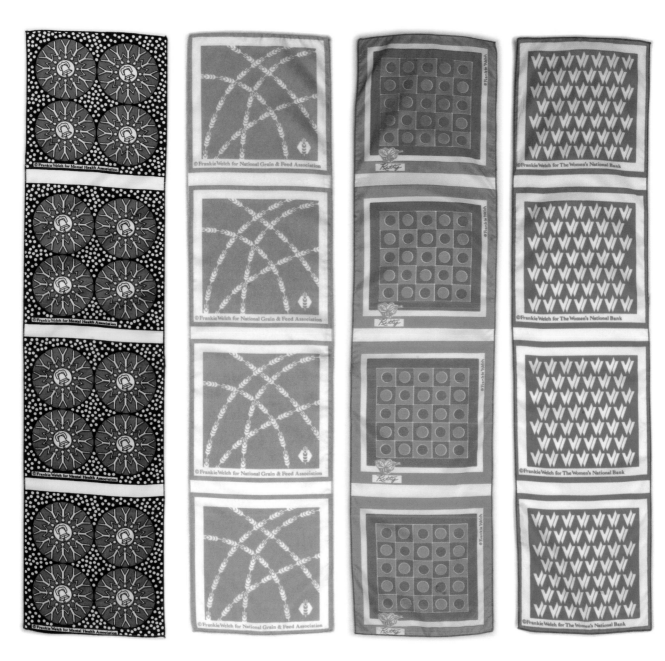

LEFT TO RIGHT:

Mental Health Association scarf, 1977, Qiana, photo by Mary Linnemann, Hargrett Rare Book and Manuscript Library; collection of Frankie Welch, Peggy Welch Williams, and Genie Welch Leisure.

National Grain and Feed Association scarf, 1977, Qiana, photo by Mary Linnemann, Hargrett Rare Book and Manuscript Library; Frankie Welch Textile Collection, Hargrett Rare Book and Manuscript Library, University of Georgia Libraries.

Kitty Rotruck scarf, 1977, Qiana, photo by Mary Linnemann, Hargrett Rare Book and Manuscript Library; Frankie Welch Textile Collection, Hargrett Rare Book and Manuscript Library, University of Georgia Libraries.

Women's National Bank scarf, 1977, Qiana, photo by Mary Linnemann, Hargrett Rare Book and Manuscript Library; Frankie Welch Textile Collection, Hargrett Rare Book and Manuscript Library, University of Georgia Libraries.

LEFT: Mount Vernon College scarf, 1977, Qiana, photo by Mary Linnemann, Hargrett Rare Book and Manuscript Library; Frankie Welch Textile Collection, Hargrett Rare Book and Manuscript Library, University of Georgia Libraries.

RIGHT: University of Virginia scarf, 1977, Qiana, photo by Mary Linnemann, Hargrett Rare Book and Manuscript Library; Frankie Welch Textile Collection, Hargrett Rare Book and Manuscript Library, University of Georgia Libraries.

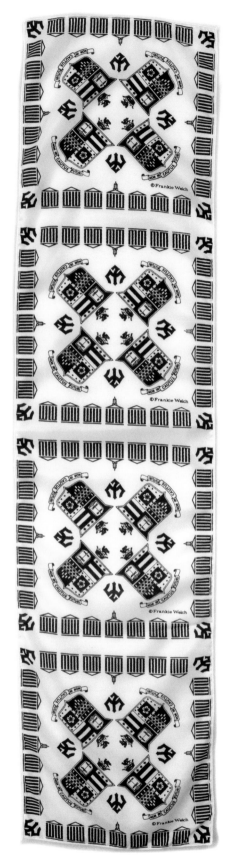

Washington and Lee scarf advertisement from Washington and Lee's _Alumni Magazine_, September 1978; Courtesy of Special Collections, Washington and Lee University.

Washington and Lee scarf, 1978, Qiana, photo by Mary Linnemann, Hargrett Rare Book and Manuscript Library; Frankie Welch Textile Collection, Hargrett Rare Book and Manuscript Library, University of Georgia Libraries.

University of Alabama napachief, 1978, cotton, photo by Mary Linnemann,
Hargrett Rare Book and Manuscript Library; Frankie Welch Textile Collection,
Hargrett Rare Book and Manuscript Library, University of Georgia Libraries.

LEFT TO RIGHT:

Tobacco Institute scarf, 1978, cotton, photo by Mary Linnemann, Hargrett Rare Book and Manuscript Library;
Frankie Welch Textile Collection, Hargrett Rare Book and Manuscript Library, University of Georgia Libraries.

Women's Auxiliary to the Texas Dental Association scarf, 1978, polyester, photo by Mary Linnemann,
Hargrett Rare Book and Manuscript Library; Frankie Welch Textile Collection, Hargrett Rare Book and Manuscript
Library, University of Georgia Libraries.

Atlanta Dogwood Festival scarf, 1978, Qiana, photo by Mary Linnemann, Hargrett Rare Book and Manuscript Library;
Frankie Welch Textile Collection, Hargrett Rare Book and Manuscript Library, University of Georgia Libraries.

United Virginia Bank scarf, 1978, polyester, photo by Mary Linnemann, Hargrett Rare Book and Manuscript Library;
Frankie Welch Textile Collection, Hargrett Rare Book and Manuscript Library, University of Georgia Libraries.

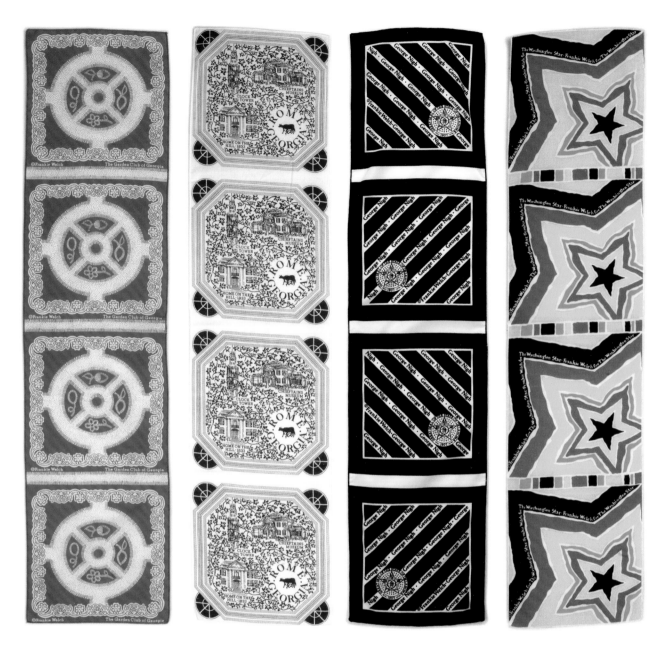

LEFT TO RIGHT:

Garden Club of Georgia scarf, 1978, polyester, photo by Mary Linnemann, Hargrett Rare Book and Manuscript Library; Frankie Welch Textile Collection, Hargrett Rare Book and Manuscript Library, University of Georgia Libraries.

Rome, Georgia, scarf, 1978, cotton, photo by Mary Linnemann, Hargrett Rare Book and Manuscript Library; Frankie Welch Textile Collection, Hargrett Rare Book and Manuscript Library, University of Georgia Libraries.

George Nigh campaign for governor of Oklahoma scarf, 1978, Qiana, photo by Mary Linnemann, Hargrett Rare Book and Manuscript Library; collection of Frankie Welch, Peggy Welch Williams, and Genie Welch Leisure.

Washington Star scarf, 1979, cotton, photo by Mary Linnemann, Hargrett Rare Book and Manuscript Library; collection of Frankie Welch, Peggy Welch Williams, and Genie Welch Leisure.

the S.A.M.E. SCARF by FRANKIE WELCH

At last something really special for our S.A.M.E. ladies. FRANKIE WELCH is a widely recognized fabric and scarf designer whose clientele has included four of our first ladies. She has now designed a symbolic S.A.M.E. scarf consisting of four identical squares—each square containing a group of subtle but distinguishable S.A.M.E. logos in a field of wreaths and crests in true engineer red on a white field. The scarf is 8" by 34."

The ideal gift for the S.A.M.E. wife or girl friend—and super for Lady S.A.M.E. members. Special "package" offer to Posts and Regions ordering in quantity.

Mail to: The Society of American Military Engineers, 740 15th St., N.W., Suite 905, Washington, DC 20005 (202) 638-4010

Please send _____ Scarves at $10.00 each.

Name _____
Street _____
City _____
State/Zip _____

THE MILITARY ENGINEER, NO. 460

Society of American Military Engineers scarf flyer, 1979; Frankie Welch Collection, Rome Area History Center.

St. Luke's Episcopal Church (Alexandria, Va.) scarf, 1979, polyester, photo by Mary Linnemann, Hargrett Rare Book and Manuscript Library; Frankie Welch Collection, Historic Clothing and Textile Collection, College of Family and Consumer Sciences, University of Georgia.

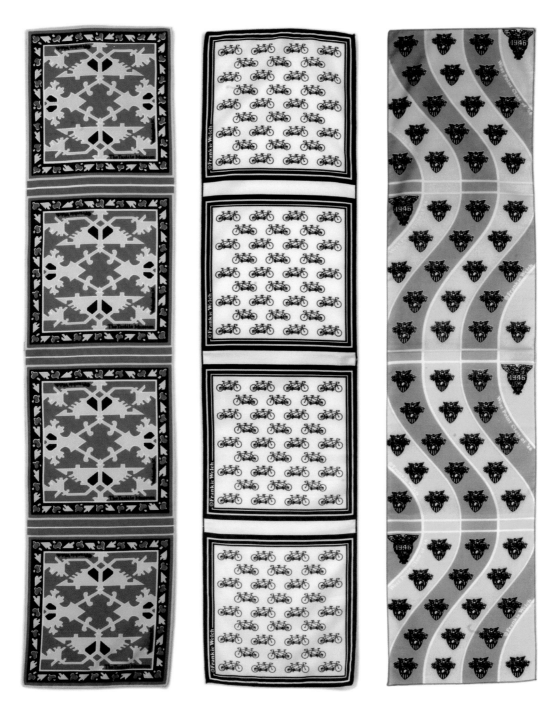

Textile Museum (Washington, D.C.) scarf, 1980, polyester, photo by Mary Linnemann, Hargrett Rare Book and Manuscript Library; Frankie Welch Textile Collection, Hargrett Rare Book and Manuscript Library, University of Georgia Libraries.

Tandem Computers (California) scarf, 1981, polyester, photo by Mary Linnemann, Hargrett Rare Book and Manuscript Library; Frankie Welch Textile Collection, Hargrett Rare Book and Manuscript Library, University of Georgia Libraries.

West Point Class of '46 scarf, 1981, polyester, photo by Mary Linnemann, Hargrett Rare Book and Manuscript Library; Frankie Welch Textile Collection, Hargrett Rare Book and Manuscript Library, University of Georgia Libraries.

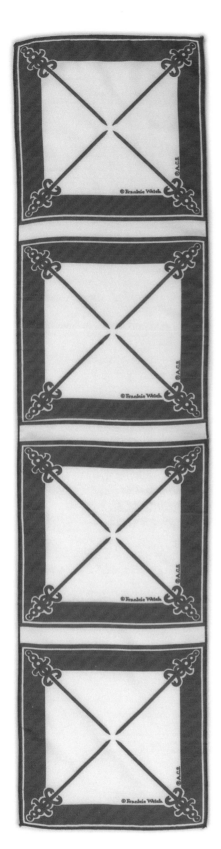

Frankie Welch with Elizabeth Taylor and Barbara Bush at an American Cancer Society event at the Tysons Corner Marriott Hotel (*left to right*: Joe Thiesmann, Eddy Dalton, Frankie Welch, Elizabeth Taylor, Barbara Bush, unidentified), 1981; Frankie Welch Collection, Rome Area History Center.

American Cancer Society scarf, 1981, polyester, photo by Mary Linnemann, Hargrett Rare Book and Manuscript Library; collection of Frankie Welch, Peggy Welch Williams, and Genie Welch Leisure.

Fourteenth Centennial of Islam napachief 1982, unidentified synthetic fabric,
photo by Mary Linnemann, Hargrett Rare Book and Manuscript Library; collection
of Frankie Welch, Peggy Welch Williams, and Genie Welch Leisure.

Berry College napachief, 1983, polyester, photo by Mary Linnemann,
Hargrett Rare Book and Manuscript Library; Frankie Welch Collection,
Rome Area History Center.

Georgia College scarf, 1984, polyester, photo by Mary Linnemann, Hargrett Rare Book and Manuscript Library; Frankie Welch Collection, Historic Clothing and Textile Collection, College of Family and Consumer Sciences, University of Georgia.

Chapter 4
Americana Scarves and Garments

As early as 1969, a reporter for a California newspaper called Frankie Welch's contributions to fashion "uniquely Americana."[1] In the ensuing years, the designation was repeatedly applied to Welch's work, including by the Smithsonian's Museum of History and Technology (now the National Museum of American History), which in 1979 featured many of her scarves from its collection in the book *Threads of History: Americana Recorded on Cloth, 1775 to the Present* by Herbert Ridgeway Collins, showing them as the newest in a long line of Americana textiles. Though always somewhat nebulous in meaning, in the 1960s and 1970s the term "Americana" generally suggested early American antiques, folk art, colonial revival designs, or simply anything in a red, white, and blue color scheme. In fashion it could mean inspiration from the military, the trappers of the frontier era, Native Americans, or iconic pastimes like baseball, as well as the use of fabrics associated with the Old West such as denim, calico, and gingham.[2] The term typically indicated patriotism and nostalgia. While "Americana" encompassed nearly all of Welch's scarves, including ones related to politics and branding, it was most closely linked to her Native American–influenced designs and her creations for the U.S. Bicentennial.

One of Welch's early and distinctly Americana scarves, though, was not for the Bicentennial or inspired by Native American designs. Instead, for her Fifty State Flowers scarf, she took inspiration from a keenly American source that was itself described as "pure Americana": the White House china ordered by Lady Bird Johnson from Tiffany & Co. in 1967 that features wildflowers from the United States bordering the dinner plates and state flowers painted on the dessert plates.[3] Though most of the flowers on her scarf are clustered in bunches, Welch placed the Cherokee rose, Georgia's state flower, alone in the center, honoring her own heritage. At first the scarf appears as a straightforward, pretty floral design, but

OPPOSITE: Fifty State Flowers dress, ca. 1970, photo by Michael McKelvey, courtesy of the Hargrett Rare Book and Manuscript Library; Frankie Welch Collection, Rome Area History Center.

RIGHT: Photo by Mary Linnemann, Hargrett Rare Book and Manuscript Library; private collection.

Fifty State Flowers scarf, 1970, Supima cotton, photo by Mary Linnemann, Hargrett Rare Book and Manuscript Library; collection of Frankie Welch, Peggy Welch Williams, and Genie Welch Leisure.

Welch's references to the White House, the nation's flora, and her home state elevate it to a clear expression of Americana. The *Oakland (Calif.) Tribune* even described both Welch and Supima, the luxury cotton from the Southwest on which the scarf was printed, as "pure Americana," and the scarf as an example of "the gentlest, prettiest patriotic flag-waving seen to date."[4]

Heightening its Americana-ness, the Fifty State Flowers scarf was introduced to the garden clubs of Washington, D.C., on May Day 1970 at the annual Flower Mart at Washington National Cathedral, and the wife of the secretary of the interior, Ermalee Hickel, received the first one.[5] Also, as with many of her scarf designs, Welch made dresses of the fabric, and the event's chairperson, Sally Parkinson, wore one for the occasion, while Hickel ordered one to have as a summer evening dress.[6] A surviving dress, with its long skirt and slightly puffed shoulders, reflects the era's desire for romantic, pastoral-style clothing.

Like the Cherokee rose in the center of the Fifty State Flowers scarf, the Cherokee Alphabet scarf, for Welch, reflected her country's history and fit the Americana theme. It remained her bestseller, and she had it reprinted at least forty-five times in a variety of colors on different fabrics, in slight modifications to the original design as well as in a vertically oriented version referred to in business records as Running Cherokee.[7] Welch's personal fondness for the design was reflected in the interior of her shop, where she lined the walls of the entrance hall with 513 of the scarves.[8] In this small space, Welch also used the print as curtains, upholstery, and a tablecloth, demonstrating the design's flexibility and her creativity.

The Cherokee Alphabet design adapted well to clothing, and Welch used it for coat linings, dresses, and a bathing suit, and she printed it on tote bags.[9] Frances Cawthon of the *Atlanta Constitution* wrote that she "once observed that the most elegant woman in a chic gambling casino on the French Riviera" was wearing a Cherokee Alphabet Frankie.[10] By June 1970 Welch offered Cherokee Alphabet short dresses and pantsuits in polyester for fifty or seventy-five dollars.[11] Wearing pants was still a little edgy for some of her customers in the early 1970s, and she did not recommend them for every occasion, noting, "I still use discretion in wearing a pants suit." Welch acknowledged, though, as journalist Helen Thomas reported, that "the young secretaries on Capitol Hill [were] beginning to buy pants suits for the office."[12] One of

Model wearing a Fifty State Flowers dress, ca. 1970; Frankie Welch Collection, Rome Area History Center.

Peggy Welch Williams with a Cherokee Alphabet tote bag, 1977; collection of Frankie Welch, Peggy Welch Williams, and Genie Welch Leisure.

Genie Welch and Peggy Welch Williams wearing Cherokee Alphabet Frankies, 1977; collection of Frankie Welch, Peggy Welch Williams, and Genie Welch Leisure.

Running Cherokee scarf, designed ca. 1971, silk, photo by Mary Linnemann, Hargrett Rare Book and Manuscript Library; Frankie Welch Collection, Historic Clothing and Textile Collection, College of Family and Consumer Sciences, University of Georgia.

OPPOSITE: Frankie Welch in the entrance hall of Frankie Welch of Virginia, 1971, photo by Harry Naltchayan; collection of Frankie Welch, Peggy Welch Williams, and Genie Welch Leisure.

Nancy Ziegler (wife of President Nixon's press secretary, Ron Ziegler) wearing a Cherokee Alphabet pantsuit, 1970, *Washington Star* photograph, reprinted with permission of the D.C. Public Library, Star Collection © *Washington Post*; Frankie Welch Collection, Rome Area History Center.

OPPOSITE: Cherokee Alphabet pantsuits, ca. 1970, photo by Michael McKelvey, courtesy of the Hargrett Rare Book and Manuscript Library; (*left*) private collection and (*right*) Frankie Welch Collection, Rome Area History Center.

her Cherokee Alphabet pantsuits, paired with a long scarf, appeared in *Vogue* in November 1970 on a model in an advertisement for the liqueur Bénédictine.[13] Closer to home, Miss Georgia U.S.A. wore a Cherokee Alphabet top and hot pants with tall boots in 1971, and Welch designed a custom uniform for the drum majorette of the West Rome High School's marching band in 1974, with a jacket made from Cherokee Alphabet, white wool shorts, tall boots, and a Cherokee Alphabet scarf.[14]

In another fashion achievement for Welch, Le Drugstore, a trendy American-themed boutique and eatery on the Champs-Élysées near the Arc de Triomphe in Paris, sold her Cherokee Alphabet scarves.[15] The *Washington Post and Times Herald* described the Cherokee Alphabet wares as "Pioneer gear" featuring "authentic American Indian characters," and Eleni in the *Washington Star* added that Le Drugstore could not "keep enough of the Cherokee scarves in stock to satisfy a Wild

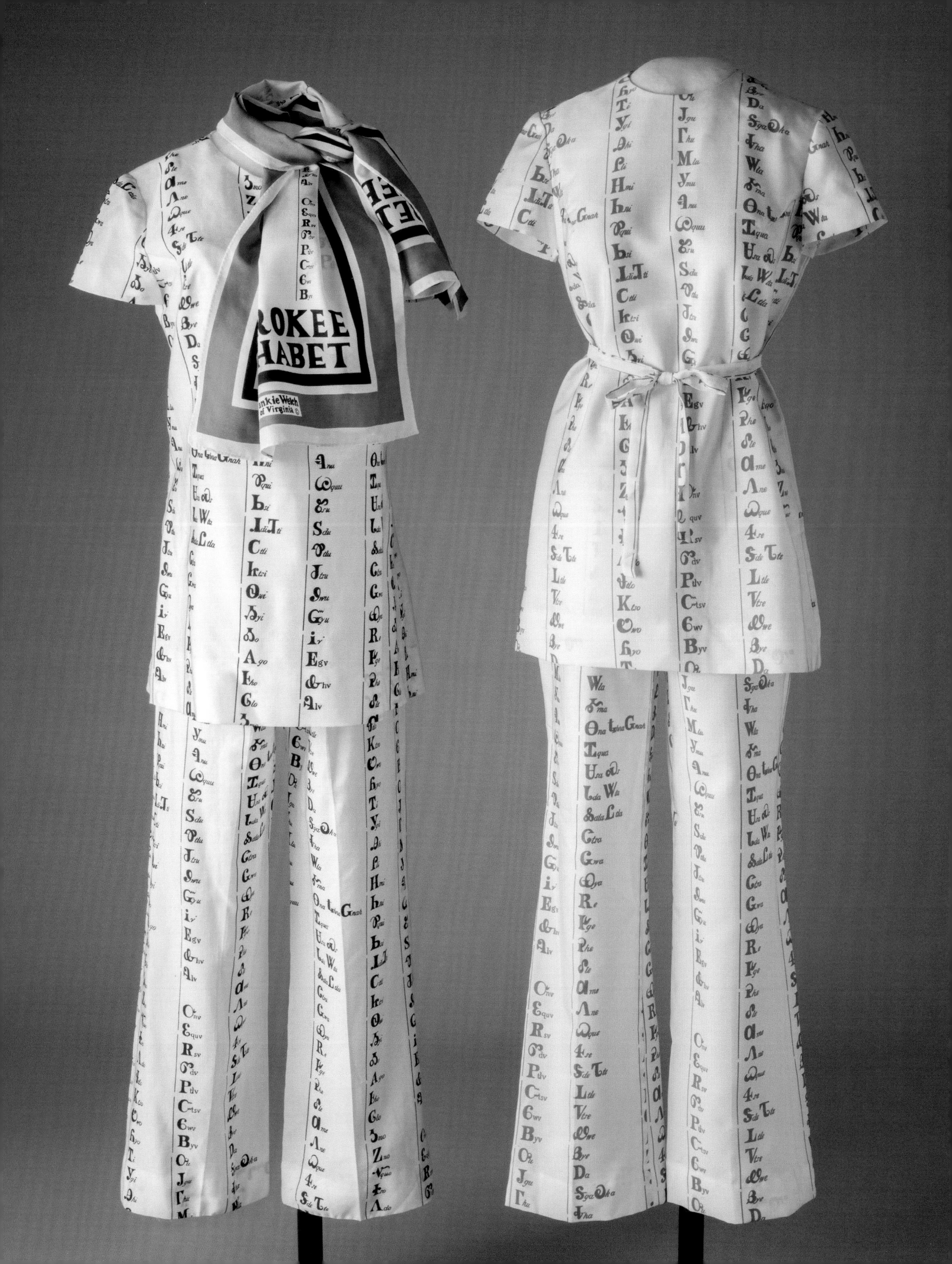
ROKEE
HABET
ankie Welch
of Virginia

LaDonna and Fred Harris on
The Dick Cavett Show, July 13, 1970.

West-loving Gallic public," clearly demonstrating that the design qualified as Americana abroad too.[16]

One important relationship for Welch regarding her Cherokee Alphabet design was with LaDonna Harris, a prominent Native American rights activist and then-wife of the Oklahoma senator Fred Harris (in office 1964–73). When Harris first met Welch during a visit to the shop in Alexandria with a few other congressional wives in the mid-1960s, Welch was thrilled to learn that Harris is Comanche. Harris recalls, "She just got very, very excited and we became friends instantly."[17] Harris modeled at Welch's show of Vera Maxwell's Native American–inspired fashion in 1966, and, when Welch was preparing to design her original Cherokee Alphabet scarf, Harris helped her find a clear copy of the syllabary.

Harris wore several Cherokee Alphabet outfits, including a Cherokee Alphabet top (with the borders forming an X across the front) and skirt to a party before the Democratic National Convention in Chicago in 1968 hosted by Mr. and Mrs. Jules Lederer (columnist Ann Landers).[18] In 1970 she donned a Cherokee Alphabet pantsuit and a Cherokee Alphabet scarf with a brown border to a party she and her husband helped host in Manhattan honoring American Indians.[19] Harris wore the pantsuit again on the *Dick Cavett Show*, making a grand fashion statement with the eye-catching black-and-white design paired with a long turquoise-bordered Cherokee Alphabet scarf that billowed elegantly as she and her husband walked onto the set.[20]

Harris received many compliments when she wore Cherokee Alphabet garments, and she recognized that the imagery intrigued people and provided her with a way to start talking with them, and educating them, about

Indian issues. Harris explained that expanding education about Native Americans was and is one of her passions, and that Welch "just fed into it" and felt the same way. Harris added, "We had an uphill climb for everything we tried to do for Native Americans, but that [Cherokee Alphabet design] really helped me because it was such a conversation piece."[21]

Other prominent Native Americans wore Welch's Cherokee Alphabet designs as well. In photographs from the Twenty-First Annual Cherokee National Holiday in Tahlequah, Oklahoma, in 1973, published in the *Cherokee Nation News*, Principal Chief W. W. Keeler appears wearing a Cherokee Alphabet robe or jacket and prominent pastor and teacher Sam Hider is shown wearing a Cherokee Alphabet shirt.[22] Decades later, Wilma Mankiller, the first female principal chief of the Cherokee Nation, was photographed wearing a long Cherokee Alphabet scarf, an image that accompanied her obituary in *Time* magazine in 2010.[23]

With the success of her Cherokee Alphabet designs, Welch continued to include Native American–inspired elements in her work. By late 1971 she introduced a turtle design based on a piece of pottery found in Arizona.[24] She repeated the turtle motif in a four-by-four grid with a modified Greek key border to create a standard module for scarves, and she printed yardage that she used for garments including Frankie dresses, nightgowns, pajamas, bikini pants, and bras.[25] Welch often, at least through the mid-1970s, included a turtle or two with her signature, much as Vera Neumann used a ladybug with hers.[26] Rather than drawing on the spiritual meanings of the turtle among Native Americans, Welch viewed the turtle as a symbol of travelers and printed posters of the turtle with the words, "Behold the turtle! He makes progress only when he sticks his neck out," meaning that it is necessary to take chances in order to move forward.[27]

Cherokee Alphabet and Turtles were two of the fabrics, along with the Genie design and solid colors, that Welch used when she promoted Frankies nationally in 1971, working with a factory in Tennessee to have them made for both women and girls.[28] The first department store to order Frankies was Rich's in Atlanta, which sold them in all eight of its locations and created dedicated areas to display Welch's wares.[29] Joel Goldberg, senior vice president and general merchandise manager for Rich's, praised the collection as something that he believed would be popular in the Atlanta market, adding, "Her kind of chic conforms to the natural elegance of the Southern way of life."[30] As a native Georgian, Welch found it meaningful to have the famous southern store appreciate her designs.[31] Her authority as a southern voice in fashion was underscored at the time by her role as fashion editor for *Southern Living* magazine.[32]

LaDonna Harris and Fred R. Harris voting in the presidential election, 1968; LaDonna Harris Papers and Americans for Indian Opportunity Records, University of New Mexico Center for Southwest Research.

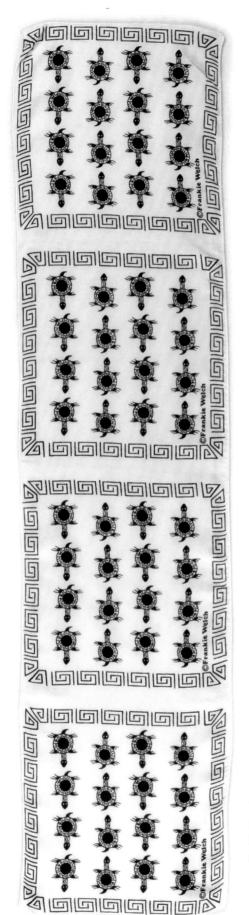

Models wearing Turtles and Cherokee Alphabet Frankies, ca. 1971,
photo by Nolen E. Williamson, Austin, Texas; collection of Frankie Welch,
Peggy Welch Williams, and Genie Welch Leisure.

Turtles scarf, designed ca. 1971, Qiana, photo by
Mary Linnemann, Hargrett Rare Book and Manuscript
Library; collection of Frankie Welch, Peggy Welch Williams,
and Genie Welch Leisure.

Adele Furin and Katie Jewell modeling Turtles Frankies, 1971; Frankie Welch Collection, Rome Area History Center.

Woman wearing a Frankie with the Genie design, ca. 1971; Frankie Welch Collection, Rome Area History Center.

SHORT CHEROKEE PRINT
WITH WHITE TOP IN
SIZES 4 TO 8, 16.00

BLACK OR
BROWN
TURTLES
IN WHITE
SIZES 4 TO 8
18.00

INTRODUCING
LITTLE
FRANKIE

THE
LITTLE FRANKIE
TIES JUST LIKE
THE BIG FRANKIE—
IN 8 DIFFERENT
WAYS

LEFT: Hightower advertisement, from the *Daily Oklahoman*, April 24, 1972; Frankie Welch Collection, Rome Area History Center.

RIGHT: Folded tag for "Little Frankie," ca. 1971; collection of Frankie Welch, Peggy Welch Williams, and Genie Welch Leisure.

Frankie Welch display in Rich's Department Store, Atlanta, Georgia, 1971; collection of Frankie Welch, Peggy Welch Williams, and Genie Welch Leisure.

Rena Peck modeling a red wool Frankie for Rich's Department Store, Atlanta, Georgia, 1971;
Frankie Welch Collection, Rome Area History Center.

Models at the Woman's Club Fiesta Flower and Fashion Show, San Antonio, Texas, presented by Joske's, 1972, photo by Nolen W. Williamson, Austin, Texas; Frankie Welch Collection, Rome Area History Center.

Model (Del) at the Woman's Club Fiesta Flower and Fashion Show, San Antonio, Texas, presented by Joske's, 1972, photo by Ron Jones, *San Antonio News*; Frankie Welch Collection, Rome Area History Center.

Welch soon had her Frankies featured in one hundred boutiques and department stores across the South, including Joske's of San Antonio, Texas. For the Woman's Club Fiesta Flower and Fashion Show in San Antonio in 1972, presented by Joske's, Welch designed special Frankies with confetti and balloon appliqués inspired by the city's annual fiesta—again using elements that her contemporaries would have interpreted as Americana.[33] Another early fashion show, notable because numerous snapshots of it survive, took place in Willemstad, Curaçao, at the U.S. Consulate General, in 1971, with models wearing various Frankie dresses and assorted garments with the Turtles design.

In 1973, after considering the idea for two years and consulting with a representative of the Goldwaters department stores in Arizona, Welch launched four additional American Indian–inspired scarf designs—Thunderbird, Roadrunner, Basket Weave, and Squash Blossom—as well as new fashions, a line of jewelry, and a book titled *Indian Jewelry*.[34]

OPPOSITE: Anne Oliver modeling the Genie Frankie in front of the super graphics in Rich's Park, 1971, Atlanta, Georgia; Frankie Welch Collection, Rome Area History Center.

Fashion show in Willemstad, Curaçao, at the
U.S. Consulate General (Frankie Welch at the
microphone), 1971; Frankie Welch Collection,
Rome Area History Center.

Fashion show in Willemstad, Curaçao, at the U.S. Consulate
General (Frankie Welch front row, second from left), 1971;
collection of Frankie Welch, Peggy Welch Williams, and
Genie Welch Leisure.

Fashion show in Willemstad, Curaçao, at the U.S. Consulate General, 1971; collection of Frankie Welch, Peggy Welch Williams, and Genie Welch Leisure.

Fashion show in Willemstad, Curaçao, at the U.S. Consulate General, 1971; Frankie Welch Collection, Rome Area History Center.

Model in Curaçao wearing a dress with a Turtles design, 1971; collection of
Frankie Welch, Peggy Welch Williams, and Genie Welch Leisure.

Model in Curaçao wearing a Genie Frankie with a matching pillow and handbag, 1971,
collection of Frankie Welch, Peggy Welch Williams, and Genie Welch Leisure.

Frankie Welch with Cherokee baskets in Frankie Welch of Virginia, 1973, *Alexandria Gazette* staff photo, courtesy *Alexandria Gazette Packet*; collection of Frankie Welch, Peggy Welch Williams, and Genie Welch Leisure.

LEFT: Thunderbird scarf, 1973, cotton, photo by Mary Linnemann, Hargrett Rare Book and Manuscript Library; collection of Frankie Welch, Peggy Welch Williams, and Genie Welch Leisure.

RIGHT: Basket Weave scarf, 1973, silk, photo by Mary Linnemann, Hargrett Rare Book and Manuscript Library; collection of Frankie Welch, Peggy Welch Williams, and Genie Welch Leisure.

Roadrunner napachief, 1973, cotton, photo by Mary
Linnemann, Hargrett Rare Book and Manuscript Library;
Frankie Welch Collection, Rome Area History Center.

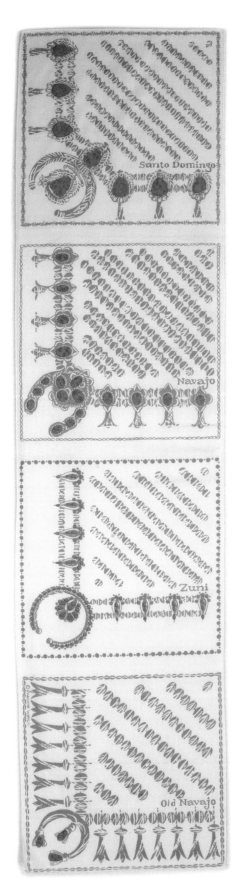

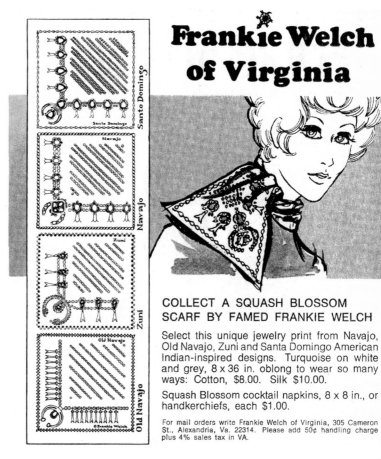

Squash Blossom scarf advertisement, 1973 (ran in *Washingtonian*, July 1973, 47);
Frankie Welch Collection, Rome Area History Center.

Squash Blossom scarf, 1973, cotton, photo by Mary
Linnemann, Hargrett Rare Book and Manuscript Library;
collection of Frankie Welch, Peggy Welch Williams,
and Genie Welch Leisure.

The nationally famous Washington designer, Frankie Welch, helps Hightower celebrate the Arts Festival with her new summer collection and will be in the store

Frankie's Back in Town!

Friday. Come enjoy with us her vivid evocations of American Indian motifs in the famed "Frankie" dresses and accessories. Wonderful colors, new prints—the Thunderbird, Squash Blossom, Roadrunner. And Frankie, the inimitable . . . all at Hightower. Frankie Fashions will be modeled in the store and at lunch in our Cellar Restaurant. Shown: the tie-it-eight-ways Frankie; orange or turquoise, patchwork Thunderbird appliqué, 90.00.

HIGHTOWER
COLCORD STREET AT HUDSON ON CIVIC CENTER

Hightower advertisement from the *Daily Oklahoman*, April 13, 1973; Frankie Welch Collection, Rome Area History Center.

OPPOSITE: Basket Weave Frankie and Turtles Frankie, n.d., photo by Michael McKelvey, courtesy of the Hargrett Rare Book and Manuscript Library; Frankie Welch Textile Collection, Hargrett Rare Book and Manuscript Library, University of Georgia Libraries.

The Basket Weave design depicts four woven patterns of Cherokee baskets (Peace Pipe, Box, Single Diamond, and Jacob's Ladder), while the Squash Blossom scarf shows four variations of the iconic silver and turquoise Squash Blossom necklaces (Santo Domingo, Navajo, Zuni, and Old Navajo)—one in each module.[35]

Welch premiered her new designs at the Annual Cherry Blossom Luncheon (coordinated each year by the Washington Fashion Group as part of the Cherry Blossom Festival) in 1973 in Washington, where attendees included First Lady Pat Nixon and Second Lady Judy Agnew.[36] The theme was Native American dress and jewelry, and the event featured Native Americans in traditional dress, fashion and jewelry by Native Americans, and Native American–inspired designs by Welch and other American designers such as Betsey Johnson, Halston, Donald Brooks, and Pierre Cardin.[37] Susan Goldwater (then-wife of California representative Barry Goldwater Jr.) was one of the models, and Goldwaters, which her husband's grandfather founded, sponsored the luncheon.

Welch then traveled west to present her summer fashion collection at Goldwaters in Phoenix, which advertised her designs as "inspired by Arizona and our Indian culture."[38] Goldwaters hosted a series of events to promote Welch's designs, including fashion shows at their stores, the local country club, and the Arizona Costume Institute at the Phoenix Art Museum.[39] Goldwaters used the Squash Blossom fabric as a wall covering in a boutique corner it created to feature her designs.[40] She also showed her designs at Hightower, an upscale shop in Oklahoma City, Oklahoma, where her fashions were modeled in the store and during lunch in the store's gourmet Cellar Restaurant.[41]

The garments Welch presented at these events included a Frankie with a patchwork appliquéd thunderbird "in Arizona colors of orange and white or all turquoise," a long dress in turquoise or white with a high and wide waistband, and a short "wrap-and-tie apron dress" with the Cherokee Alphabet in turquoise, as well as Frankies of the scarf patterns.[42] The fashion reporter for the *Arizona Republic*, Ellie Schultz, described one event: "Mrs. Welch's contribution to the showing of her creations locally (at the Phoenix Country Club) was to patter along the runway herself, tie and untie the Frankie dress, show her ideas on tying scarves, and to send out good feelings to the women present." She quoted Welch explaining, "If you send out good feelings . . . others will receive them and be happy and good to you in return."[43]

Of her line of jewelry, manufactured by the costume jeweler Freirich, Welch explained, "Each design . . . is based on an ancient Indian piece. All the components are real—steel, ivory, bone, leather, wood, copper." Welch's view of these preindustrial materials

Woman wearing a necklace designed by Frankie Welch, 1974; collection of Frankie Welch, Peggy Welch Williams, and Genie Welch Leisure.

Woman wearing a necklace designed by Frankie Welch, 1974; collection of Frankie Welch, Peggy Welch Williams, and Genie Welch Leisure.

Necklace designed by Frankie Welch, manufactured by Freirich, 1973, photo by Mary Linnemann, Hargrett Rare Book and Manuscript Library; collection of Frankie Welch, Peggy Welch Williams, and Genie Welch Leisure.

as "real" and therefore "Indian" was part of a common approach to objects at the time that equated historic Native American artifacts with cultural authenticity.[44] With her typical ebullience, Welch shared, "This jewelry is a symptom of my own excitement over these old Indian designs," adding, "It makes me happy to share them with other women."[45] At least two prominent Native American women in Washington wore her jewelry: reporter Wauhillau La Hay, who donned one of Welch's necklaces "inspired by Pre-Columbian Indian jewelry" with a dress by Welch when she was photographed with needlework pillows of her own design (which she showed at Welch's shop), and LaDonna Harris, who wore a necklace "patterned after a Plains Indian male breastplate" by Welch with a white Frankie when *Ladies' Home Journal* named her as one of eight Women of the Year in 1973 at a Kennedy Center event that was televised nationwide.[46]

Frankie Welch wearing one of her necklaces, ca. 1973, Craig Photography; collection of Frankie Welch, Peggy Welch Williams, and Genie Welch Leisure.

Wauhillau La Hay wearing a necklace and dress designed by Frankie Welch (with embroidered pillows of her own design), ca. 1973, Craig Photography; collection of Frankie Welch, Peggy Welch Williams, and Genie Welch Leisure.

That November, Welch released her petite and attractive book, *Indian Jewelry: How to Wear, Buy and Treasure America's First Fashion Pieces*, with one of the designs from the Basket Weave scarf on the cover. In it she discusses her own experiences with Native American history and objects, gives tips on collecting, explains the meanings of select Native American motifs, and suggests ways to incorporate Native American jewelry into wardrobes and interior settings. She addresses the Americana theme directly, writing about how Indian artifacts had given her "a new pride in America," and about the current "craze for Americana," which she explains as a nostalgia for the past that was growing as people moved to cities.[47] While the book's text makes clear that she talked to experts and traveled to many museums to examine artifacts, Welch avoided the dark realities of Native American history and instead focused on its picturesque aspects,

Frankie Welch, *Indian Jewelry: How to Wear, Buy and Treasure America's First Fashion Pieces* (McLean, Va.: EPM, 1973).

Frankie Welch and Betty Ford at the party celebrating the publication of *Indian Jewelry*, 1973, UPI photo, courtesy UPI/Newscom; collection of Frankie Welch, Peggy Welch Williams, and Genie Welch Leisure.

idealizing Native Americans as closely connected to the earth. Reviewing the book for *Wassaja* (a Native American newspaper), Cory Arnet stated that Welch's ideas about wearing Indian jewelry "would not be acceptable to most Indian women (and men)" but acknowledged her appreciation of and respect for Indian jewelry and deemed the book useful for "fashion-conscious [white] people who are learning to admire" and collect Native American jewelry.[48]

Coverage of the book's release party at Duvall House, which took place during the Watergate scandal, focused as much on the politics surrounding the many Washington notables in attendance as on the book. The prominent partygoers included Liz Carpenter, Lady Bird Johnson's press secretary and a women's rights advocate; Betty Ford, who responded that she did not think Congress would impeach Nixon when asked if she might become first lady; and Nancy Ziegler, whose husband, Ron, was White House press secretary.[49] Solomon McComb, a Creek artist from Oklahoma whose paintings hung in Duvall House, attended wearing a Roadrunner necktie, and Betty Ford wore one of Welch's Native American–inspired necklaces.[50]

During the event, models, including Susan Ford (Betty's daughter), Patricia Lott (wife of Congressman Trent Lott from Mississippi), and Jerry Wilson (wife of Congressman Charles Wilson from Texas), wandered informally among the crowd.[51]

Through her interests in Native American history, Welch developed strong ties to Oklahoma, where many Cherokee were forcibly relocated under policies resulting from the Indian Removal Act of 1830. Welch, again taking a romanticized view of history, shared with a reporter from Oklahoma a family story that her "great-great-great-grandfather had come to Oklahoma on the Trail of Tears and then returned to Georgia."[52] Though nearly four thousand Cherokee died on the compulsory march in the fall and winter of 1838 and 1839, Welch's interest was in establishing a personal connection, as she understood her family's history, to the Cherokee and therefore to Oklahoma. One link she had to the state was through her friend Martha Griffin (later White), who helped found the Five Civilized Tribes Museum in Muskogee, Oklahoma, which focused on the tribes Europeans deemed "civilized" (Cherokee, Chickasaw, Choctaw, Creek/Muscogee, and Seminole). Welch gave the museum an early Cherokee Alphabet scarf for its collection and designed a custom scarf for the museum.[53]

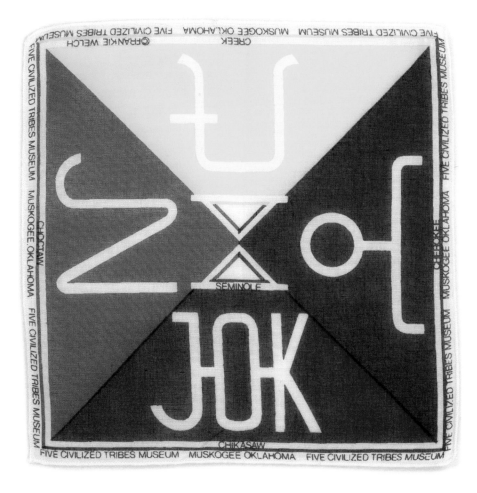

Five Civilized Tribes napachief, n.d., cotton, photo by Mary Linnemann, Hargrett Rare Book and Manuscript Library; collection of Frankie Welch, Peggy Welch Williams, and Genie Welch Leisure.

Though today Welch's Native American–inspired designs raise issues of cultural appropriation, a sensitive topic in contemporary fashion, she genuinely considered the designs as Americana and as reflective of her own family's background.[54] Prominent individuals of Indigenous heritage wore and enjoyed her designs, which increased their legitimacy. Welch's designs were also in line with trends at the time, fitting a larger vogue for American Indian–inspired fashions in the late 1960s and early 1970s (though more conservative than the leather fringe and feathers favored by hippies).[55] She appreciated the craftsmanship of Native Americans, acquiring original Native American jewelry—especially squash blossom necklaces—as she traveled, and in 1979 she purchased a quantity of hand-dyed fabric from the Cherokee Nation to use for unspecified projects.[56]

The Americana theme in Welch's work reached new heights with her creations for the country's two-hundredth anniversary in 1976. Her first Bicentennial design was commissioned by the Bicentennial Council of the Thirteen Original States (a nonprofit group organized in 1970) and based on a button created for George Washington's inauguration in 1789 that she had seen at the Smithsonian Institution.[57] Her design, like the button, features Washington's monogram in the middle, surrounded by linked ovals with the initials of each original state. The scarf is bordered by circles of thirteen stars. She offered this Thirteen Original States design as tea towels in red, blue, and white and as scarves and Frankies in either red, blue, and white or beige, coral, and white.

This design, and six others, became officially licensed products for the American Revolution Bicentennial Administration (ARBA), a group created by Congress in 1973. One of the new designs featured the ARBA logo, in either blue or red on white, while the remaining five related to presidents. Welch based each of them on historic textiles.[58] The scarf for George Washington, a spare design with Washington on horseback in one corner, was inspired by a kerchief from 1889 celebrating the centennial of his inauguration.[59] The scarf for John Adams, with a delicate floral pattern, recalls a blue-and-white bandana from 1825, though she printed her Bicentennial version in a variety of colors.[60] For Abraham Lincoln, she looked to an 1864 campaign scarf, replacing the central image of Lincoln's face with a picturesque split-rail fence.[61] Theodore Roosevelt's scarf reproduces the design from a campaign bandana made by the Progressive Party in 1912, with a Rough Rider hat in the center, his initials repeated in a grid around it, and a border of him wearing a hat, glasses, and a bandana.[62] (She reprised the Roosevelt design as a larger bandana for an exhibition at the Library of Congress, *The American Cowboy*, in 1983, where President Ronald Reagan was presented with one.)[63] For Lyndon Johnson, Welch recreated her Discover America design as an eight-by-eight-inch module. Although she had a design for Richard Nixon that she could reuse as well, she decided not to because, in the post-Watergate years, she did not think it would sell.[64] The designs she did produce, though, sold very well. She

Woman wearing a Thirteen Original States Frankie at a Bicentennial Council of the Original 13 States booth, ca. 1976; photo by Stephen Top[illegible] (possibly Cherry Hill, New Jersey); Frankie Welch Collection, Rome Area History Center.

Thirteen Original States scarf, designed 1975, Qiana, photo by Mary Linnemann, Hargrett Rare Book and Manuscript Library; collection of Frankie Welch, Peggy Welch Williams, and Genie Welch Leisure.

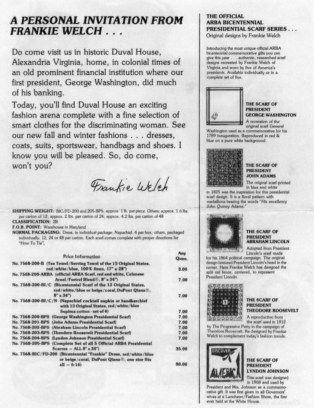

Frankie Welch Bicentennial flyer (front and back), ca. 1975; Frankie Welch Textile Collection, Hargrett Rare Book and Manuscript Library, University of Georgia Libraries.

replied to one inquiry about her Bicentennial items that she had been "so besieged with requests for the catalog sheet" that she was temporarily out.[65] Her friend Al Neher recalled that the Army and Air Force Exchange Service even ordered thousands of her scarves to be sold at exchanges on military bases around the world.[66]

Welch created several designs for the Bicentennial in addition to the ones officially associated with ARBA, including a scarf for the American Freedom Train, which traveled the country with a dozen display cars filled with American treasures (including George Washington's copy of the U.S. Constitution, Alan Shepard's Apollo space suit, Martin Luther King Jr.'s pulpit, and Judy Garland's "Dorothy" dress from *The Wizard of Oz*), and a scarf of landmarks in Alexandria—including Duvall House.[67] She also offered a red, blue, and white module version of a scarf she had designed for First Lady Betty Ford, an association that enhanced her credibility as a purveyor of Americana and led to several seminal moments in her career.

LEFT TO RIGHT:

American Revolution Bicentennial Administration scarf, ca. 1976, triacetate and nylon blend, photo by Mary Linnemann, Hargrett Rare Book and Manuscript Library; Frankie Welch Collection, Rome Area History Center.

George Washington Bicentennial scarf, designed 1975, triacetate and nylon blend, photo by Mary Linnemann, Hargrett Rare Book and Manuscript Library; Frankie Welch Collection, Rome Area History Center.

John Adams Bicentennial scarf, designed 1975, silk, photo by Mary Linnemann, Hargrett Rare Book and Manuscript Library; private collection.

Abraham Lincoln Bicentennial scarf, designed 1975, Qiana, photo by Mary Linnemann, Hargrett Rare Book and Manuscript Library; Frankie Welch Collection, Rome Area History Center.

LEFT TO RIGHT:

Theodore Roosevelt Bicentennial scarf (unhemmed on the ends), designed 1975, Qiana, photo by Mary Linnemann, Hargrett Rare Book and Manuscript Library; Frankie Welch Textile Collection, Hargrett Rare Book and Manuscript Library, University of Georgia Libraries.

Lyndon Johnson Bicentennial scarf, designed 1975, unidentified fabric, photo by Mary Linnemann, Hargrett Rare Book and Manuscript Library; Frankie Welch Collection, Historic Clothing and Textile Collection, College of Family and Consumer Sciences, University of Georgia.

American Freedom Train scarf, ca. 1976, Qiana, photo by Mary Linnemann, Hargrett Rare Book and Manuscript Library; private collection.

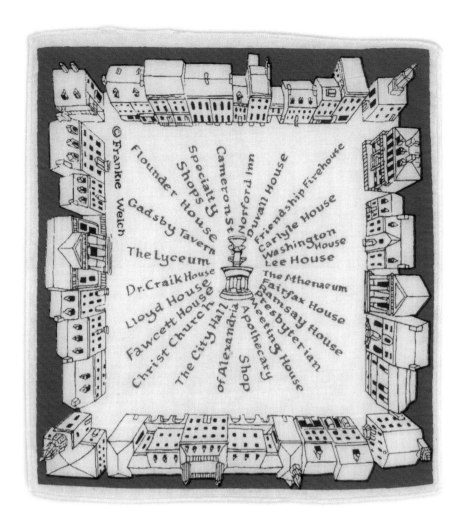

Alexandria Historic Landmarks napachief, ca. 1974, cotton, photo by Mary Linnemann, Hargrett Rare Book and Manuscript Library; private collection.

Alexandria Historic Landmarks scarf advertisement, 1974; collection of Frankie Welch, Peggy Welch Williams, and Genie Welch Leisure.

Chapter 5
First Ladies and Fashion

Frankie Welch's renown increased significantly when her friend Betty Ford became first lady in August 1974. Betty and Gerald Ford had moved from Grand Rapids, Michigan, to Washington, D.C., in 1949 when he was elected to serve in the House of Representatives. They relocated across the Potomac River to Alexandria in 1951. Betty Ford and Frankie Welch, both young mothers, attended the same church, Immanuel Church-on-the-Hill, and became neighborhood friends.[1] Ford had worked as a model, dancer, and fashion coordinator before marrying Gerald, and the two women bonded through their interest in clothing. Ford was an early customer at Welch's shop and continued to purchase clothes there throughout her husband's political rise. Gerald Ford served as House minority leader from 1965 to 1973, as vice president from 1973 to 1974 following Spiro Agnew's resignation, and as president from 1974 to 1977 after Richard Nixon resigned.

Betty Ford was with Welch when she debuted her Cherokee Alphabet scarf in 1967, and Welch later wrote to her, "I'm still so sentimental about the day you helped me unveil my first scarf."[2] In 1968 Ford, requesting equal time for the Republicans, had encouraged Welch to design a fabric for the Republican National Convention that was used for a variety of hostess dresses.[3] She also attended the launch of Welch's book *Indian Jewelry* at a time when national media interest in her spiked: following her husband's nomination to be vice president and preceding the approval of his nomination. Betty Beale, society columnist for the *Washington Star*, correctly predicted that if Betty Ford became first lady, "the fashion spotlight will land on creative designer and shopowner Frankie Welch," as Ford "buys almost everything she wears at Frankie's shop."[4] For example, when Betty Ford accompanied her husband on an official trip to China in 1972, she purchased numerous outfits from Welch, including a long rose-colored dress for a dinner with Premier Zhou Enlai; a Frankie; and three shirt-waist dresses in Welch's custom designs—Fifty State Flowers, Turtles, and

OPPOSITE: Betty Ford in the Yellow Oval Room of the White House, 1975, photograph by Horst P Horst for *Vogue*, Horst P Horst/Condé Nast/Shutterstock.

RIGHT: From collection of Frankie Welch, Peggy Welch Williams, and Genie Welch Leisure.

Betty Ford wearing a Cherokee Alphabet shirtwaist dress while she packs for move from her home in Alexandria, Virginia, to the White House, 1974, AP photo by Bob Daugherty; collection of Frankie Welch, Peggy Welch Williams, and Genie Welch Leisure.

Cherokee Alphabet.[5] The media's attention certainly did shine on Welch, even leading to an article on her in *People* magazine.[6]

After Nixon's nationally televised announcement on August 8, 1974, that he intended to resign the presidency at noon the following day, Betty Ford emerged from her home in Alexandria, in the rain, to greet reporters wearing the Fifty State Flowers cotton shirtwaist dress, a thoughtful choice for the soon-to-be first lady considering that it represented all states, was based on White House china, and was by an American designer.[7] She also invited Welch to her home for fashion advice, and the *New York Times* ran the headline, "Mrs. Ford Sees Dress Designer Instead of Her Doctor."[8] The next morning, Ford had "her friend," as the *New York Times* described Welch, come over in the morning with Ford's favorite dress, a light-blue jersey knit that had been dry-cleaned overnight, for her to wear to the inauguration later in the day.[9] Welch and her husband were invited to attend the event, for which Welch donned an Adolfo hat, described by Elaine Tait of the *Philadelphia Inquirer* as "a trademark of the vivacious retailer."[10] Welch's older daughter Peggy was married the following day, and Welch admitted to her hometown newspaper in Rome that "it was a bit hectic . . . but also great fun."[11]

Betty Ford and Frankie Welch in the alterations room at Frankie Welch of Virginia, 1974; collection of Frankie Welch, Peggy Welch Williams, and Genie Welch Leisure.

Betty Ford in the alterations room at Frankie Welch of Virginia, 1974; collection of Frankie Welch, Peggy Welch Williams, and Genie Welch Leisure.

Seamstresses (on the right is Mariko Marshall) working on a dress for Betty Ford at Frankie Welch of Virginia, 1974; collection of Frankie Welch, Peggy Welch Williams, and Genie Welch Leisure.

First Lady Betty Ford and President Gerald R. Ford following the swearing-in ceremony in the East Room of the White House, 1974, photo by Robert L. Knudsen, courtesy of the Gerald R. Ford Library.

Betty Ford was known for wearing simple, comfortable, practical clothes with traditional accessories. She favored scarves, and Welch told one reporter, "Mrs. Ford has 60 of my scarves and she knows how to tie them and wear them."[12] Nancy Howe, Ford's personal assistant, averred, "The thing that works best in Mrs. Ford's wardrobe is definitely scarves."[13] Even a decade later, a writer for the *Washington Post Magazine* listed scarves as the fashion item with which Ford would always be associated in the memories of Americans.[14]

Though Welch was adamant about keeping confidences private and did not discuss garments Ford had not yet worn in public, she did share some details with the media about Ford's fashion preferences.[15] Welch observed, "She tends to lean lines, but selects things that will go up and down stairs gracefully, and will sit and travel well."[16] She described Ford's look as "casual elegance," and, though Welch sometimes was called Ford's fashion adviser, she praised Ford's own fashion know-how.[17] From Welch, Ford primarily purchased affordable ready-to-wear designs by American designers including Kaspar, Jim Baldwin, Justin McCarty, Ciao Knits, Mollie Parnis Boutique, Halston, Geoffrey Beene, Diane von Furstenberg, and Anne Klein.[18] Welch remarked, "Betty Ford will wear a $40 dress if it looks great," adding, "She's her own person. She doesn't have to have designer things."[19] Welch also revealed that Gerald Ford shopped for his wife at Frankie Welch of Virginia.

The Fords entered the White House at a time of increasing inflation and high unemployment, so Betty Ford sought to be both style- and economy-conscious with her fashions.[20] She caused some controversy in the fashion world in late 1974 when she announced to reporters that

OPPOSITE: Betty Ford greeting reporters outside of her home in Alexandria after learning she would become first lady, wearing a Fifty State Flowers dress, 1974, AP photo by Paul Vathis.

Betty Ford wearing a Veterans
Administration scarf as her husband
speaks before the Seventy-Fifth
Annual Veterans of Foreign Wars
Convention at the Conrad Hilton Hotel
in Chicago, 1974, official White House
photo; collection of Frankie Welch,
Peggy Welch Williams, and Genie
Welch Leisure.

Betty Ford wearing a
Member of Congress scarf
in the Oval Office as her
husband nominates Nelson
Rockefeller (*right*) to be
his vice president (Henry
Kissinger, *left*), 1974, official
White House photo by
Bill Fitz-Patrick; collection
of Frankie Welch, Peggy
Welch Williams, and Genie
Welch Leisure.

Betty Ford wearing an
Indianapolis Motor
Speedway scarf, ca. 1975;
Frankie Welch Collection,
Rome Area History Center.

she would "cut back on her purchase of new, expensive designer dresses for White House functions because of current economic conditions."[21] However, she quickly made a personal call to Welch to reassure her that she just was not going to buy the expensive dresses, which she had not been buying anyway.[22] Even for her first state dinner, for King Hussein bin Talal and Queen Alia Bahauddin Toukan of Jordan, Ford purchased an off-the-rack dress from Welch.[23] The media and public favorably received Ford's fashions, and she made the International Best-Dressed List in 1975.[24] Welch later recalled, "She was very conscious of being well-dressed and that was good for me, good for her, and good for fashion."[25]

Welch's daughter Peggy remembers that, especially early in her time at the White House, Ford often called Welch to bring clothes or come visit, and Welch wrote once about what a thrill it was to drive up to the main entrance of the White House.[26] In a 1984 interview Welch shared, "We talked nearly every day when she was in the White House," and she later explained, "Well, you know, we were so close. It was like sister to sister."[27] When Welch's husband died in April 1975, after a year of illness, Betty Ford, while first lady, attended his funeral in Alexandria.[28] The following year, Ford included Welch in a White House dinner for the prime minister of Australia, Malcolm Fraser, and his wife Tamara, a kind gesture and special invitation that Peggy says made her mother feel good during a difficult time.[29]

Betty Ford supported women's rights, was pro-choice, and was forthright about her own health issues with breast cancer. Following a series of particularly candid interviews, in which she acknowledged, among other things, that contrary to White House tradition she and her husband shared a bed, and the subsequent public backlash, one of Ford's staff reported to her that "Frankie . . . wants you to know that she is thinking of you. You have the support of her and her entire staff. They are with you."[30]

In early 1975 Welch designed a scarf for Betty Ford to use as gifts to White House visitors. She made this scarf especially personal, using one of Ford's favorite flowers, the petunia; hues that matched her favorite turtleneck shirts—pink, orange, purple, and green; polka dots, which she liked; and her handwritten signature.[31] The two women posed with the scarf for media photographs that appeared in newspapers across the country. In a public talk in 1991, Welch shared a story about the photo session: one trick Welch often suggested to her customers was that they stand slightly behind someone else in photographs to appear slimmer, and of this photo she explained, "We really had to jockey for positions. Mrs. Ford said, 'Frankie, I'm standing behind you,' and I said, 'I know you are first lady, and I know you deserve to, but I invented this.' So we both had to hide behind the scarf."[32]

The Fords first presented the design as gifts at a governors' dinner in February 1975. The president even acknowledged the scarves in his toast, stating,

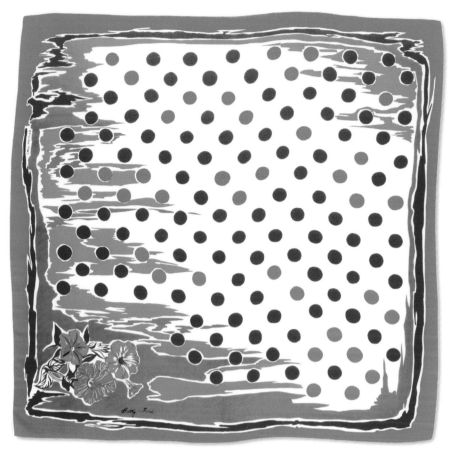

Betty Ford scarf, 1975, Qiana, photo by Mary Linnemann,
Hargrett Rare Book and Manuscript Library; collection
of Frankie Welch, Peggy Welch Williams, and
Genie Welch Leisure.

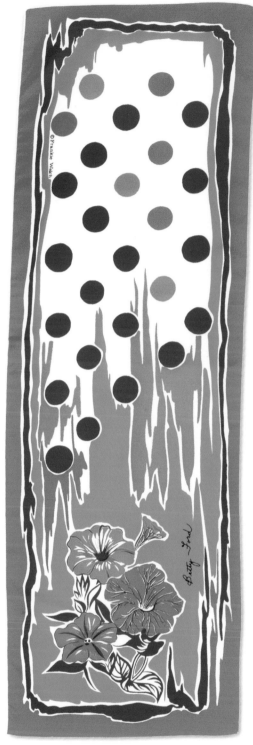

Betty Ford scarf, 1975, Qiana, photo by
Mary Linnemann, Hargrett Rare Book
and Manuscript Library; collection of
Frankie Welch, Peggy Welch Williams,
and Genie Welch Leisure.

Betty Ford and
Frankie Welch with
the Betty Ford scarf,
1975, official White
House photo by
Karl Schumacher.

Betty Ford wearing a Frankie of the Betty Ford scarf design with Gerald Ford, ca. 1976; Frankie Welch Collection, Rome Area History Center.

We do appreciate the honor of your visit, and as a small souvenir, it's my understanding Betty would like the ladies to have this first edition of a very special scarf she has designed with Frankie Welch over in Alexandria. I believe you found them on your chairs as you came in. Betty and I hope that even in the chilliest of days ahead they will prove, or provide you, I should say, with the warm memories of this particular evening.[33]

(Diana McLellan, famous Washington gossip columnist, once remarked about this event that Welch was "the only chickie who ever got Jerry Ford to do a commercial for her.")[34] The scarf elicited positive media to balance the negative reactions Betty Ford received for supporting the Equal Rights Amendment.[35]

Welch produced the scarf originally in large squares and long rectangles of Qiana. In addition to giving them as White House gifts, Ford allowed Welch to sell them in her shop, with 5 percent of the wholesale sales going to the White House Historical Association.[36] Ford wore a Frankie of the design as well, to several dinners between 1975 and 1977.[37] Welch reprinted the design as a module version in red, blue, and white for the Bicentennial, along with a version in blue, green, and white, and one in pink, green, and white, in various fabrics.[38]

The friends made fashion headlines again in June 1976 when Betty Ford donated a dress designed by Frankie Welch to represent her in the Smithsonian Institution's First Ladies Collection. Most first ladies donate their inaugural gowns, but Ford's husband did not have formal inaugural celebrations. Instead, she selected her "favorite" dress, one she considered "timeless and not gimmicky."[39] The floor-length, long-sleeved, princess-cut dress with a mandarin collar and a narrow, plunging neckline has a "swingy" skirt so that she could dance in it.[40] Welch used a light-green nylon chiffon embroidered with chrysanthemums and sequins of the same color over a heavier fabric (probably silk), making it the first dress with a synthetic material to enter the First Ladies Collection.[41] Demonstrating her attachment to the gown, Ford requested that Welch make her a duplicate of it before she donated the original.[42]

Welch created several related dresses for Ford, including an earlier gown with a narrower skirt but similar top—made from red silk brocade she had received on a trip to China—that she wore to an exhibition of Chinese archeological finds in December 1974 at the National Gallery of Art; a green dress made from Chinese silk with embroidered flowers and a silhouette nearly identical to that of the Smithsonian gown that Ford wore for both a photo shoot by Horst P Horst for *Vogue* in 1975 and an official photographic portrait in the White House's Treaty Room in 1975; and a pink-and-white-striped dress without a collar.[43]

Betty Ford and Frankie Welch at the Smithsonian for the unveiling of the dress Ford donated to the Smithsonian's First Ladies Collection, 1976; collection of Frankie Welch, Peggy Welch Williams, and Genie Welch Leisure.

Frankie Welch and Betty Ford at the Smithsonian, with the dress Ford donated to the First Ladies Collection, 1976; collection Frankie Welch Collection, Rome Area History Center.

Betty Ford's copy of the dress designed by Frankie Welch that she donated to the Smithsonian Institution's First Ladies Collection, 1976; Gerald R. Ford Presidential Library and Museum, 1983.88.3, gift of Betty Ford.

The official portrait dress is the only one acknowledged in the media as made by Japanese-born seamstress Mariko Horii Marshall, who worked for Welch, though she likely constructed, or at least worked on, all of these dresses.[44] Dorothy Marks, with the Women's News Service, credited Ford with helping design the "Chinese-style dresses."[45] Ford wore the dress she later donated to the Smithsonian to numerous official functions, including state dinners for the shah and shahbanu (Mohammad Reza Pahlavi and Farah Pahlavi) of Iran in May 1975 and King Juan Carlos and Queen Sophia of Spain in June 1976.

The donation by Betty Ford of a dress Welch designed to the Smithsonian was a landmark event in Welch's life. She invited not only her daughters and son-in-law to the celebration but also people special to her from her childhood in Rome: her second-grade sewing teacher, Martha Moore Quarles; her high-school home economics teacher, Sue Griffith; her friend Margaret Gaines; and Pope McDonald, the first boy to take her on a date (during which she wore the first party dress she designed and made for herself).[46] Guests to the event received a version of the Betty Ford scarf as gifts.[47] Later, around 1990, Welch joined the group Friends of First Ladies as it sought to raise $2 million to conserve the First Ladies gowns at the Smithsonian.[48]

In a close vote, Gerald Ford lost the presidential election in 1976 to Jimmy Carter, ending the Fords' time in the Washington area. Though Betty Ford and Welch did not see each other frequently in the following years, they remained friends. In an interview in 1984, Welch described Ford as a "very close friend" and stated, "I consider her a friend forever."[49] In 1998 Welch even spoke at an event in Grand Rapids celebrating Betty Ford's eightieth birthday.[50] That same year, on the occasion of a party celebrating thirty years of Welch's designs, Ford praised Welch, writing, "Frankie made me look so good when I was First Lady. Her colorful scarves were particularly meaningful to me. What a great friend."[51] Many of Welch's dresses for Betty Ford are preserved in the collection of the Gerald R. Ford Presidential Library and Museum in Ann Arbor, Michigan.

Though Welch's close friend left the White House, she shared a special connection with the next first couple: their home state of Georgia. Joan Nielsen McHale, a friend of Welch's from Alexandria and former *Miami News* fashion editor and social columnist, acknowledged the importance of the regional link, recalling, "Naturally, the Georgia Mafia, as Jimmy Carter's coterie was called, loved one of their own . . . and that whole contingent shopped Frankie Welch's boutiques just as each regime had done."[52] About five weeks before the Carter administration took office, LaBelle Lance took her family to a Christmas party at Welch's shop, explaining, "I think I'll be spending a lot of time here, so I thought my husband should know where I am."[53] (LaBelle Lance's husband Bert, for whom Welch had earlier designed two scarves, one for his Calhoun [Georgia] National Bank and another for his unsuccessful campaign for governor of Georgia, was incoming director of the Office of Management and Budget.) Nina Hyde, in the *Washington Post*, noted that many local women bought dresses for the inaugural events from Welch.[54]

First Lady Betty Ford and President Gerald Ford, December 17, 1974, in the Blue Room of the White House, in front of a Christmas tree during the Christmas Ball for Members of Congress, Gerald R. Ford White House Photographs.

Gown designed by Frankie Welch for First Lady Betty Ford, 1974; Gerald R. Ford Presidential Library and Museum, 1983.88.3, gift of Betty Ford.

Mariko Marshall, 1974; collection of Frankie Welch, Peggy Welch Williams, and Genie Welch Leisure.

President and Mrs. Ford with King Juan Carlos and Queen Sophia of Spain, 1976, official White House photo; collection of Frankie Welch, Peggy Welch Williams, and Genie Welch Leisure.

Farah Pahlavi, shahbanu of Iran, and Betty Ford, 1975, official White House photo; collection of Frankie Welch, Peggy Welch Williams, and Genie Welch Leisure.

OPPOSITE: Photographic portrait of First Lady Betty Ford in the White House Treaty Room, ca. December 24, 1975, photograph by David Hume Kennerly; courtesy Gerald R. Ford Library.

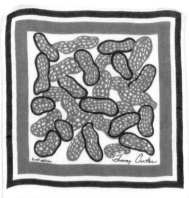
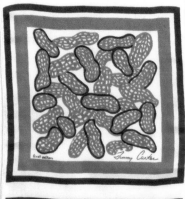
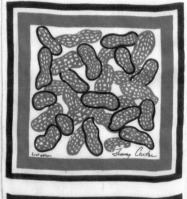
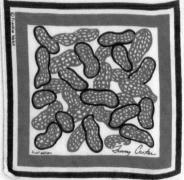

Peanut scarf for Governor and Mrs. Jimmy Carter, 1973, silk, photo by Mary Linnemann, Hargrett Rare Book and Manuscript Library; private collection.

Welch's ties to the Carters went back several years before the presidential transition, to 1973 when Welch designed a scarf for them to use as gifts while Jimmy was governor of Georgia. Welch met Rosalynn Carter and her daughter Amy when she rode with them to Atlanta after speaking at an event at New Echota, a historic capital of the Cherokee Nation in northwestern Georgia.[55] Though initially interested in a quilt pattern, Carter agreed to a peanut motif because of her husband's family business.[56] The dynamic design in tan and brown on a creamy white suggests an overhead view of a basket full of Georgia's famous legumes.

Welch made a Frankie of the peanut fabric as well, and Rosalynn Carter appeared in a photograph in the *Atlanta Constitution* wearing it with the caption, "Nutty but Nice."[57] In 1974 Welch reprinted the peanut scarves on cotton (the original ones were on silk) and wrote to Mrs. Carter: "'Peanuts' was such a delightful scarf to make and I am so pleased to be re-running that design for you. I know it must make a tremendous hit with the people who receive them. It is such a marvelous way to advertise products of your own home state + especially your very own product—peanuts."[58] While Jimmy Carter's signature is on every module, Welch's name only appears on one of every four.

Welch designed a second peanut scarf in 1976 when Jimmy Carter became a presidential candidate. The Democratic National Committee asked her for a campaign scarf, and she explained, "I called Mrs. Carter at the time and we decided to come up with a different peanut scarf because they liked the original one as a collector's item. People really do hang onto that one."[59] For this design she used diagonal rows of peanuts and printed them in either green or brown on white for both scarves and neckties. These do not have Carter's signature, but include ©Frankie Welch on every module.[60]

Rosalynn Carter appeared in public numerous times wearing scarves by Frankie Welch, both during the campaign and after becoming first lady. For example, she is wearing the first peanut scarf while watching the primary returns in May 1976 in a photograph on the front page of the *Washington Post*; the Thirteen Original States scarf during an Easter sunrise service in Plains, Georgia, in a color photograph that ran in a *Newsweek* feature in May 1976; and a Basket Weave scarf in August 1980 while she and her husband observed the sixtieth anniversary of women's right to vote.[61] She also wore Welch's Mental Health Association scarf, designed in 1977, multiple times.[62] For her first public event following her husband's inauguration, Carter attended a meeting of the Woman's National Democratic Club, where she was named Woman of the Year and presented with a commemorative scarf by Welch (slightly wider than the standard eight-by-eight-inch module) featuring a lace design with "RSC," for Rosalynn Smith Carter, in the middle.[63] (She wore this scarf when the Carters visited Brazil in 1978.)[64] Carter, as had first ladies before her, included Frankie Welch of Virginia in her activities. One notable event that brought her to the shop's Washington, D.C., location was a book signing in

Rosalynn Carter wearing a Frankie of the peanut pattern with Frankie Welch in the Governor's Mansion, Atlanta, Georgia, 1973; collection of Frankie Welch, Peggy Welch Williams, and Genie Welch Leisure.

Peanut Frankie, 1973, photo by Michael McKelvey, courtesy of the Hargrett Rare Book and Manuscript Library; Frankie Welch Collection, Historic Clothing and Textile Collection, College of Family and Consumer Sciences, University of Georgia.

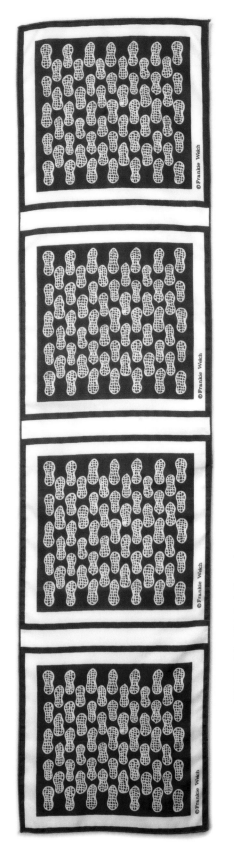

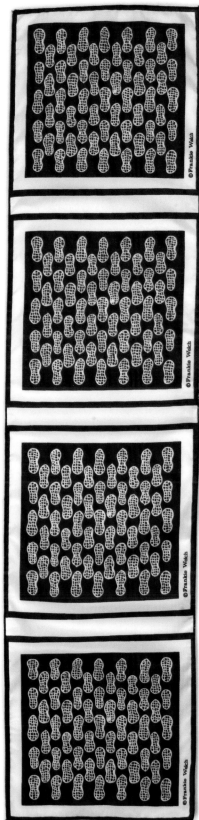

Page Williams wearing a peanut tie, 1977; collection of Frankie Welch, Peggy Welch Williams, and Genie Welch Leisure.

LEFT: Peanut scarf for Jimmy Carter's presidential campaign, 1976, Qiana, photo by Mary Linnemann, Hargrett Rare Book and Manuscript Library; private collection.

RIGHT: Peanut scarf for Jimmy Carter's presidential campaign, 1976, Qiana, photo by Mary Linnemann, Hargrett Rare Book and Manuscript Library; Frankie Welch Textile Collection, Hargrett Rare Book and Manuscript Library, University of Georgia Libraries.

Rosalynn Carter wearing a Cherokee Alphabet scarf, n.d.; collection of Frankie Welch, Peggy Welch Williams, and Genie Welch Leisure.

The Carter Family in Plains, Georgia, with Rosalynn Carter wearing a peanut scarf, signed by Rosalynn Carter, 1976, AP photo by Bob Daugherty; collection of Frankie Welch, Peggy Welch Williams, and Genie Welch Leisure.

1980 for Edna Langford and Linda Maddox's biography *Rosalynn: Friend and First Lady.*[65]

Following the Carter administration, Welch continued to create designs related to presidents and their wives, including numerous scarves and other items for presidential inaugurations: scarves, neckties, and umbrellas in red or blue on white with repeated encircled "RBS" for the 1981 inauguration of Ronald Reagan and George H. W. Bush; a red, white, and blue plaid, called "Reagan Plaid," for scarves and tote bags for Reagan's second inauguration in 1985; versions of her Washington, D.C., design for both George H. W. Bush and Dan Quayle's inaugural in 1989, and Bill Clinton and Al Gore's first inaugural in 1993; and neckties for Clinton's second inauguration.[66] She also designed a scarf in 1986 for the second annual Nancy Reagan Tennis Benefit to raise funds to end drug abuse, and a small tote bag for Barbara Bush with one of the Basket Weave designs. Her last scarf connected to a first family was a large silk square with a painterly image of vegetables, commissioned by the Senate Wives for a First Lady's Luncheon honoring Hillary Clinton in 1993.[67] By this time, though still known primarily as a scarf mogul, Welch engaged in many other creative efforts.

Rosalynn Carter and Frankie Welch at a meeting of the Woman's National Democratic Club, 1977; collection of Frankie Welch, Peggy Welch Williams, and Genie Welch Leisure.

Woman's National Democratic Club scarf for Rosalynn Carter, 1977, Qiana, photo by Mary Linnemann, Hargrett Rare Book and Manuscript Library; collection of Frankie Welch, Peggy Welch Williams, and Genie Welch Leisure.

Genie Welch, Peggy Welch Williams, Frankie Welch, and Rosalynn Carter at the Rosalynn Carter book event at Frankie Welch's shop, Washington, D.C., 1980; collection of Frankie Welch, Peggy Welch Williams, and Genie Welch Leisure.

Rosalynn Carter and Edna Langford signing books at Frankie Welch's shop, Washington, D.C., 1980; collection of Frankie Welch, Peggy Welch Williams, and Genie Welch Leisure.

Frankie Welch, Peggy Welch Williams, Genie Welch, Peggy's daughter Lindsay, and unidentified woman at the Rosalynn Carter book event at Frankie Welch's shop, Washington, D.C., 1980; collection of Frankie Welch, Peggy Welch Williams, and Genie Welch Leisure.

Necktie for the inauguration of Ronald Reagan and George H. W. Bush, 1980, photo by Mary Linnemann, Hargrett Rare Book and Manuscript Library; Frankie Welch Textile Collection, Hargrett Rare Book and Manuscript Library, University of Georgia Libraries.

Frankie Welch at her drawing table with the Reagan/Bush inaugural designs, 1980, Julia Gaines, *Washington Star* photograph, reprinted with permission of the D.C. Public Library, Star Collection © *Washington Post*; Frankie Welch Collection, Rome Area History Center.

Scarf for the inauguration of Ronald Reagan and George H. W. Bush, 1980, polyester, photo by Mary Linnemann, Hargrett Rare Book and Manuscript Library; Frankie Welch Textile Collection, Hargrett Rare Book and Manuscript Library, University of Georgia Libraries.

Reagan Plaid napachief, 1985, silk, photo by Mary Linnemann,
Hargrett Rare Book and Manuscript Library; collection of Frankie
Welch, Peggy Welch Williams, and Genie Welch Leisure.

Scarf for George H. W. Bush and Dan Quayle inauguration, 1989, silk, photo by Mary Linnemann, Hargrett Rare Book and Manuscript Library; collection of Frankie Welch, Peggy Welch Williams, and Genie Welch Leisure.

Bandana for Bill Clinton and Al Gore inauguration showing the bus trip from Charlottesville to Washington, D.C., for the inaugural festivities, 1993, cotton, photo by Mary Linnemann, Hargrett Rare Book and Manuscript Library; private collection.

First Lady's Luncheon for Hillary Rodham Clinton scarf, 1993, silk, photo by
Mary Linnemann, Hargrett Rare Book and Manuscript Library; collection of
Frankie Welch, Peggy Welch Williams, and Genie Welch Leisure.

Chapter 6
Frankie Welch beyond the Scarf

Frankie Welch was an irrepressible entrepreneur; she expanded her brand in numerous ways and proposed a steady stream of new ideas. She opened several additional shop venues in the Southeast in the 1970s, and she also worked in the fields of interior design and corporate consulting, largely as extensions of her textile design. By the 1980s Welch enjoyed prominent standing in Washington society and was a local celebrity, burnishing her reputation by frequently attending and hosting social events and supporting charitable organizations. Even as her activities expanded, though, her shop in Alexandria—which had its own constant swirl of events—and her scarves remained the centers of her attention and renown.[1]

With her adept staff at Frankie Welch of Virginia, including assistants Jane Hearn in the late 1960s and 1970s and D. D. Bozek in the 1980s, fashion coordinator and model Opal Beverly, and her younger daughter Genie, who began working in the shop full time in 1978, Welch served the fashion needs of countless Washington women.[2] One reporter noted in 1975 that "many political wives wouldn't purchase a necklace without consulting Frankie first."[3] LaDonna Harris recalled that Welch would "figure out some wonderful thing" for her to wear if she knew that Harris would be in the public eye, and she appreciated the kindness and affection with which Welch guided her wardrobe choices, adding, "I didn't dress well until I met her. . . . She made me care about what I wore."[4] Opal Beverly's daughter, Jamie Waldrop, who spent a lot of time in the shop as a child (often playing under the dress racks), noted the devotion between Welch and her customers, saying, "People who were her customers, were her customers for life."[5] For many years, the shop kept cards on all of its customers with their sizes and lists of clothes they had purchased there so that, as Welch explained, "if they call looking for a particular blouse, we can tell them what we have available in their size, and what it will go with in their wardrobe."[6]

Sometimes the shop needed to respond quickly, like when a client suddenly had to travel overseas; Welch noted that in such a situation,

OPPOSITE: Duvall House, 1979; collection of Frankie Welch, Peggy Welch Williams, and Genie Welch Leisure.

RIGHT: From the Frankie Welch Textile Collection, Hargrett Rare Book and Manuscript Library, University of Georgia Libraries.

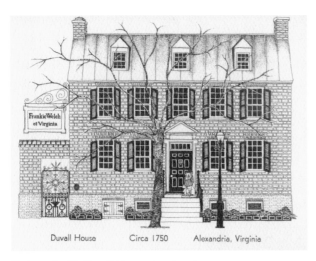

Notecard with Duvall House drawing, by 1972;
Frankie Welch Textile Collection, Hargrett Rare Book and
Manuscript Library, University of Georgia Libraries.

Postcard of Frankie Welch of Virginia in Alexandria, with Genie
Welch in the foreground and Frankie Welch in the midground, 1983;
collection of Frankie Welch, Peggy Welch Williams, and Genie
Welch Leisure.

they could "get together a completely coordinated wardrobe in about an hour."[7] A 1976 press release from the shop describes the typical level of activity: "On Tuesday of a recent week Mrs. Lyndon Johnson, visiting the Washington area, stopped in to add a few items to her wardrobe. Next day Susan Ford, daughter of the president, came for a bathing suit. At the same time, fashion assistants were packing clothes to send Helen Smith [assistant to Ambassador Elliott Richardson and former White House press secretary to Pat Nixon] at the U.S. Embassy in London," all while the other customers received their own courteous personal assistance and Welch saw to her business and designing responsibilities.[8]

Welch's early dress design, the Frankie, was a mainstay of her shop for more than twenty years. Journalist Frances Cawthon in Atlanta mused that it was "the ONE dress" that had been to more White House dinners than any other, and Marian McBride in the *Milwaukee Sentinel* reported that fashionable women did not mind encountering other Frankies at the same party because each was so different.[9] Virginia Rusk had one made of a Chinese fabric given to her by Soong Mei-ling, wife of Chinese president Chiang Kai-shek; Wauhillau La Hay wore one when she became president of the Washington Press Club; and Patricia Park, the first sanctioned female Episcopal priest in the Washington area, wore one in black cotton when she was ordained.[10] Welch even designed a line of wedding Frankies with coordinated bridesmaids' dresses in the early 1970s.[11]

Frankie flyer, ca. 1971; Frankie Welch Textile Collection, Hargrett Rare Book and Manuscript Library, University of Georgia Libraries.

Frankie flyer, ca. 1979; Frankie Welch Textile Collection, Hargrett Rare Book and Manuscript Library, University of Georgia Libraries.

Frankie flyer, ca. 1975; collection of Frankie Welch, Peggy Welch Williams, and Genie Welch Leisure.

Frankie Welch with an unidentified interviewer in Frankie Welch of Virginia in front of racks of Frankies and other dresses, ca. 1974; collection of Frankie Welch, Peggy Welch Williams, and Genie Welch Leisure.

OPPOSITE: Peggy Welch modeling a wedding dress Frankie, ca. 1972, photo by Joan Larson; collection of Frankie Welch, Peggy Welch Williams, and Genie Welch Leisure.

Throughout the 1970s, Welch hired Helen Kirby of Louelen Garments in Maryland to sew the one-size-fits-all dresses for her shop.[12] Each full-length Frankie required three and a half yards of plain or small-print fabric or four yards of a design that needed to be matched along the seams.[13] Some had one side (front or back) of a patterned fabric with a solid color or contrasting pattern on the other side, to create striking effects when tied different ways. Welch called it her "ever-changing, multipurpose dress perennial," and she advised her customers that it traveled well and could easily be rolled up and placed in a small carry-on bag when flying.[14] In fact, when Betty Ford traveled to China, Welch encouraged her to do this in case her luggage got lost; it did, and Ford was able to wear the Frankie to a dinner party.[15]

Though the Welch family lived in Duvall House when Frankie Welch of Virginia opened, around 1970 they moved to a townhouse on Cameron Mews, two blocks away. In 1976 Welch, a savvy real estate investor, acquired nearby historic Gilpin House on King Street and lived there for a while before using it as a rental property.[16]

Duvall House underwent numerous renovations and reconfigurations as the needs of the shop changed. When Welch redecorated it in 1976, she designed a commemorative fabric—in white and a powdery peach that resembled the old brick of the house—with an image of the exterior and text

Frankie Welch with two models wearing Frankies, ca. 1971, photo by Don Arnold of Drinnon, Inc., Macon, Georgia; courtesy of the Drinnon/Macon Telegraph Collection, Middle Georgia Archives, Macon, Georgia; Frankie Welch Collection, Rome Area History Center.

Frankie Welch tying a Frankie on a model, ca. 1971, photo by Don Arnold of Drinnon, Inc., Macon, Georgia; courtesy of the Drinnon/Macon Telegraph Collection, Middle Georgia Archives, Macon, Georgia; Frankie Welch Collection, Rome Area History Center.

Margo Jurgensen, wife of Sonny Jurgensen (quarterback for the Washington Redskins), wearing a Frankie, ca. 1972, photo by Tappy Phillips; Frankie Welch Collection, Rome Area History Center.

Frankie Welch adjusting a Frankie on Mitzi Hoyle, 1972; Frankie Welch Collection, Rome Area History Center.

Genie Welch, Frankie Welch, and
Peggy Welch Williams wearing Frankies,
1976; Frankie Welch Collection,
Rome Area History Center.

OPPOSITE: Three Frankie dresses, n.d., photo by
Michael McKelvey, courtesy of the Hargrett Rare Book and
Manuscript Library; *left to right*: Frankie Welch Collection,
Rome Area History Center; Frankie Welch Collection,
Rome Area History Center; private collection.

recognizing important events that occurred there to celebrate its history.[17] In 1988 she renamed Duvall House as Welch House, using a length of Cherokee Alphabet scarves for the ribbon-cutting ceremony.[18]

Welch, in 2011, recalled the shop's interior: "We had lovely racks built in three rooms [on the first floor] and the fourth quadrant included the dressing rooms. There was a ballroom upstairs, running the entire right hand side of the building, which was unusual for that era, and we used that space for small fashion shows, [and] special events such as introducing other designers or my *Indian Jewelry* book, for example."[19] Welch created many cozy areas where she could provide a quiet space for high-profile customers or a comfortable nook for visiting with special friends. In particular, she often used one of the rooms in the two-story flounder house (a historic architectural form with a single-sloped roof) attached to the back to entertain clients and guests.[20] For a while, the dressing rooms and a bathroom were decorated with the Republican National Convention daisy fabric, and later the dressing rooms featured the Turtles design.[21] She also had teas and held photo shoots in the small garden behind the shop.

One bit of advice Welch offered about merchandising was "Keep something exciting going on all the time," giving the example of how she would invite shoppers to bid on garments displayed on a specific rack, then sell them for the highest offers at the end of the week.[22] She also scheduled countless events such as trunk shows, book parties, and product launches "to generate excitement, get people into the shop, and certainly for press coverage."[23] Welch held regular fashion show luncheons at the Sheraton-Carlton Hotel, two blocks north of the White House, in the early to mid-1970s. The printed programs typically listed the guests at her table and the names of the guest models, often congressional wives or secretaries—a feature of her fashion shows that likely made the clothes more relatable to the attendees and the events more intimate.[24] Typically for the fashion shows, whether at big hotels or popular luncheon spots, her fashion co-ordinator, Opal Beverly, would select the garments and arrange for the models, and if the models were inexperienced, she would instruct them in how to walk down a runway and advise them on what shoes to wear.[25] A longtime customer, Val Anderson, said, "Frankie is always coming up with something new, exciting and different. . . . She has a gathering of friends and it makes it very personal."[26]

Welch partnered with the Campbell Soup Company in fall 1972 to present Frankies for a promotional program titled "After the Game."[27] These cotton Frankies—in stripes with checks, stripes with flowers, a football player print, and solid colors or paired football colors—each came with a hangtag-sized booklet with simple recipes from Campbell's, such as Touchdown Tacos, Gridiron Gazpacho, and Frankie's Special: Chicken with Curried Rice, which included beef, chicken, and Campbell's cream of mushroom soup.[28] One of the department stores that featured this new

Duvall House Frankie, 1976, photo by
Michael McKelvey, courtesy of the
Hargrett Rare Book and Manuscript
Library; collection of Frankie Welch,
Peggy Welch Williams, and Genie
Welch Leisure.

Frankie Welch of Virginia, ca. 1970; collection of Frankie Welch, Peggy Welch Williams, and Genie Welch Leisure.

Frankie Welch in Frankie Welch of Virginia, mid-1970s; collection of Frankie Welch, Peggy Welch Williams, and Genie Welch Leisure.

Frankie Welch in Frankie Welch of Virginia, ca. 1977; collection of Frankie Welch,
Peggy Welch Williams, and Genie Welch Leisure.

LEFT: Bathroom at Frankie Welch of Virginia with Republican National Convention design, n.d.; collection of Frankie Welch, Peggy Welch Williams, and Genie Welch Leisure.

RIGHT: Dressing room at Frankie Welch of Virginia with Turtles design, 1974; collection of Frankie Welch, Peggy Welch Williams, and Genie Welch Leisure.

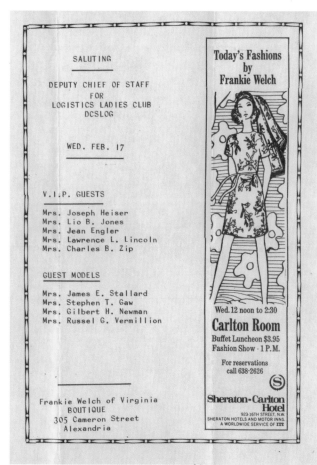

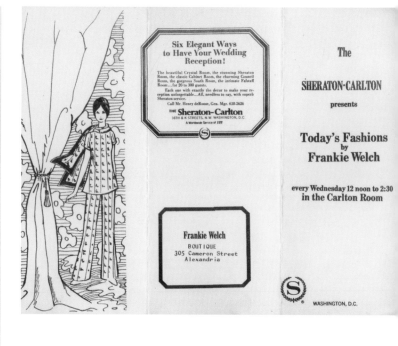

Today's Fashions by Frankie Welch, Sheraton-Carlton program, 1971; Frankie Welch Collection, Rome Area History Center.

Opal Beverly (right) modeling for Frankie Welch at the Sheraton-Carlton Hotel, Washington, D.C., ca. 1971, Capitol and Glogau photo, probably by Ed Segal; collection of Jamie Beverly Waldrop.

Wednesday
April 28, 1971

GUESTS AT FRANKIE'S TABLE

Mrs. Gene Anderson

Mrs. Sam Martin, Jr.

Trudie Johnson

Mrs. Wm. Sydnor

Mrs. Barney Martin

Turban style

rf designed by FRANKIE WELCH of Virginia.
305 Cameron St. Alexandria

TODAY'S FASHIONS

1.	Red & white gingham hot pants with matching blouse	$14. 14.
2.	Red Alligator hot pants & top	36.
3.	Blue polka dot hot pants with matching jacket	16. 14.
4.	Yellow Alligator pants suit	60.
5.	Beige & white check Alligator dress	34.
6.	Navy pants suit	85.
7.	Purple & white plaid dress	40.
8.	Beige dress with knit top	95.
9.	Red ensemble with striped blouse	68.
10.	Brown & white checked dress	70.
11.	Red & white print dress with stole	95.
12.	Navy all-weather coat	75.
13.	Red all-weather coat	95.
14.	Red, white & blue coat	75.
15.	Yellow print Frankie	25.
16.	Cherokee pants suit	75.
17.	Garden club pants suit	75.
18.	Yello print skirt with matching blouse	20. 16.
19.	Red long dress with purple, black & turquoise trim	80.
20.	Red, white & blue hot pants with overskirt	95.
21.	Plaid evening pants and trop	75.
22.	Multi-print long dress	36.
23.	Red, white & blue hot pants with over skirt & blouse	55.
24.	Multi-color hot pants with ruffles	68.
25.	Multi-color print long dress with yellow top	110.
26.	Red long dress with white embroidery	95.

TODAY'S MODELS

Kathy McCourt - White House Secretary

Cindy Colucci
Patsy Miller - Students at Marjorie Webster Jr. Col.

Alison Van Metra - Student Corcoran Art Gallery

Erica Lowery - Professional Model

Rebecca Moore - Secretary Cong. G.V. Montgomery

Opal Beverly - Frankie Welch House Model

As a pillow

CHEROKEE ALPHABET

Today's Fashions by Frankie Welch, Sheraton-Carlton program (outside and inside), 1971; Frankie Welch Collection, Rome Area History Center.

Cover of the "After the Game" recipe booklet with Campbell Soup Company, 1972; collection of Frankie Welch, Peggy Welch Williams, and Genie Welch Leisure.

group of Frankies, Thalhimers in Richmond, Virginia, promoted them alongside her Native American–inspired jewelry.[29]

Welch also designed garments of Ultrasuede, the popular ultra-microfiber, nonwoven synthetic fabric invented in Japan in 1970 that is closely associated with the designer Halston. Initially, she sold Ultrasuede garments by other designers, including a wine-colored shirtdress by Halston to Lynda Johnson Robb and a suit and a dress by Gino Rossi of Chicago's Wilson Garment Company to Betty Ford.[30] By 1977 Welch introduced her own designs, which were manufactured with the Skinner Fabrics division of Spring Mills.[31] Her line followed classic 1970s conservative silhouettes, with items including below-the-knee skirts, fitted blazers, a V-neck jumper, and a safari-style jacket she conceived while on a trip to Paris, all produced in a broad range of colors.[32] She sold her Ultrasuede line until at least 1984.

Welch established branches of her shop in several other cities in the 1970s. Her shop in Birmingham, Alabama, opened at 2018 Eleventh Avenue, in "an older district," in 1974 with Margaret H. Yeates as manager; the following year it changed to Margaret's of Birmingham, which went

Center spread of the "After the Game" recipe booklet with Campbell Soup Company, 1972; collection of Frankie Welch, Peggy Welch Williams, and Genie Welch Leisure.

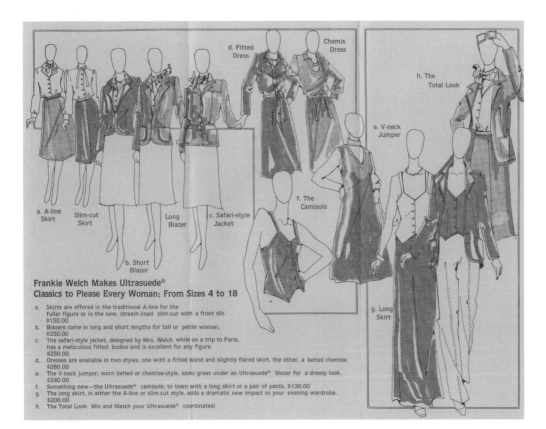

Frankie Welch Makes Ultrasuede®
Classics to Please Every Woman; From Sizes 4 to 18

a. Skirts are offered in the traditional A-line for the
    fuller figure or in the new, stream-lined slim-cut with a front slit.
    $150.00
b. Blazers come in long and short lengths for tall or petite women.
    $250.00
c. The safari-style jacket, designed by Mrs. Welch while on a trip to Paris,
    has a meticulous fitted bodice and is excellent for any figure.
    $250.00
d. Dresses are available in two styles, one with a fitted waist and slightly flared skirt, the other, a belted chemise.
    $280.00
e. The V-neck jumper, worn belted or chemise-style, looks great under an Ultrasuede® blazer for a dressy look.
    $240.00
f. Something new—the Ultrasuede® camisole, to team with a long skirt or a pair of pants. $130.00
g. The long skirt, in either the A-line or slim-cut style, adds a dramatic new impact to your evening wardrobe.
    $200.00
h. The Total Look- Mix and Match your Ultrasuede® coordinates!

Frankie Welch
Ultrasuede brochure,
n.d.; Frankie Welch
Collection, Rome Area
History Center.

Betty Ford wearing
an Ultrasuede dress
and scarf from Frankie
Welch of Virginia, 1975,
official White House
photo; collection of
Frankie Welch, Peggy
Welch Williams, and
Genie Welch Leisure.

My daughter Genie and I invite you to select from our spectacular
Spring fashions and from my latest ULTRASUEDE® designs!

Frankie Welch

Joanne Jacobson, Manager
305 Cameron Street, Alexandria, Va. 22314
(549-0104)
Mon.-Sat. 9:30 to 5:30, Thurs. 'til 7:30

Genie Welch Roberts, Manager
1702 G. St., N.W., Washington, D.C. 20006
(466-8900)
Mon.-Fri. 10:00 to 6:00

Major Credit Cards Accepted

Frankie Welch and Genie Welch wearing
Ultrasuede in a Frankie Welch advertisement,
Washington Dossier, June 1980, courtesy of
Washington Dossier editor David Adler; Frankie
Welch Textile Collection, Hargrett Rare Book
and Manuscript Library, University of
Georgia Libraries.

Frankie Welch wearing Ultrasuede,
ca. 1978; collection of Frankie Welch,
Peggy Welch Williams, and Genie
Welch Leisure.

out of business in late 1976 or early 1977.[33] Next, in 1977, she opened a store
in Atlanta in the upscale Omni International Complex, which originally
included a hotel, office space, shops, a movie theater, an arcade, and an
ice-skating rink and now is home to CNN Center. There she offered scarves,
clothing, and accessories along a "designers' row," near stores for Hermès,
Givenchy, and Pucci.[34] Evalyn Garner, who managed the store, described
it as "geared to working women," with fashionable, fun, and formal clothes
and both luxury and affordable scarves.[35] This remained open until around
1980. Finally, Welch established Frankie Welch of the Capital in 1978 in
Washington at 1702 G Street NW, on Liberty Plaza across from the Old
Executive Office Building.[36] Of that location, she explained, "I'm bringing
my business to my clients."[37] The Washington venue closed around 1984.[38]

Though the reasons these shops closed are not recorded, they probably
reflect circumstances beyond Welch's control. For example, the opening
of the Birmingham store took place while Welch's husband was ill, which
likely impacted her willingness to travel there often. Also, the Omni

Frankie Welch of Virginia in Birmingham store,
ca. 1974; collection of Frankie Welch, Peggy Welch
Williams, and Genie Welch Leisure.

Frankie Welch of Virginia in Birmingham
store, ca. 1974; Frankie Welch Collection,
Rome Area History Center.

International Complex was financially plagued—barely avoiding foreclosure shortly after Welch opened her store there—and challenged by its downtown Atlanta location, which many white, middle-class shoppers at the time viewed as unsafe. The shop in Washington lasted the longest, perhaps because she could be there in person more often. Throughout these expansions, the Alexandria location remained the heart of Welch's enterprise. Even though her younger daughter Genie took over management of the retail business in 1982, Welch remained the figure most prominently associated with it.[39]

Using her skills with fashion, color, and composition, in the late 1970s Welch focused part of her efforts on interiors, highlighting her textile designs. She viewed fashion and interior design as closely connected, and she even described clothes as "an extension of one's home," observing that her customers often "gravitat[ed] toward colors that match[ed] their living rooms."[40] She also believed that being able to coordinate a wardrobe should translate to being able to coordinate interior accessories in a home.[41]

Frankie Welch store at the Omni International Complex in Atlanta, ca. 1977; collection of Frankie Welch, Peggy Welch Williams, and Genie Welch Leisure.

Postcard of the Omni International Complex in Atlanta, with Frankie Welch's shop near the center on the second floor, n.d., photo by J. H. Robinson, Scenic South Card Co., Bessemer, Alabama; private collection.

Frankie Welch store at the Omni International Complex in Atlanta, ca. 1977; collection of Frankie Welch, Peggy Welch Williams, and Genie Welch Leisure.

Model in front of the Frankie Welch shop in Washington, D.C., ca. 1980; Frankie Welch Collection, Rome Area History Center.

Postcard of Frankie Welch shop in Washington, D.C., with Genie Welch (in the foreground) and Frankie Welch (in the midground), 1983; collection of Frankie Welch, Peggy Welch Williams, and Genie Welch Leisure.

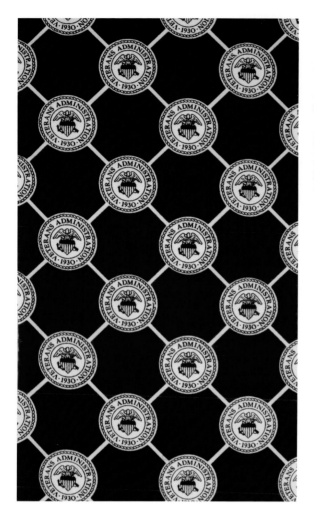

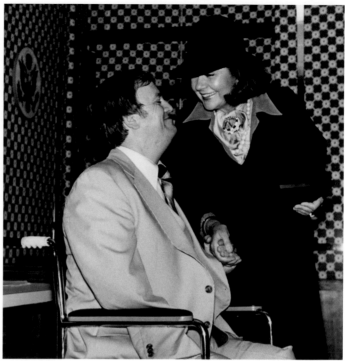

Max Cleland and Frankie Welch at the Veterans Administration, ca. 1978; Frankie Welch Collection, Rome Area History Center.

Veterans Administration fabric by Frankie Welch, 1978, cotton, photo by Mary Linnemann, Hargrett Rare Book and Manuscript Library; Frankie Welch Textile Collection, Hargrett Rare Book and Manuscript Library, University of Georgia Libraries.

In 1978 the Veterans Administration, headed at the time by fellow Georgian (and friend) Max Cleland, hired her to redo its offices.[42] After signing the contract, she announced that instead of accepting the fee, she would do the job as a donation in memory of her husband, who was the director of congressional liaison for the VA for many years.[43] The most prominent element of her work there was a custom wall covering of blue-and-white fabric with the seal of the VA repeated against a diagonal grid. Similarly, when she redecorated Second Lady Joan Mondale's office in the Old Executive Office Building in 1979, she also focused on fabric-covered wall panels, this time with a design based on the historic building's architectural moldings.[44]

Welch demonstrated the interior design potential of her fabrics again when she decorated her apartments at the Watergate complex in Washington, D.C. She moved there in 1977, first renting a small apartment to try out the location, then purchasing a large condo on the twelfth floor, where she lived until she downsized to another unit in 1988, all in

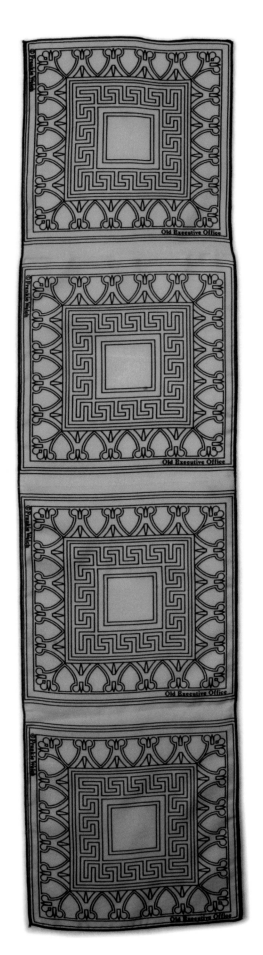

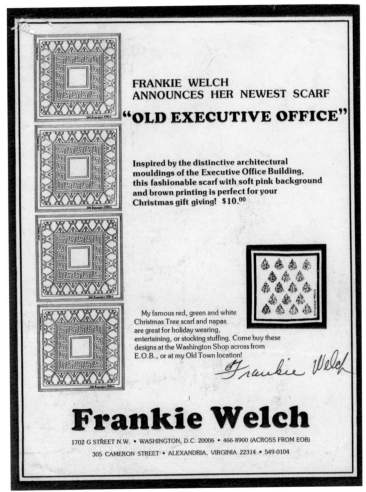

Old Executive Office Building scarf, 1979, polyester, photo
by Mary Linnemann, Hargrett Rare Book and Manuscript
Library; Frankie Welch Textile Collection, Hargrett Rare Book
and Manuscript Library, University of Georgia Libraries.

203

Frankie Welch's Watergate condo, ca. 1981, photo by Glen Leach; collection of Frankie Welch, Peggy Welch Williams, and Genie Welch Leisure.

Frankie Welch's Watergate condo, ca. 1981, photo by Glen Leach; collection of Frankie Welch, Peggy Welch Williams, and Genie Welch Leisure.

Aerial view of the Watergate Complex, 1984, photo by Mickey Sanborn, U.S. National Archives, Combined Military Service Digital Photographic Files.

Frankie Welch demonstrating how her fabric-covered boards work, 1980; collection of Frankie Welch, Peggy Welch Williams, and Genie Welch Leisure.

Watergate South.[45] A two-part feature in the *Washington Post* in 1980 detailed how she used modular fabric-covered panels to flexibly incorporate her designs throughout the large condo.[46] She attached her printed fabrics to quarter-inch-thick boards that could be mounted to the wall or hinged together and used as freestanding screens, and that could serve as insulation, provided easy cover-ups for damaged areas, and were convenient to move when the owner relocated. She appreciated the portability of the fabric panels both for their appropriateness for the Washington routine of changing offices every four to eight years and because they allowed for easy seasonal interior design changes.[47]

The primary fabric she used throughout her Watergate condo was a maze pattern in an eight-by-eight-inch module that she had designed as a scarf for the Folger Shakespeare Library. Besides using it in the fabric wall panels, she incorporated it as bed linens, as coverings for the bed's headboard and footboard, gathered on the ceiling of the foyer like the inside of a tent, and as napkins.[48] She used a second maze design for the Folger on pillows. She framed and hung the screens used to print the Folger designs as art on the walls of the living room.[49]

The interior colors, including lavender, mauve, and apricot, in addition to being popular for that era, reflected the changing hues of the sunset sky Welch could see through her large windows when she returned home from working in Alexandria.[50] Her fifty-foot balcony overlooked the Potomac River and Theodore Roosevelt Island bird sanctuary and was decorated with potted hemlocks, herbs, geraniums, seasonal flowers, and floral-themed scarves.[51]

LEFT: Folger Shakespeare Library scarf, 1978, Qiana, photo by Mary Linnemann, Hargrett Rare Book and Manuscript Library; Frankie Welch Textile Collection, Hargrett Rare Book and Manuscript Library, University of Georgia Libraries.

RIGHT: Folger Shakespeare Library scarf, 1978, Qiana, photo by Mary Linnemann, Hargrett Rare Book and Manuscript Library; Frankie Welch Textile Collection, Hargrett Rare Book and Manuscript Library, University of Georgia Libraries.

Washington Home and Garden featured her third Watergate apartment, where she reused the portable fabric-covered panels and again incorporated scarves throughout.[52] She covered an entrance wall in a grid of framed scarves and propped one large framed scarf in front of the television. Particularly notable was her use of lattice on the large terrace, which could accommodate one hundred guests, to create arches that framed mirrors reflecting the abundant potted plants and giving the illusion of extensive gardens.

Combining her fashion-advising experience with the knowledge that she had gained through working with corporate clients on scarves, Welch began offering national and international corporate image consulting services in the late 1970s. She advised on all areas, "from the specific corporate gift to the general level of taste," beginning with the reception area and the receptionist. Welch also presented talks and fashion shows for political groups, corporate groups, and students.[53]

The year 1983 marked the twentieth anniversary of Frankie Welch of Virginia. Welch organized numerous events and launched a custom fragrance, named "Frankie," that was described as "a mix of roses, violets and lavender," like "a stroll in a Virginia garden."[54] She presented it in a mini-tote bag in the same colors, purple and white, as bags she had made for the actress Elizabeth Taylor (then-wife of five-term Republican senator John Warner of Virginia) to give in celebration of a revival of Lillian Hellman's *The Little Foxes*, which ran at the Kennedy Center in 1981 before moving to Broadway.[55] She also introduced a special paisley-patterned Frankie to mark the anniversary.[56]

The *Washington Dossier*, a magazine that chronicled Washington society from 1975 to 1991, regularly mentioned Welch—listing her fashion events in its calendar, citing her successful dieting efforts, describing her fitness routine (ten minutes of daily exercise and two or three massages a week), detailing one of her Sunday brunches, and noting parties she attended, including a benefit movie premiere at the Kennedy Center Opera House in 1977 and a benefit for the D.C. Society for Crippled Children in 1982.[57] In 1981, just after Ronald Reagan became president, the *Washington Dossier* quoted her on popular colors in fashion, saying, "For sportswear, lots and lots of red—red jackets, red sweaters, and I'm calling it Nancy Red."[58]

Other society writers reported on her activities as well, including Diana McLellan, who christened her "designer to the divine" and "Scarfmaker to the Splendid Ones."[59] Characters, a modeling agency established in 1987 by Rosetta McPherson for nontraditional models, even enlisted her as one of its celebrity models.[60] The Foundry, a chic restaurant in Georgetown, named a booth in Welch's honor.[61] She regularly donated scarves to charitable organizations to be used in auctions and other fundraisers.[62]

The *Washington Dossier* described her approach to party planning: "Frankie Welch, with the aid of her invaluable Chinese housekeeper-cook

Frankie Welch on her terrace
at the Watergate, ca. 1990,
Lautman Photography
Washington; collection of Frankie
Welch, Peggy Welch Williams,
and Genie Welch Leisure.

OPPOSITE: Frankie Welch's third Watergate condo,
ca. 1990, Lautman Photography Washington;
collection of Frankie Welch, Peggy Welch
Williams, and Genie Welch Leisure.

Birthday party for Frankie Welch's granddaughter, Lindsay (*center*) on her terrace at the Watergate, 1991; collection of Frankie Welch, Peggy Welch Williams, and Genie Welch Leisure.

[Dannie Lowe], pulls together a sparkling brunch or dinner in one day, even via long distance," explaining that she always chose from one of three set menus to make the process easier.[63] (She favored corn pudding, honey-apple glazed ham, spinach quiche, and green pea salad, or her chicken with creamed chipped beef from the Campbell's soup promotion over rice with a Bibb lettuce salad and green beans.)[64] Welch was a popular hostess. *People* magazine described her as the Perle Mesta of designers, referring to the Washington socialite and ambassador famous in the 1940s and 1950s for her lavish parties (and subsequently a customer of Frankie Welch of Virginia).[65] Welch preferred a casual, though not haphazard, approach to entertaining. She followed specific protocol, not serving drinks "more than 45 minutes before dinner," and keeping everything punctual because Washington was such a busy town. Regarding her guest list, she explained, "If I talk to people during the week whom it would be fun to see again, I invite them to brunch on Sunday."[66] She also reinvited guests "who spar-kle[d] and contribute[d] to the party."[67]

In the midst of these many professional activities and social recognitions, a major change occurred for Welch—her shop in Alexandria, which she had opened in 1963, closed its doors. While shops typically fade into obscurity when they close, Frankie Welch of Virginia instead made headlines. In February 1990 the *Washington Post* proclaimed, "Alexandria Shop Ends a Fashionable Era" and reported that "former first ladies, the wives of governors and native Washingtonians were stunned and saddened." Lady Bird Johnson called Welch to reminisce when she heard the news, and one of Genie's friends, who had just left Washington for her home in Houston, Texas, immediately flew back.[68] Welch, though, appears to have taken the change in stride and continued working in Duvall House with her ongoing design business, which she had branded as Frankie Welch Designs by the early to mid-1980s.[69]

In addition to scarves, Welch designed custom tote bags (in a variety of sizes) and large statement umbrellas, as well as occasional tiles, plates, T-shirts, and paperweights. The tote bags in particular were a signature item for her, and she often carried one (or more) with her to advertise her business. Her totes were especially popular and at the leading edge of the vogue for branded tote bags.[70] Welch also had many ideas that never materialized but reflect her ambition and confidence. For example, when she spoke to an audience at the Smithsonian's National Museum of American History in 1991, she proposed starting a line of home fabrics to rival Laura Ashley, the British textile and fashion company known for its romantic floral prints, casually mentioning the need for $20 million to get started.[71] In 1993 she talked about transferring scarf designs to rugs and writing a book on design.[72] Welch once told a visitor, "I have so many ideas I can't sleep. . . . I'm making plans for the next three years."[73]

As an independently successful female entrepreneur, Welch was a role model during the era of the women's liberation movement. In particular, many young women worked for her—especially through paid internships or summer jobs—and were inspired by her creativity and business success, including Inge Oliveria, a Brazilian immigrant who managed the shop while Welch's husband was ill, then started her own dress business; the late Caroline Ragsdale Reutter, who founded the now-famous southern sweets business, Caroline's Cakes; and Ginger Howard, who opened her own dress shop (Ginger Howard Selections) in the upscale Buckhead district of Atlanta. Howard recognized Welch as a trailblazer and has followed Welch's model in how she provides custom service to high-profile political clients.[74] Another young employee, Chris Tucker Haggerty, who sketched some of Welch's scarf designs for her and went on to have a career as an artist, was fascinated by Welch's "all-pervasive creativity" and credits Welch as her inspiration, saying, "It was she who first showed me that art could spawn a career."[75]

Welch's views on feminism, though, were relatively traditional. When she spoke in 1975 at a luncheon for women in management positions, she presented a carefully balanced approach. She eschewed the hard sell and stated, "I am feminine. I feel like a woman and I think being a woman is the most wonderful thing in the world," but acknowledged that it was okay to be determined and motivated, adding, "I was motivated by money and still am."[76] When interviewed in 1984, she expressed her belief that women should achieve success through style and a sense of humor, while avoiding a confrontational attitude. She further explained her position on feminism:

> I have not been an activist. I don't like the Jane Fonda approach. I've not been discriminated against because I am a woman. I think good manners and kindnesses prevail. . . . I know there are discriminations, but my approach is that I feel that a lot of the movement has been towards a lot of mixed up people. . . . I do know that I want equal pay for women, and I have had equal pay and more.[77]

As with her nonpartisan political stance, this moderate view of feminism likely allowed her to appeal to a broad clientele base and contributed to her professional and financial success.

Though Welch expanded her activities beyond scarves, she never abandoned them, continuing to create custom scarves through the 1990s. By the mid-1980s, she had begun moving away from the eight-by-eight-inch module and returned to large silk squares and occasional long, narrow scarves (though she often had one-by-four module scarves printed next to the large silk squares in order to use the full width of the yardage). Some of the large silk square scarves recall designs from Hermès, the iconic luxury brand from Paris that she held in particularly high regard at this time, and were promoted as her most valuable offerings.[78] Many of her late scarves featured architectural motifs.[79] For example, she began a National Treasures series by 1993 with details from historic artifacts and historic buildings including Mount Vernon and Drayton Hall in Charleston, and a design for the Republican Senatorial Trust employs elements from the Minton tiles installed in the Senate Capitol extension in the mid-nineteenth century.[80] She favored designs with images of large tassels, as seen on her U.S. Naval Academy's scarf for the thirtieth reunion of the Class of 1960, noting in a talk at the Smithsonian in 1991, "I'm in my tassel period now."[81] She continued to create bold, individualized scarves for a variety of clients. Also, from the mid-1980s into the mid-1990s, she designed many medium-sized, more casual cotton squares, variously called—and used as—bandanas, scarves, and napkins.

Neither Welch nor her staff maintained a master list of her scarf designs, and there is no official record of how many scarves she produced. The numbers quoted in the media—approximations and best guesses supplied by Welch and her staff—suggest that she had designed more than three hundred scarves by spring 1972, seven hundred by fall 1974, and 2,800 by 1980.[82] The highest count reported was four thousand.[83] Regardless of the exact number, scarves remain her signature accomplishment in a successful career full of creative business endeavors.

National Treasures (Mount Vernon) scarf, commissioned by Holly Coors, 1993, silk, photo by Mary Linnemann, Hargrett Rare Book and Manuscript Library; collection of Frankie Welch, Peggy Welch Williams, and Genie Welch Leisure.

National Treasures Series version of Squash Blossoms, 1993, silk, photo by Mary Linnemann,
Hargrett Rare Book and Manuscript Library; collection of Frankie Welch, Peggy Welch Williams,
and Genie Welch Leisure.

Senatorial Trust scarf, n.d., silk, photo by Mary Linnemann, Hargrett Rare Book and Manuscript Library; collection of Frankie Welch, Peggy Welch Williams, and Genie Welch Leisure.

United States Naval Academy scarf, 30th reunion of the Class of
1960, 1990, silk, photo by Mary Linnemann, Hargrett Rare Book and
Manuscript Library; private collection.

Manhattan Jaguar (Rockville, Maryland) scarf, 1987, silk, photo by Mary Linnemann, Hargrett Rare Book and Manuscript Library; collection of Frankie Welch, Peggy Welch Williams, and Genie Welch Leisure.

Moore Cadillac Company (Virginia), ca. 1984, silk, photo by
Mary Linnemann, Hargrett Rare Book and Manuscript Library; collection
of Frankie Welch, Peggy Welch Williams, and Genie Welch Leisure.

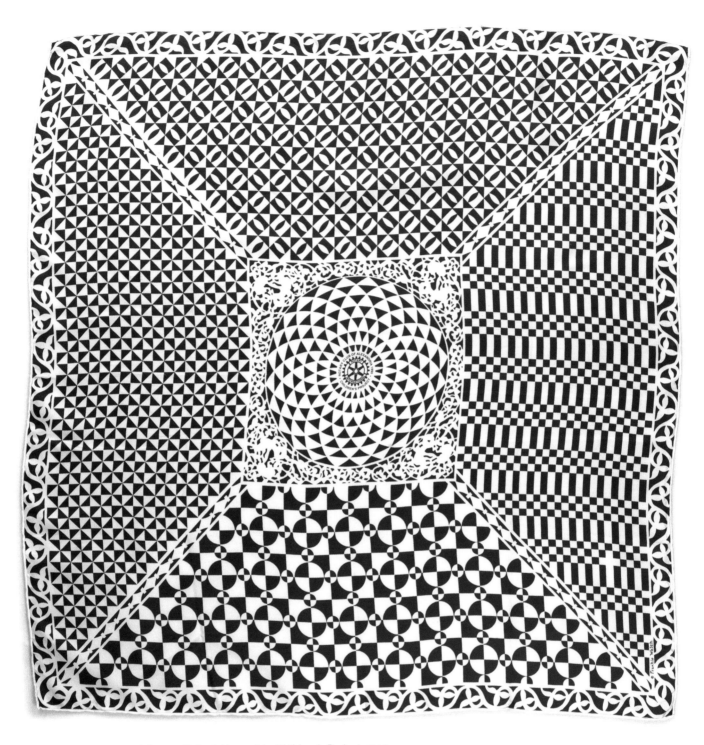

Rotary International, Rotary Club of Alexandria, Children's Project, 1995,
silk, photo by Mary Linnemann, Hargrett Rare Book and Manuscript Library;
collection of Frankie Welch, Peggy Welch Williams, and Genie Welch Leisure.

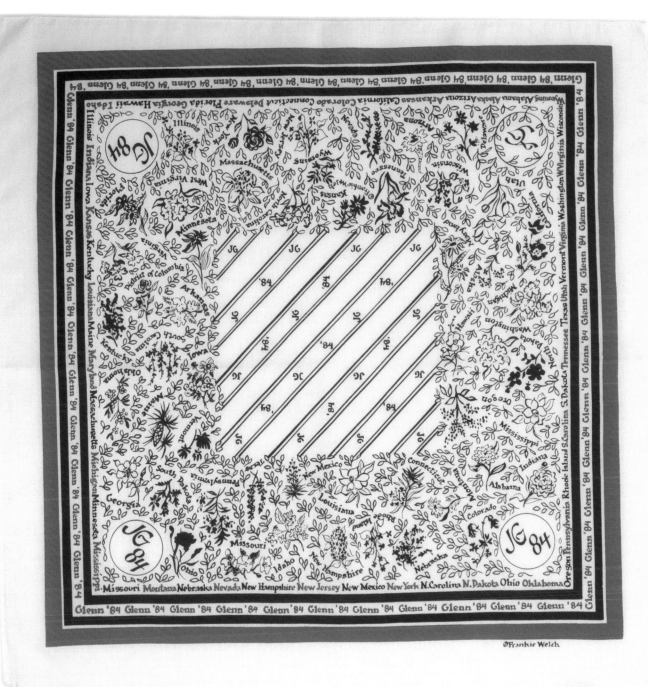

John Glenn presidential campaign bandana, 1983, cotton, photo
by Mary Linnemann, Hargrett Rare Book and Manuscript Library;
Frankie Welch Collection, Rome Area History Center.

(*left to right*) John Glenn, Frankie Welch, Genie Welch, ca. 1984;
Frankie Welch Collection, Rome Area History Center.

Mothers Embracing Nuclear Disarmament (MEND) bandana, 1987, cotton, photo
by Mary Linnemann, Hargrett Rare Book and Manuscript Library; collection of
Frankie Welch, Peggy Welch Williams, and Genie Welch Leisure.

Shell Details on 18th-Century Furniture from the Diplomatic Rooms of the State Department of the United States of America bandana, n.d., cotton, photo by Mary Linnemann, Hargrett Rare Book and Manuscript Library; collection of Frankie Welch, Peggy Welch Williams, and Genie Welch Leisure.

Daughters of the American Revolution Centennial Celebration bandana, 1990, cotton, photo by Mary Linnemann, Hargrett Rare Book and Manuscript Library; collection of Frankie Welch, Peggy Welch Williams, and Genie Welch Leisure.

Architectural Details from National Cathedral, Washington, D.C., bandana, n.d., cotton, photo by Mary Linnemann, Hargrett Rare Book and Manuscript Library; collection of Frankie Welch, Peggy Welch Williams, and Genie Welch Leisure.

BB&T bandana, n.d., cotton, photo by Mary Linnemann, Hargrett Rare Book and Manuscript Library; collection of Frankie Welch, Peggy Welch Williams, and Genie Welch Leisure.

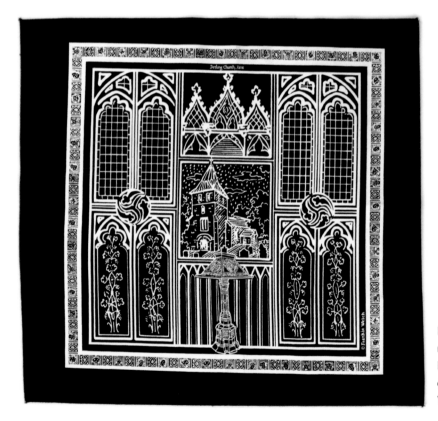

Detling Church, Kent, U.K., bandana, n.d., cotton, photo by Mary Linnemann, Hargrett Rare Book and Manuscript Library; collection of Frankie Welch, Peggy Welch Williams, and Genie Welch Leisure.

Bandana fun with Frankie flyer, n.d.; collection of Frankie Welch, Peggy Welch Williams, and Genie Welch Leisure.

Conclusion
Frankie Welch's Legacy

By the mid-1990s—she turned seventy in 1994—Frankie Welch began to slow down. She also began to experience issues with her memory. The initial changes were subtle, though, and she covered lapses well.[1] Welch moved from the Watergate to a high-rise condo in Alexandria House in Old Town (the historic neighborhood where she had lived and worked for so many years) in 1995, and in 2001 she relocated to Westminster-Canterbury of the Blue Ridge, a senior living community in Charlottesville, Virginia, near her daughter Peggy. By that time, Welch already had taken steps to ensure her legacy, in particular donating collections of her work to colleges and universities, and her achievements had been recognized through exhibitions and honors for more than two decades. Welch resided for many years in the Memory Wing of Westminster until her death in 2021. Both of her daughters continue to enjoy, protect, and share their mother's legacy.

The first major exhibition of her work, *Frankie Welch Designs for American Industry*, took place at the Textile Museum in Washington, D.C., in 1980 and was cosponsored by Time Life Books, which rented part of Gilpin House (the property she owned near Duvall House) from her, and Clyde's, a restaurant in Georgetown. For this show, Welch displayed many finished scarves along with the screens that were used to print them, emphasizing the industrial process through which they were produced and highlighting her combination of art and business. The show included two designs she created for Time Life, one of which was for the company's twentieth anniversary.[2] The Textile Museum also commissioned designs for scarves (based on a lotto carpet in its collection) and umbrellas (based on a Star Ushak carpet also in its collection), which were prominent during the well-attended event; the umbrellas were used to keep guests dry as they arrived at the opening reception during a rainstorm.[3]

OPPOSITE: Frankie Welch's studio, n.d.; collection of Frankie Welch, Peggy Welch Williams, and Genie Welch Leisure.

RIGHT: Photo by Mary Linnemann; Frankie Welch Textile Collection, Hargrett Rare Book and Manuscript Library, University of Georgia Libraries.

229

To Frankie
my love
Betty Ford

Genie Welch Leisure, Frankie Welch, and Peggy Welch Williams in Rome, Georgia, for Frankie Welch Day, 2010; collection of Frankie Welch, Peggy Welch Williams, and Genie Welch Leisure.

OPPOSITE: Peggy Welch Williams, Frankie Welch, and Genie Welch at the White House, signed by Betty Ford, 1976; collection of Frankie Welch, Peggy Welch Williams, and Genie Welch Leisure.

Frankie Welch with two unidentified people at the Textile Museum, Washington, D.C., 1980; Frankie Welch Collection, Rome Area History Center.

Frankie Welch at the Textile Museum, Washington, D.C., 1980; collection of Frankie Welch, Peggy Welch Williams, and Genie Welch Leisure.

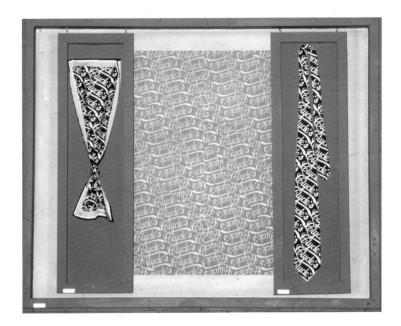

Display of Clyde's scarf, screen, and tie, 1980; collection of Frankie Welch, Peggy Welch Williams, and Genie Welch Leisure.

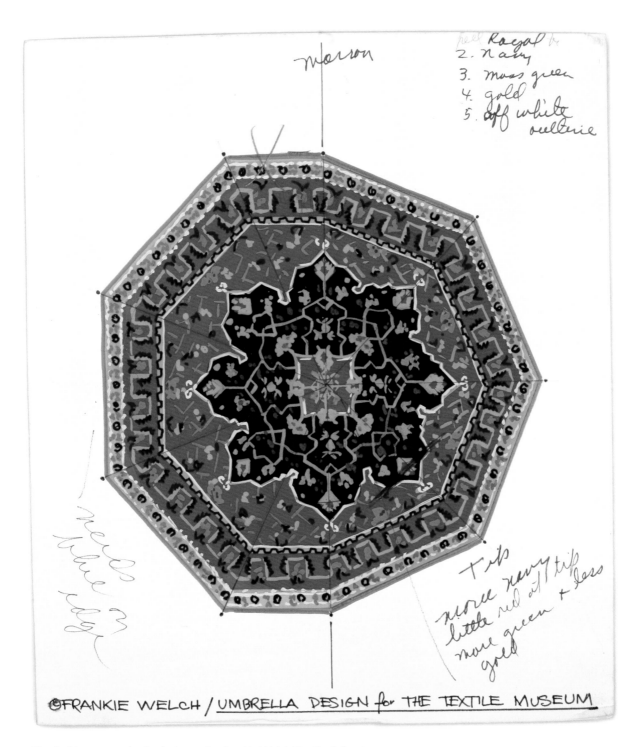

maroon

1. red Royal b[?]
2. navy
3. moss green
4. gold
5. off white outline

need blue sky

rib
more navy tip
little red at tip
more green + less
gold

©FRANKIE WELCH / UMBRELLA DESIGN for THE TEXTILE MUSEUM

Textile Museum umbrella design, 1980; Frankie Welch Textile Collection,
Hargrett Rare Book and Manuscript Library, University of Georgia Libraries.

Frankie Welch and Mary Ellen Brooks of the Hargrett Rare Book and Manuscript Library at the Frankie Welch exhibition at the University of Georgia, 1982; Frankie Welch Textile Collection, Hargrett Rare Book and Manuscript Library, University of Georgia Libraries.

Dr. and Mrs. Irv Wofford at the Frankie Welch exhibition at the University of Georgia, 1982; Frankie Welch Textile Collection, Hargrett Rare Book and Manuscript Library, University of Georgia Libraries.

In 1982 the University of Georgia, where she had taken summer classes to earn her teacher certification in the mid-1940s, presented an exhibition of her work called *Frankie Welch Designs*.[4] At this time she donated a large collection of her scarves and papers to the university and designed a scarf for the university's Presidents Club, a patrons group of which she was a charter member, based on Greek revival architectural details from the ceiling of the university's mid-nineteenth-century President's House. She sometimes joked that this was her most expensive scarf because it cost $10,000—the membership level for the Presidents Club at that time—to get one.[5]

When the Lyndon Baines Johnson Library and Museum presented *Frankie Welch: American Designer* in 1984, her friend Lady Bird Johnson hosted a luncheon in her honor.[6] The Athenaeum (which had hosted the event debuting her Cherokee Alphabet scarf) in Alexandria celebrated twenty years of her scarf designs with an exhibition in 1987 called *Frankie Welch: A Design Retrospective*, with Betty Ford as the show's honorary chairman.[7] In October 1993 Auburn University in Alabama presented a retrospective with more than two hundred scarves.[8] Welch's hometown has held several exhibitions of her work, including at the Rome Area History Museum in 1999 and 2010 and the Chieftains Museum in 2019–20.[9] The University of Georgia's Hargrett Rare Book and Manuscript Library is presenting a major exhibition on her designs, coinciding with the publication of this book, in early 2022. Additionally, in 2015–17 the traveling exhibition *Native Fashion Now*, organized by the Peabody Essex

Frankie Welch giving a talk at the University of Georgia, 1982,
photo by Wingate Downs, Athens, Georgia; Frankie Welch
Collection, Rome Area History Center.

Museum in Salem, Massachusetts, included two works by Welch—her
iconic Cherokee Alphabet scarf and the red dress she designed for Betty
Ford—and recognized her as a Native American designer.[10]

Welch received numerous honors and recognitions during her career. One
of the earliest took place in 1968, when Lady Bird Johnson included her in
a Women Doers Luncheon.[11] In 1975 the International Fine Arts College
in Miami, Florida (now the Miami International University of Art and
Design), bestowed an honorary doctorate on Welch.[12] The city of Alexandria
declared a Frankie Welch Day on March 29, 1992 (her birthday), and Mayor
Patsy Ticer proclaimed, "Frankie Welch is a philanthropist, entrepreneur
and teacher who has given generously of her time, talent and personal
savings to the City of Alexandria."[13] She received a Distinguished Woman
Award from Northwood University in Michigan in 1997.[14]

President George H. W. Bush appointed Welch to the Department of
Defense's Textiles and Clothing Board in 1991.[15] She was the only female
on the board, which otherwise comprised a dozen male generals and ad-
mirals. They met several times at Duvall/Welch House, and one of their
tasks was to consider and approve designs and materials for military
forces to use during Operation Desert Storm.[16]

Welch served on the boards of Furman University, Auburn University,
Marymount College in Arlington, the International Fine Arts College
in Miami, the Francis Scott Key Foundation, the National Women's
Economic Alliance, and Women of Our Hemisphere, and on advisory

Entrance of the Athenaeum in Alexandria, Virginia, draped with fabrics during the Frankie Welch exhibition, 1987; collection of Frankie Welch, Peggy Welch Williams, and Genie Welch Leisure.

Frankie Welch exhibition at the Athenaeum in Alexandria, Virginia, 1987; collection of Frankie Welch, Peggy Welch Williams, and Genie Welch Leisure.

committees of Virginia Polytechnic Institute and State University's Textile Department as well as Mount Vernon College's Department of Business.[17]

In honor of Welch's thirtieth anniversary in design, in 1998 Helen Thomas, White House UPI correspondent (and longtime Welch family friend); Judith Terra, an art philanthropist from Chicago; and Holly Coors, a former ambassador-at-large and conservative political activist (and close personal friend of Welch's), cohosted a celebration at Duvall/Welch House.[18] During the series of predinner tributes, Thomas described Welch as "the First Lady of American Design" and recalled how when they and their husbands used to vacation together in the Shenandoah mountains, Welch would use her southern charm to soothe everyone's feelings after Helen and Bill inevitably argued about politics.[19] Also for this anniversary, Senator Fritz Hollings of South Carolina recognized her in the Congressional Record of the Senate with a "Tribute to Frankie Welch," praising her as "no ordinary fashion designer," and for using her talents "to produce patriotic garments" and designs that demonstrated "an exemplary love of our country."[20] The exhibitions and honors reflect an on-going interest in Welch's work and have helped maintain awareness of her accomplishments.

Frankie Welch with her granddaughter
Lindsay wearing a McDonald's Frankie
at the Athenaeum, 1987; collection of
Frankie Welch, Peggy Welch Williams,
and Genie Welch Leisure.

Frankie Welch at an exhibition of her designs at the Rome
Area History Museum, 2010; collection of Frankie Welch,
Peggy Welch Williams, and Genie Welch Leisure.

Welch donated collections of her scarves and archival materials (business records, newspaper clippings, photographs, and original designs) to numerous schools in the 1980s and early 1990s, including:

University of Georgia in Athens, Georgia
Berry College near Rome, Georgia
Winthrop College in Rock Hill, South Carolina
Goldie Paley Design Center at the Philadelphia College of Textiles and
     Science (now the Textile and Costume Collection at Thomas Jefferson
     University—East Falls)
University of Texas at Austin
University of Rhode Island (housed in the Historic Textile and Costume
     Collection in the Department of Textiles, Fashion Merchandising and
     Design; College of Business)
University of Missouri-Columbia, Department of Clothing and Textiles,
     College of Home Economics (now the Missouri Historic Costume and
     Textile Collection, Department of Textile and Apparel Management)
Auburn University[21]

She repeatedly expressed her love of teaching, and, by placing her work
in academic institutions, she hoped that students could learn from her

designs. She often gave talks, was commissioned to design scarves, or developed connections with the merchandising and consumer sciences areas to engage with the student communities of these institutions. For example, with Winthrop, she was the Distinguished Visiting Professor of Merchandising and Design for the School of Consumer Science from 1982 to 1985; lectured to individual classes and joined a Fashion Club luncheon in fall 1982; and presented a fashion show in 1984.[22] The presence of her designs in so many university collections will continue to engage new audiences.

Welch's work also is well represented in the Smithsonian Institution. The Museum of History and Technology (now the National Museum of American History) acquired a group of her scarves in the 1970s as well as the dress she designed for First Lady Betty Ford. Recently, the Cooper Hewitt, Smithsonian Design Museum in New York added a group of Welch's scarves to its collection through a donation from her daughters.

Welch's friend Eleni, the Washington fashion reporter who first wrote about her distinctive Frankie dresses in 1964, offered a tribute in 1990, saying, "What I like most about Frankie Welch is that she is a true original. She has created a life that many envy with its travel, its stimulation, and loveliness. She has a grace about her. She shares her happiness in finding her place in this exciting world of ours that includes more than clothes."[23]

Frankie Welch's positive outlook and joy in life were authentic and enduring. She pursued her passion for fashion and design with determination and spread her enthusiasm and knowledge to those around her. While her designs stand as a testament to her profound understanding of fashion's trajectory, the business of dress, and the attraction of scarves, she was more than just a designer.

Welch combined fashion and design with an acute business sense, emphatically nonpartisan political stance, and awareness of the marketability of her own persona that anticipated the lifestyle brand approach of people like Martha Stewart and today's influencer culture. Her shop filled a need in the Washington area for clear fashion guidance; her Frankie dress—though a simple form developed for an educational purpose—was so expertly promoted that it remained an "in" garment for decades; and her scarf designs, which debuted on the crest of the signature scarf craze, defined and satisfied a niche market for limited-edition custom scarves. The scarves, while embodying the evolution of fashion from the late 1960s through the 1990s, also are a remarkable record of businesses and institutions, private weddings and annual conferences, schools and associations. Her scarves constitute a unique body of work in the history of American fashion, standing apart from exclusively design- or art-based scarves because of Welch's embrace of their commercial and documentary possibilities. Welch's scarves are a distinct and delightful expression of Americana.

OPPOSITE: Frankie Welch in front of Duvall House, ca. 1972, photo by Joan Larson; Frankie Welch Collection, Rome Area History Center.

American Alphabet, 1969, cotton, photo by Mary Linnemann,
Hargrett Rare Book and Manuscript Library; private collection.

Appendix
Partial List of Scarves, Tote Bags, and Neckties by Frankie Welch

This list is intended to provide a general impression of the expansiveness of Welch's roster of clients and to help with the identification of less obvious designs. It is not a complete record of every design Welch produced, and it likely contains errors. Sometimes only the client (and not the type of item) is known. The information is based on records in her various archives (which themselves contain dating inconsistencies), observation of Welch items that have appeared in online auctions for the past decade, and examination of scarves and other items in her archives and with her family. Welch also sold numerous conventional scarves with simple geometric or floral designs that are not included here.

Description	Date	Type of item
4-H	1980	module scarf
82nd Airborne Division (Airborne AA)	n.d.	module scarf
101st Airborne Division	n.d.	module scarf
President John Adams (U.S. Bicentennial)	1975	module scarf
The African Room, The John F. Kennedy Center for the Performing Arts	n.d.	tote
A. G. Edwards, Inc.	n.d.	tote
Agnes Scott Alumnae Association	1982	module scarf
Airclaims (London) (navy, red, and white, with red arrow form over globe)	ca. 1981	module scarf
Air Force Debutante Ball	1989	bandana
Air Force Officers' Wives' Club	1975, 1978, 1981	module scarf
Air Force Sergeants Association (AFSA)	n.d.	module scarf and tote
Air National Guard	n.d.	module scarf
Alexandria Historic Landmarks (houses around edge with names radiating from center)	by 1974	module scarf
Alexandria Junior Woman's Club Embassy Tour	1977	module scarf
Alexandria National Bank of Northern Virginia	n.d.	module scarf
Algonquin Hotel (with signature of Ben C. Bodne, owner)	ca. 1969	large silk square scarf
Alpha Delta Kappa	1987	module scarf and tote
Altomar Collection	n.d.	tote
American Alliance for Health, Physical Education, Recreation and Dance (AAHPERD)	n.d.	necktie
American Alphabet	1969	square cotton scarf
American Association of University Women centennial (AAUW, 1881–1981)	1981	module scarf
American Cancer Society (ACS)	1981	module scarf
American Consulting Engineers Council (ACEC)	1981	module scarf
American Diabetes Association	n.d.	tote
American Family Insurance	n.d.	module scarf
American Family Life Assurance (Columbus, Ga.)	1979	module scarf
American Film Institute (possibly filmstrip with star design)	n.d.	tote, bandana, and apron
American Freedom Train	ca. 1976	module scarf
American Horticultural Society	n.d.	module scarf
American Institute of Architects (AIA)	n.d.	module scarf, bandana, and tote
American Medical Association, Educational Research Fund (AMA-ERF) (blue, green, and yellow, with dogwoods)	1973	long rectangle scarf
American Medical Association, Educational Research Fund (AMA-ERF) (brown and black with buildings)	n.d.	module scarf
American Revolution Bicentennial Administration (ARBA)	ca. 1976	module scarf and necktie
American Road and Transportation Builders Association (ARTBA)	n.d.	module scarf
American Short Line Railroad Association	1979, 1980, 1981	module scarves

Description	Date	Type of item
American Trucking Associations (trucks design)	ca. 1976	module scarf
American University	n.d.	large silk square scarf
American Water Works Association (red droplets enclosing stick figures with blue droplet heads, "Willie the Water Drop")	ca. 1970	long rectangle scarf with continuous design and necktie
Apollo 11 Landing, twentieth anniversary (1969–1989)	1989	bandana
Appleseed Ridge Girl Scout Council	1981	module scarf
Arabic Alphabet: see Fourteenth Centennial of Islam		
Architectural Woodwork Association, New Orleans Convention	n.d.	
Arizona Thunderbirds tourism group (variation of Thunderbird design)	n.d.	module scarf
Army and Navy Club, on Farragut Square, Washington, D.C.	n.d.	tote
Army National Guard	n.d.	module scarf
Army Wives Are Special	n.d.	bandana
Aspen Music Festival	n.d.	
Associated General Contractors of America	1979	module scarf
Associated General Contractors of America (AGC), Hawaii '80	1980	module scarf
Associated General Contractors of America	n.d.	tote
Association of American Railroads (trains design)	n.d.	module scarf
Atlanta Dogwood Festival	1978	module scarf
Auburn University	ca. 1993	bandana
Auto-Train	early 1970s	module scarf
Baltimore Museum of Art	1974	module scarf
Bankers Life of Nebraska (golfer with "Maui 1980")	1980	module scarf
Bank for Cooperatives, Iowa, 50th anniversary	n.d.	
Bank of Virginia (for opening of branch in Alexandria), the Money Bag	n.d.	tote
Banks for Cooperatives (Denver, Colo.) ("50" and wheat)	ca. 1983	module scarf
Barbara Sinatra Children's Center	n.d.	bandana
Basil (restaurant)	n.d.	module scarf
Basket Weave design (Box, Peace Pipe, Single Diamond, Jacob's Ladder)	1973	module scarf
William C. Battle (campaign for governor of Virginia)	1969	square cotton scarf
Bayles and Wallace Ranches, Jack and Donna, California (variation of Christmas trees design)	1989	napachief
BB&T	n.d.	bandana
Begg, Inc. (real estate company)	1979	module scarf and tote
Begg International, 35th anniversary	n.d.	bandana and tote
Bell System Home Consultant	ca. 1980	napachief
Bendix, Paris Air Show	1982	yardage
Benedictine Health Foundation, Inc. (letters around circle: S.M.Q.L.I.V.B. V.R.S.N.S.M.V.; letters in cross: NDSMD, CSSML with middle S used in both; letters in small circles: CSPB)	1979	module scarf
Benihana Corporation	n.d.	necktie

Description	Date	Type of item
Berkshire Playhouse, Berkshire Theater Festival (Stockbridge, Mass.)	n.d.	module scarf
Berry College	1983	module scarf
Bicentennial Council of the Thirteen Original States	1975	module scarf and tea towel
Birmingham Centennial (Alabama)	1971–72	module scarf
Stephen Howard Blount and Linda Falvey Rowland wedding, Austin, Texas	1987	module scarf
Blount International (Alabama construction company) (with the words "Blount" and "Camellia")	1981	module scarf
Boar's Head Inn and Sports Club (Charlottesville, Va.)	n.d.	module scarf
Bonnets design: see Salvation Army		
Sandy Liddy Bourne, A New Voice for Mount Vernon	n.d.	bandana
Bozell & Jacobs, Inc. (Nebraska design firm)	1978	module scarf
Bridge design (created as cover for *Bridge Made Easy* by Caroline Sydnor then used as shop stock)	ca. 1975	module scarf
Brown Construction Co. (variation of Christmas trees design)	n.d.	napachief
Samuel A. Brunelli and Robin Read wedding, St. Petersburg, Florida	1989	napachief
Burke & Herbert Bank (Alexandria, Va.) (green with parrot, dollar signs, and two signatures)	1979	module scarf
B. Burris	n.d.	
Barbara Bush (Basket Weave design)	n.d.	tote
George H. W. Bush and Dan Quayle inauguration	1989	tote, umbrella, wine bottle bag, and scarf
Business and Professional Women's Clubs, District of Columbia Federation	1979	module scarf
Butterflies design: see Dorothy Gray Cosmetics		
Cabaret (show opening in Johannesburg, South Africa) (with signature of Taubie Kushlick)	1969	large square scarf
Caduceus design: see Pan American Medical Women's Alliance		
Calhoun National Bank (Bert Lance's bank in Calhoun, Ga.)	probably by 1974 or earlier	large square scarf
Camp Greystone (Tuxedo, N.C.)	ca. 1984	module scarf
Cancer Institute of the Washington Hospital Center	n.d.	bandana
Capital City Club (private club in Atlanta) (CCC, Carpe Diem, 1883–1983)	1983	module scarf
CarrPark (parking garage in Washington, D.C.)	n.d.	necktie
Jimmy Carter (while governor of Georgia) (overhead view of peanuts)	1972, 1974	module scarf
Jimmy Carter (for presidential campaign) (peanuts in a checkerboard pattern in brown or green)	1976	module scarf and necktie
Ceilings of the White House	n.d.	bandana and napachief
Central Fidelity Bank (Charlottesville, Va.)	n.d.	tote
Central Intelligence Agency, fiftieth anniversary	1997	bandana
Certified Personnel Consultant, NAPC	n.d.	bandana and napachief
Certified Professional Secretaries (CPS with burning oil lamp logo)	n.d.	module scarf
Challenge (with wheelchair symbol)	1985	module scarf

Description	Date	Type of item
Chas. R. Hooff Realtors	by 1977	module scarf
Chemonics	n.d.	tote
Cherokee Alphabet	designed 1967	scarves in a variety of fabrics and formats, bandanas, neckties, and totes
Cheshire, a Xerox Company	ca. 1977	module scarf and/or napachief
Chi-Chi's (Washington, D.C., area chain of Mexican restaurants)	1983	module scarf
Children's Medical Center of the University of Virginia	n.d.	square scarf
Christ Church (Alexandria, Va.)	n.d.	tote
Christmas Greetings 1969: see National Tuberculosis and Respiratory Disease Association		
Christmas trees design	ca. 1970, reprinted numerous times	module scarf, napachief, and tote
Circus Saints and Sinners	ca. 1979	module scarf
The Citadel, the Military College of South Carolina	ca. 1975 and 1978	module scarf
City of Alexandria, Virginia (same border design as Alexandria Historic Landmarks plus ship and scales silhouette in circle)	n.d.	module scarf and bandana
City of Alexandria, Virginia (ship and scales silhouette in circle)	n.d.	module scarf and/or napachief
Clemson University	1981	tote
Bill Clinton and Al Gore inauguration (depicting bus trip from Monticello in Charlottesville, Va., to Washington, D.C.)	1993	bandana
Hillary Clinton: see First Lady's Luncheon for Hillary Rodham Clinton		
The Cloister (Sea Island, Ga.)	ca. 1982	napachief and possibly module scarf
Clyde's (restaurant in Georgetown) (blue, green, purple)	ca. 1973	large square and long rectangle scarves
Clyde's (navy and yellow)	ca. 1976	necktie and large square and long rectangle scarves
College of Home Economics (CHE) (University of Georgia)	1982	module scarf
College of William and Mary	ca. 1971	module scarf
Colonial Parking (Washington, D.C.)	1978	module scarf, necktie, and bowtie
Colonial Williamsburg (drawings of buildings)	n.d.	module scarf
Colonial Williamsburg (leafy drawing with sites)	n.d.	module scarf
Columbia (Md.)	by 1977	module scarf
Commanderie de Bordeaux	n.d.	
COMSAT	n.d. (early design)	module scarf
Terence M. Considine and Elizabeth Walton Callaway wedding, Callaway Gardens, Pine Mountain, Georgia	1976	napachief

Description	Date	Type of item
Continental Quilting Conference	1979	module scarf
Converse College	by 1975	large square scarf
Corcoran Gallery of Art	by 1987	module scarf
Country Curtains for Jack and Jane Fitzpatrick (Stockbridge, Mass.)	1976	module scarf
DACOR Bacon House	n.d.	large square scarf
Eddy and John Dalton, first lady and governor of Virginia	1978	module scarf
Les Dames d'Escoffier	1984	module scarf
Daughters of the American Revolution, Centennial Celebration	1990	bandana
Daughters of the American Revolution (hearts and Georgane Love signature)	1999	long silk rectangle scarf
Decorating Den	n.d.	module scarf
Degesch America, Inc.	1976	module scarf
Delaware American Revolution Bicentennial	1976	module scarf
Delta Kappa Gamma (professional society for women educators)	1977	module scarf
Delta Sigma Theta (historically African American sorority)	1977	module scarf
Department of State, Roselyne Chroman Swig, Director of Art in Embassies	1994	napachief and bandana
Department of the Army, United States of America	n.d.	module scarf
Detling Church, Kent (United Kingdom)	1989	bandana
DG (script in blue dots on white)	n.d. (early)	square scarf
Discover America	1968	originally hand-painted and screen-printed silk square for first White House fashion show, subsequently printed in many variations
Dogwood Ball, Floyd County Medical Center (Rome, Ga.)	1986	bandana
Dogwood Daddy (Rome, Ga.)	n.d.	napachief
Dogwood Stable (near Aiken, S.C.)	n.d.	module scarf
Doll Club (dolls design)	1980	long rectangular scarf and napachief
Dolphin design	by 1976	scarf for shop stock
Dolphin Corporation	n.d.	large square scarf
Dorothy Gray Cosmetics (abstract butterflies design in orange and pink)	ca. 1969	silk square scarf
Drayton Hall	ca. 1979	module scarf
Ducks design (for Nathan Brenner)	n.d.	module scarf
Duvall House (Alexandria, Va.)	1976	documentary fabric and module scarf
Duvall House (Alexandria, Va.) (large tassel design border and architectural details)	ca. 1990	large square silk scarf
Duvall House American Ironwork (used as gifts by the State Department)	ca. 1976	module scarf
Dynamic (script "D")	n.d.	module scarf and necktie
Eagles (for Republican donor group for 1989 inauguration of George H. W. Bush and Dan Quayle)	1989	umbrella
Early Churches of Rome, Georgia	n.d.	tote

Description	Date	Type of item
Eastern Airlines	n.d.	module scarf
Eastern Orthopaedic Association	n.d.	module scarf
Eastern Star (red, white, and blue, Marion N. Sheffield, W. G. M. 1976–77, Clifford C. Grotz W. G. P. 1976–77) (Virginia Masonic Orders)	ca. 1977	module scarf
Elephants design: see Republican National Convention		
El Tumi	by 1978	module scarf
Episcopal High School (Alexandria, Va.)	n.d.	module scarf
Executive Jet Aviation	1972 and 1973	module scarf
Expo 74, USA Pavilion ("the earth does not belong to man" quote)	ca. 1974	long rectangle scarf
Exxon	by 1980	
Falls Church Village Preservation and Improvement Society Centennial (variation of trees design)	1985	tote
Federal Emergency Management Agency, United States Fire Administration	ca. 1979	module scarf
Fifty State Flowers	1970	large square and long rectangle scarves in a variety of fabrics and colorways
First Lady's Luncheon for Hillary Rodham Clinton	1993	large silk square scarf
Jeffrey Fisher and Frances Spell wedding, Fisher Island	1998	large silk square scarf
Fisher Island	n.d.	bandana
Five Civilized Tribes Museum (Muskogee, Okla.)	n.d.	bandana
Five Civilized Tribes Museum (Muskogee, Okla.)	n.d.	module scarf
Scott Fletcher and Sarah Goettsche wedding, Stonewall, Texas	1989	module scarf
Folger Shakespeare Library (angular maze)	1978	module scarf
Folger Shakespeare Library (square maze)	1978	module scarf
Folger Theatre, Washington, D.C., 15th Anniversary Season, 1984–85	ca. 1984	bandana and tote
Following Seas	n.d.	bandana
Betty Ford	1975	initially large Qiana square and long rectangle scarves, then module scarf
Foremost McKesson (California PR firm)	1979	module scarf
The Foundry (restaurant in Georgetown)	1977	module scarf
Four Seasons Hotel	n.d.	umbrella
Fourteenth Centennial of Islam (Arabic alphabet around edge)	1982	module scarf
Foxcroft School	n.d.	umbrella
Frankie Welch of Virginia	1969	large silk square scarf and medium silk square scarf for shop stock
Frankie Welch of Virginia	1984	tote
Frederick Memorial Hospital (Maryland) (FMH)	n.d.	tote
Free (General Federation of Women's Clubs)	n.d.	tote

Description	Date	Type of item
Friends of the First Ladies Tea to benefit the First Ladies Gown Collection (with Betty Ford and Discover America designs)	n.d.	bandana that could be hemmed as napachiefs
Friends of the State Historical Society of Wisconsin	1985	module scarf
Bill Frogale, Lazy Corners (private yacht)	1976	module scarf
Furman University	1969	medium silk square scarf and later large silk square scarf
Future Farmers of America	1977	module scarf
Future Homemakers of America	ca. 1979	module scarf
Futuros para la Niñez	n.d.	bandana and mini-tote
Garden Club of Georgia	1978	module scarf
Gavel design (Rome, Ga.)	ca. 1989	necktie
General Federation of Women's Clubs (GFWC), Unity in Diversity	n.d.	tote
Genie (design created by Genie Welch for her parents' 25th anniversary)	1969	printed in multiple scarf formats on a variety of fabrics
Georgetown, est. 1751	n.d.	bandana
Georgetown Alumni Association	1976	scarf
Georgetown Citizens Association	n.d.	bandana or large square scarf
Georgetown University	n.d.	large silk square scarf
Georgetown University	n.d.	necktie
Georgetown University bicentennial	1989	bandana
Georgetown University Hoya	n.d.	module scarf
George Washington Parkway Classic	n.d.	bandana
Georgia College (Milledgeville)	1984	module scarf
Georgia Federation of Women's Clubs	1984	module scarf
Georgia Home Economics Association (GHEA)	ca. 1979	module scarf
Georgia Library Association (books around the edge, call numbers in the center)	1971	module scarf
Ghirardelli Square (San Francisco PR business)	1972 or 1975	module scarf
John Glenn 84 (presidential campaign)	1983	napachief and bandana
"go": see RCA		
Katherine Godwin, first lady of Virginia	ca. 1974 and 1976	module scarf
Rube Goldberg exhibition, National Museum of History and Technology, Smithsonian Institution	1970	small cotton rectangle scarf
Golden Door (spa resort)	1985	module scarf
Good Housekeeping centennial	1985	module scarf
Graham family (Rome, Ga.)	ca. 1969	large silk square scarf
Grand Hotel, Mackinac Island	n.d.	module scarf
Granny's Place (Old Town Alexandria) (variation of Peggy design)	n.d.	tote
Great Dane Trailers, Inc.	by 1978	module scarf
Great Lakes Aircraft Company	by 1977	module scarf
Greek Alphabet	1969	large silk square scarf

Description	Date	Type of item
Greek Alphabet	ca. 1978	module scarf
Grocery Manufacturers of America (GMA) (navy and dark red linear design on white, Etch-a-Sketch style "GMA" as plus sign in center)	1978	module scarf
Guantanamo Bay, Cuba	1983	module scarf
Gum Drop Square (store in Stockbridge, Mass.)	ca. 1976	module scarf
Hagley Museum	1974	module scarf
Harlequin design (four triangles outlined in white)	n.d.	module scarf for shop stock
Hazel Family (Broad Run, Va.) (floral with names and images on a tree)	n.d.	napachief
Health Industry Manufacturers Association	n.d.	umbrella
Christina Healy (variation of shells design)	ca. 1976	napachief
Hecht's (line drawing of waterfront)	n.d.	module scarf and tote
Hexagon Benefit for Second Genesis	probably 1976 or 1980	module scarf
Higbee's (department store in Indianapolis), Come to a Party	n.d.	long rectangle scarf
Higbee's, Signature	n.d.	large square and long rectangle scarves
Higbee's (concentric rectangles in burgundy, tan, and purple on white)	ca. 1968	large square and long rectangle scarves
Omer L. Hirst	1971	long silk rectangle scarf
Ambassador and Mrs. Glen Holden (Kingston, Jamaica) (variation of Christmas trees design)	1989	napachief
Hotel/Motel Association (now American Hotel and Lodging Association) (ordered through the Washington WhirlAround) (variation of the Washington, D.C., design)	n.d.	tote
House of Representatives	n.d.	large square scarf
Houston Museum of Natural Science	n.d.	module scarf
Hubert H. Humphrey (presidential campaign)	1968	large square scarf
Hyatt Regency Washington	ca. 1974	module scarf
Iberian Imports (Alexandria, Va., shop owned by Caroline Abshire) (design also called Sunny Days in business records)	ca. 1969	large silk square scarf
I Love You	by 1976	napachief
Indianapolis Life Insurance Company	1979	module scarf
Indianapolis Motor Speedway, L.S. Ayres & Co.	1974	module scarf
Industrial College of the Armed Forces	1969	large silk square scarf
In Focus (both with "In Focus" and with logo only, possibly for the Washington Fashion Group)	by 1975	napachiefs
INS (red triangle with letters and dots, possibly the Atlanta Insurance Women's Club)	n.d.	module scarf
International Azalea Festival (Norfolk, Va.) (with signature of Tricia Nixon, festival princess)	1969	large silk square scarf
International Federation of Consulting Engineers (FIDIC)	n.d.	module scarf
International Fine Arts College (Miami, Fla.)	n.d.	module scarf
International Toastmistress Clubs	1977	module scarf

Description	Date	Type of item
Irish Georgian Society, The Obelisk, gift of Rose Saul Zalles to the Irish-Georgian Society, in memory of the Great Hugh Maguire	1979	module scarf
Jaguar, Manhattan Jaguar (Rockville, Md.)	1987	large silk square scarf and module scarf
Jeffersonian Wine Grape Growers Society (Charlottesville, Va.) (for Felicia Rogan of Oakencroft Vineyards)	early 1980s	module scarf, napachief, and tote
Jelly Beans	1981	tote
Jerusalem cross design: see Washington National Cathedral		
John and Martha Johns, president and first lady of Furman University, 1976–1994	ca. 1994	bandana
Lyndon Johnson/Discover America (U.S. Bicentennial)	1975	module scarf
Lyndon B. Johnson (LBJ) Archives	n.d.	tote
Joint Chiefs of Staff	1982	module scarf and tote
LPJ and JJJ (Mr. and Mrs. Jefferson Jones)	n.d.	module scarf
Joshelte II (for Mr. and Mrs. John Beverly Amos, Columbus, Ga.)	n.d.	napachief
Judson College	ca. 1979	module scarf
June Fete, Abington Memorial Hospital (Abington, Penn.)	ca. 1969	square scarf
Junior League Christmas Shop (Washington, D.C.)	1977	module scarf
Jurors Association of New Jersey	n.d.	module scarf
Kappa Delta Pi, "Knowledge-Duty-Power" (education honor society)	n.d.	module scarf
Kappa Kappa Gamma (sorority)	1975	module scarf
Kemper Open	1981	tote and umbrella
Kenmore 1752 (historic home in Fredericksburg, Va.)	ca. 1980	module scarf
Edward Kennedy presidential campaign ("sail against the wind" EMK '80)	1980	tote
117th Kentucky Derby luncheon, Hansel, Lazy Lane Farms (for Joe Allbritton)	1991	bandana
Christopher Leigh Stuart King and Caroline Ramsay Borgland wedding, Litchfield, Connecticut	1987	napachief
KWTV, Channel 9, Oklahoma City	by 1977	module scarf
Lace design (mix of architectural and historical elements including Jerusalem cross and pattern from John Adams scarf)	1986	large silk square scarf
Lakeland Tours (travel agency in Charlottesville, Va.) (abstract LT)	ca. 1980	necktie and possibly module scarf
Lakeside Foundation (Brockport, N.Y.)	1989	bandana
Lancaster Rose (cosmetics)	by 1978	napachief and small tote
Bert Lance for Governor of Georgia	1974	module scarf
Pierre Fernand Lapeyre and Laurie Lee Hodges wedding	1990	napachief
Erno Laszlo (Laszlo Institute skincare products)	1972	module scarf
Lear Fan (for Moya Lear)	1981	tote and long rectangle scarf
Liddy Letter, WJFK, Fairfax, Virginia (probably for radio talk show program by G. Gordon Liddy) (variation of Washington, D.C., design)	n.d.	bandana
Abraham Lincoln (U.S. Bicentennial)	1975	module scarf
Linda Benoit, Inc. (realtor in Alexandria, Va.)	1981	tote
Lindeza (motor yacht), The Bodines' Around the World Odyssey	1991	bandana

Description	Date	Type of item
Jeanie Lody's 80th birthday	1982	module scarf
Jeff Lubell and Karen Goettsche wedding, Blueberry Hill, Goshen, Vermont	1996	napachief or bandana
Lucky Leaf (Knouse Foods) (red design with apples and green design with leaf/apples)	1978	module scarves and neckties
Pat and Homer Luther (Galveston, Tex.)	1990	bandana and napachief
MAA, leaves	n.d.	
Machine Tool Builders (tools in stripes with dotted stripes)	ca. 1978	module scarf
Mac Hugh, Inc. (Gibson Girls)	n.d. (early)	large silk square scarf
MacVaugh	1980	module scarf
Andrew Maddox and Christina Rather wedding, Falls Church, Virginia	1989	bandana
Madison Hotel (Washington, D.C.) (scrolling Ms in wreathes)	n.d.	long silk scarf
Warren G. Magnuson (congressional campaign)	1968	large square scarf
Male and female symbols design	ca. 1975	module scarf
Man-Made Fiber Producers Association (diagonal stripes of various fibers)	n.d.	module scarf
March of Dimes, Gourmet Gala	1983	bandana
Mary Baldwin College	1983	module scarf
Marymount College (Arlington, Va.) (fleur-de-lis, MCV around edge)	ca. 1974	module scarf
Mayflower Hotel (Washington, D.C.)	ca. 1978	module scarf
McCormick spices (grid)	1977	module scarf
McCormick spices (floral design)	1978	module scarf and necktie
McDonald's (golden arches)	1976	module scarf
McDonald's, 4,000th store (Montreal)	1977	napachief
Medical University of South Carolina Alumni Association	n.d.	module scarf
Member of Congress (with signature block)	1969	large silk square scarf
Member of Congress (with signature block, originally sold in Senate and Congress members' stores)	ca. 1975	module scarf
Mental Health Association	1977	module scarf
Dina Merrill (for Coty)	by 1972	large silk square scarf
Andrew Miller (campaign for governor of Virginia) (with names of family members)	1976	module scarf
Mills College (Oakland, Calif.) (four pinwheel groups of Ms, blue on white)	by 1975	module scarf
Minute Man	by 1977	
Mississippi (the state of)	n.d.	module scarf
Walter Mondale campaign	n.d.	module scarf
Monsanto (Brasil design)	ca. 1978	module scarf
Monsanto (polka-dot design)	1979	module scarf
Monumental Life (M logo)	ca. 1980	necktie
Moore Cadillac Company (Virginia)	ca. 1984	large silk square and rectangle scarves
Mortar Board	ca. 1982	tote
Mothers Embracing Nuclear Disarmament (MEND)	1987	bandana

Description	Date	Type of item
Mount Vernon College (Washington, D.C.)	by 1977	module scarf
M.P.R.S. (or those letters in another order)	n.d.	bandana
Muskogee Azalea Festival (Oklahoma)	n.d.	
Myth Conceptions (with turtle)	n.d.	tote
National Air and Space Museum, Smithsonian Institution	1976	module scarf
National Association of Counties (NAC)	ca. 1981	module scarf and necktie
National Association of Secondary School Principals (NASSP)	ca. 1980	module scarf and necktie
National Cherry Blossom Festival (Washington, D.C.) (original in pink and green, later in teal and red without text)	1970	large square scarf
National Cherry Blossom Festival, 80th Anniversary of the Gift of the Trees, Jackie Wolfe, President	ca. 1992	bandana
National City Bank of Rome (Georgia) (clock tower)	1970	long rectangle and large silk square scarves
National City Bank of Rome (Georgia) (floral design with sites)	1978	module scarf and plate
National Council of Administrative Women in Education (NCAWE) (variation of male and female symbols design)	n.d.	module scarf
National Education Association (NEA) (design similar to Virginia Education Association)	1970	module scarf
National Federation of Republican Women, Dallas, Texas (elephant with Dallas skyline for RNC convention)	1984	bandana and tote
National Federation of Republican Women, Dallas, Texas (elephant without Dallas skyline for RNC convention)	1984	module scarf and necktie
National Geographic Society centennial	1988	necktie
National Grain and Feed Association	1977	module scarf
National Lumber and Building Material Dealers Association (NLBMDA) (variation of trees design)	1976	module scarf
National Museum of History and Technology, Smithsonian Institution	ca. 1973	long rectangle scarf
National Museum of Women in the Arts	1986	large silk square scarf
National Press Club	1973	necktie
National Press Club (large round logo)	1973	module scarf
National Press Club (floral design)	1977	module scarf
National Society of Professional Engineers (NSPE) (variation of Washington, D.C., design)	1984	module scarf
National Space Institute	1977	module scarf
National Treasures (also called Mount Vernon in business records)	1993	large silk square scarf
National Tuberculosis and Respiratory Disease Association, Christmas Greetings 1969 (with annual Christmas seal)	1969	square scarf
National War College	by 1969	large silk square scarf
National War College	ca. 1974	module scarf
Nautical flags design (for a marina in Maryland, flags spell out West River, later used as shop stock)	designed 1972	module scarf and necktie
Navy Nurse Corps (navy with gold oak leaves)	1982	tote and necktie

Description	Date	Type of item
New Orleans	n.d.	module scarf
New York Bank for Savings (beehives with "1st")	n.d.	module scarf
New York Jets	ca. 1978	module scarf
George Nigh (campaign for governor of Oklahoma)	1978	module scarf
Nirvana	n.d.	module scarf
Richard Nixon inauguration, Forward Together	1969	large square scarf
Northern Virginia Garden Clubs (dogwood, goldenrod, rhododendron)	ca. 1999	large silk square scarf
Northern Virginia Natural Gas (Ns forming up arrows)	1974	module scarf
Northern Virginia Special Olympics	1985	module scarf
North Texas State University	by 1978	module scarf
Northwood University, Margaret Chase Smith Rose, to celebrate thirty years of Distinguished Women at Northwood University	ca. 1999	large silk square scarf
Old Executive Office (for Joan Mondale)	1978	module scarf
Old Port Cove Marina (variation of Navy's anchor design)	n.d.	tote
Oliver T. Carr Company	n.d.	
Omni International Hotels (double rings)	1983	napachief and necktie
Order of Saint Lazarus, Atavis et armis	n.d.	large silk square scarf
Order of Saint Lazarus	1983	module scarf
Orthopaedic Research and Education Foundation Auxiliary	1978	module scarf
Overseas Private Investment Corporation	1987	large silk square scarf
Owasso Savings Bank (grid of small rounded squares with two right angles, navy on white, possibly First Bank of Owasso in Oklahoma)	ca. 1978	module scarf
Owls design (for private client, later sold as shop stock)	by 1970	long rectangle scarf
Paces Ferry Development Company (street scene with hot-air balloon)	ca. 1982	module scarf
Pan American Medical Women's Alliance (caduceus design)	n.d.	module scarf
Park Hyatt	n.d.	necktie
Peanuts design: see Jimmy Carter		
Peggy design (quilt pattern with cat)	n.d.	small tote for shop stock and stationery
Pennsylvania (the state of)	n.d.	module scarf
Pennsylvania Academy of the Fine Arts	n.d.	module scarf
Pennsylvania Association of Educational Secretaries	ca. 1982	module scarf
Peter's Restaurant	1977	module scarf and napachief
PGA Tour	ca. 1976	module scarf
PGA Tour	ca. 1977	tote
PGA Tour, TPC (golf, Tournament Players Association)	1980 or 1981	module scarf and tote
PGA Tour, TPC, Buick Open	n.d.	bandana
PGA Tour in Tokyo (for Sobu Co.)	n.d.	module scarf
PGA Tour (shield on stripes)	n.d.	tote
PGI	n.d.	necktie
Piedmont Golf Club (PGC), Charlie Yarn	1984	tote

Description	Date	Type of item
Piedmont Hospital (Atlanta)	n.d.	napachief
Piedmont Hospital (Atlanta) 75th anniversary	1980	scarf
Pink Ladies (Floyd Medical Center volunteers, Rome, Ga.) (pink dresses design)	1983	module scarf
Pioneers' Museum (Colorado Springs, Colo.)	n.d.	tote
Pisces (private club in Georgetown)	1982	tote
PNB (variation of Genie design)	n.d.	long silk scarf
Portofino (restaurant in Arlington, Va.)	n.d.	tote
Potomac House Tours (border of grapes, wheat, oak leaves, stars in purple)	1985	module scarf
President's Cup	n.d.	bandana
Princeton Club of New York	n.d.	module scarf
Princeton Club of New York	1969	large silk square scarf
Printing Industries of America (PIA on umbrella, yellow on white)	by 1978	module scarf
Queens College (New York)	n.d.	tote
Quilt pattern designs (two scarves with these modules, each of which could be hemmed into individual napachiefs: Quilt by Lottie Barnett 1840, Washington's Quilt, Royal Star, Wedding Ring; and Virginia Reel, Dolly Madison, The Kings Crown, Virginia Star)	by 1976	module scarves and napachiefs, Barnett design used as tote
Radford College	ca. 1979	module scarf
Ramsey Group	n.d.	napachief
Cortes Randell (variation of National Cherry Blossom Festival design)	ca. 1970	long rectangle scarf and large silk square
Robert D. Ray, governor of Iowa, and Billie Ray with Wild Rose	1974	module scarf
RCA (the word "go" in green and navy on white)	by 1973	irregular scarf and necktie
Reader's Digest (Pegasus in corner)	ca. 1977	square scarf
Nancy Reagan (variation of National Cherry Blossom Festival design)	n.d.	tote
Nancy Reagan Tennis Benefit	1986	module scarf
Ronald Reagan and George H. W. Bush inauguration (encircled RBs)	1980	module scarf, necktie, and umbrella
Ronald Reagan and George H. W. Bush inauguration (variation of Washington, D.C., design) (for guests at the Watergate)	1981	tote
Ronald Reagan and George H. W. Bush inauguration (Boxcar)	1981	tote
Ronald Reagan and George H. W. Bush inauguration ("Reagan Plaid")	1985	module scarf, large silk square scarf, and tote
Red Cross centennial	1980	module scarf and small tote
Reiss Coal (burgundy with black and white diagonals and one "R" in a diamond)	1979	necktie
Reiss Coal (red, black, and white diamond pattern with "R" and "100" in corner)	1979	module scarf
Republican National Convention (Miami, Fla.)	1968	documentary fabric
Republican National Convention (blue or red elephants in staggered grid)	1984	module scarf and tote
Republican Women of Capitol Hill, 25th anniversary	1988	bandana and napachief

Description	Date	Type of item
Retail Merchants Association (RMA) 65th Fall Conference	n.d.	module scarf
Vincent Ricardel and Lori Hand wedding, Washington, D.C.	1991	bandana and napachief
River Rats	n.d.	necktie
Roadrunner design	1973	continuous pattern for scarves, yardage, and neckties
Roanoke Island, 400th anniversary of settlement	ca. 1984	tote
Roanoke Voyage (North Carolina), America's 400th anniversary	ca. 1984	tote
Douglas Lamar Roberts and Eugenia Frances Welch wedding, Alexandria, Virginia	1979	napachief
Rome, Georgia, early churches	1982	tote
Rome, Georgia (with Capitoline Wolf statue)	1983	necktie
Rome, Georgia (with clock tower)	1983	umbrella
To celebrate the life of Gregory K. Rooks and benefit the Village of Childhelp East	n.d.	small silk square scarf
Theodore Roosevelt (U.S. Bicentennial)	1975	module scarf
Theodore Roosevelt design for the American Cowboy exhibition, Library of Congress	1983	bandana
Rose window design (green and red holiday design, inspired by Washington National Cathedral)	n.d.	module scarf
Roselawn	1987	module scarf
Blanka Rosenstiel, Blandemar Farm (Charlottesville, Va.)	ca. 1982	yardage for tablecloths
Rotary International, Rotary Club of Alexandria, Children's Project	1995	large square scarf
Cathy Barker Roth (with Sagebrush, Nev., and Alexandria, Va.)	n.d.	module scarf
Kitty Rotruck (teacher of the Bishop Method of Sewing) (pink and orange dots and squares with "Kitty" signature)	1977	module scarf, napachief, yardage
Linda Rowland, Driscoll Hotel (Austin, Tex.)	1985	module scarf
Royal Academy of Arts (London)	n.d.	tote
Royal wedding of His Royal Highness Prince of Wales and Lady Diana Spencer (London)	1981	tote
Runnels Drilling	ca. 1975 or 1979	module scarf
Rural Postal Carriers	ca. 1982	module scarf
Salem Academy and College	1979	module scarf
Salvation Army (bonnets design)	ca. 1980	module scarf
San Antonio, Texas (for the mayor)	ca. 1982	module scarf
San Diego Opera, 25th Celebration	probably 1990	bandana
San Francisco Cable Car Centennial	1973	module scarf
School of Foreign Service	n.d.	long rectangle scarf
Seagram Distillery	n.d.	
Sea Island Golf Club (Sea Island, Ga.)	n.d.	module scarf

Description	Date	Type of item
Sea Pines Plantation (Hilton Head Island, S.C.)	n.d.	bandana
Second Genesis Benefit, "Help Save Our Children," sponsored by Hecht's	1987	bandana
Second Panel, Sheriff's Jury (scales of justice)	1975	long rectangle scarf
Second Panel, Sheriff's Jury, New York County	1980	module scarf
See Georgia First (variation of Discover America design)	1969	square scarf
Senatorial Trust	n.d.	large square scarf
Sewing Is Chic, for Irene M. James and Nancy L. Zieman	n.d.	tote
Shamrock design	by 1976	module scarf for shop stock
Shells design	1983	module scarf for shop stock
The Ship's Scarf, Federalist Christening Celebration of the gift to George Washington from the State of Maryland	1987	bandana
Shorter College	by 1972	module scarf
Sikorsky	1978	module scarf
Silverliners	ca. 1980	long rectangle scarf
Simmons College Management Programs	n.d.	module scarf
SMACNA (variation of Jaguar design)	n.d.	bandana and napachief
Dorothy Smith to Guy Hatfield, 30th anniversary	n.d.	tote and napachief
Smith College (SC in purple diamond on white)	early 1970s	module scarf
Society for the Preservation and Encouragement of Barber Shop Quartet Singing in America, Inc. (SPEBSQSA, Keep America Singing)	ca. 1970	long rectangle scarf
Society of American Military Engineers	ca. 1979	module scarf
Southern Conference of Attorneys General	n.d.	tote
Southern Furniture Manufacturers' Association (SFMA)	ca. 1980	long rectangle scarf
Squash Blossom design (Santo Domingo, Navajo, Zuni, Old Navajo)	1973	module scarf
Squash Blossom design (or Indian Jewelry), National Treasures Series	1993	large silk square scarf
St. Agnes School (Alexandria, Va.)	by 1975	module scarf
St. Luke's Episcopal Church (Alexandria, Va.)	1979	module scarf
St. Mary's (Maryland) bicentennial	1976	module scarf
St. Mary's County	1984	module scarf
St. Paul's (Alexandria, Va.) (central cross, inner border of arched and rose windows, outer border)	1984	module scarf
St. Paul's Cathedral (London) (crosses in center and corners, rose windows in corners)	1984	module scarf and shopping bag
St. Paul's Cathedral (London) (architectural forms, border of squares)	n.d.	module scarf
Ted Stevens (probably for senate campaign)	1970	long rectangle scarf
Stockbridge, Massachusetts	n.d.	module scarf
Strategic Air Command	ca. 1973 or 1978	module scarf
Stratford Hall	n.d.	large square scarf or bandana
Straw flowers design (for Betty Ford to give as gifts during her first Christmas at the White House)	1974	large silk square scarf in multiple colorways
Paula Stringer (for a Texas real estate firm)	ca. 1975	module scarf

Description	Date	Type of item
Stuart Hall School (Staunton, Va.)	n.d.	module scarf
Stuckey's candy	by 1969	
Submarine Warfare Insignia (dolphins and top of submarine)	n.d.	module scarf
Sun Company Inaugural	n.d.	tote
Supima cotton (abstract fields of cotton with clouds, in pink, orange, and purple on white)	1975	long rectangle scarf
Swan Coach House (Atlanta, Ga.)	n.d.	tote
Syntex Washington, Inc., for Decorating Den	n.d.	
Tandem Computers (California)	1981, reordered by Frankfurt, Germany, division in 1982	module scarf and possibly necktie
Tassels design (also with "To the Greatest of Friends" variation)	n.d.	napachief for shop stock
Elizabeth Taylor, *Private Lives* at Kennedy Center	1983	small tote
Elizabeth Taylor Warner, *Little Foxes* at Kennedy Center	1981	small tote
Tennessee Walking Horse National Celebration (for a horse farm in Shelbyville, Tenn.)	ca. 1971	square scarf
Tennis design	ca. 1976	module scarf for shop stock
Texas Two-Step	n.d.	tote
Textile Museum (Washington, D.C.) (based on a lotto carpet)	1980	module scarf
Textile Museum (Washington, D.C.) (based on a Star Ushak carpet)	1980	umbrella
Thomson McKinnon Securities, Inc., 100th anniversary	1985	bandana
Thunderbird design	1973	module scarf
Time Life Books (logo repeated)	ca. 1979	module scarf
Time Life Books (books on shelves)	ca. 1980	long rectangle scarf
Timmons (TCI)	n.d.	module scarf
Tobacco Institute (TI)	1978, reprinted 1983	module scarf
TPC (golf): see PGA Tour		
Trees design	n.d.	module scarf for shop stock
Triangles design (four triangles outlined in white, points meeting in center of module): see Harlequin		
Triangles design (two striped triangles separated by white diagonal bar)	n.d.	module scarf for shop stock
Tryon Palace (New Bern, N.C.)	n.d.	bandana.
Trucks design: see American Trucking Associations		
Turtles design	1971	module scarf
Unifirst Banks	ca. 1981	module scarf
Union Warren Savings Bank	ca. 1978	module scarf
United Daughters of the Confederacy, Georgia Division	n.d.	bandana

Description	Date	Type of item
United Fresh Fruit and Vegetable Association, Fresh Approach (green or blue)	ca. 1979	module scarf
United States Air Force	ca. 1977	module scarf
United States Air Force Academy	1976	module scarf
United States Army Berlin (Berlin logo)	n.d.	module scarf
United States Army Materiel Development and Readiness Command (DARCOM)	ca. 1977	module scarf
United States Coast Guard	ca. 1977	module scarf
United States Department of Agriculture	1983	module scarf
United States Department of State, Shell Design on 18th-Century Furniture from the Diplomatic Rooms	n.d.	bandana
United States Fire Administration	n.d.	
United States Historical Society, celebrating bicentennial of the United States Capitol	1993	scarf
United States Marine Corps	ca. 1976	module scarf
United States Marine Corps Education and Development Command (Quantico, Va.), "Semper Progredi"	ca. 1981	module scarf and tote
United States Marine Corps Sergeants (eagle, anchor, globe in corners, various insignia denoting sergeant rank)	designed 1977, reordered 1979 and 1982	module scarf
United States Military Academy 1942	n.d.	module scarf
United States Military Academy, West Point Class of '45	n.d.	necktie
United States Military Academy, West Point Class of '46	1981	module scarf and bottle bag
United States Military Academy, West Point Class of '47	n.d.	necktie
United States Military Academy, West Point Class of '49	1979	module scarf
United States Military Academy, West Point Class of '51	n.d.	module scarf
United States Military Academy, West Point Class of '52	1987	large silk square scarf
United States Military Academy, West Point Class of '58	n.d.	module scarf
United States Naval Academy (USNA) (with tassels, bricks, doors, for 30th reunion of the class of 1960)	1990	large silk square scarf
United States Navy (anchors, blue and white)	by 1979	module scarf and tote
United States Navy Insignia with USS Constitution (for Naval Officers' Wives Club)	1976 and 1977	module scarf
United States Savings Bonds	ca. 1977	module scarf
United States Senate	n.d.	necktie
United States Senate (seal in center surrounded by columns and architectural details)	ca. 1983	module scarf
United Virginia Bank (U holding V in yellow on white)	ca. 1978	module scarf
United Virginia Bankshares	1978	module scarf
United Way	ca. 1976 and 1978	module scarf

Description	Date	Type of item
University of Alabama	ca. 1978	module scarf
University of Georgia (round seal repeated design)	ca. 1975	module scarf possibly with earlier related necktie
University of Georgia (bulldog design)	ca. 1977	module scarf
University of Georgia (repeated arch design)	ca. 1978	module scarf
University of Georgia (design from ceiling of the President's House for Presidents Club)	1982	module scarf and tote
University of Georgia bicentennial	1984	module scarf, tote, and related necktie
University of Maryland (possibly for the Terrapin Club)	n.d.	module scarf
University of Missouri	n.d.	module scarf
University of Missouri, 150th anniversary	ca. 1989	bandana
University of Rhode Island (URI)	1983	module scarf and tote
University of Richmond	by 1977	module scarf
University of South Carolina	n.d.	large silk square scarf
University of South Carolina at Spartanburg	n.d.	bandana
University of Texas, Austin	n.d.	tote
University of Virginia, UVA Alumni Association	1977	module scarf
University of Virginia, Darden School of Business (for opening of new campus on North Grounds, Charlottesville, Va.)	ca. 1985	bandana
USS Nimitz	1983	module scarf
Valentine Museum	1977	module scarf
Veterans Administration	1970	module scarf
Veterans Administration	1978	fabric used for wall coverings
Vienna-Falls Chorus	n.d.	bandana
Virginia Association of Extension Home Economists (VAEHE)	ca. 1979	module scarf
Virginia Association of Realtors	n.d.	tote
Virginia Automobile Dealers Association (VAEHE with cars)	n.d.	module scarf
Virginia Center for the Creative Arts	n.d.	
Virginia Education Association (VEA)	ca. 1975–76, reprinted 1978	module scarf and tote
Virginia Home Economics Association, "Flames of Home Economics"	ca. 1971–76	long rectangle scarf
Virginia Polytechnic Institute and State University	ca. 1979	module scarf
Virginia Road Builders Association, St. Thomas (probably for a conference)	1969	large square scarf
Virginia Vintage (Old Town, Alexandria, Va.)	n.d.	tote
Virginia Wines Volunteers	n.d.	tote
Virginia Women's Meeting, International Women's Year, Decade for Women	1977	module scarf
Vote Libertarian (with Statue of Liberty motif, for Edward A. Clark presidential campaign)	1980	tote
WABCO (Union Switch and Signal Division)	1977	long rectangle scarf

Description	Date	Type of item
WABCO (Union Switch and Signal Division)	1981	small tote
Wallace Ranches (for Louise Wallace)	n.d.	large silk square scarf
WASH with the Stars 97.1 FM	n.d.	module scarf
George Washington (U.S. Bicentennial)	1975	module scarf
Washington, D.C.	ca. 1978	module scarf, tote, and plate; shop stock and reworked for numerous clients
Washington College	n.d.	module scarf
Washington Convention Center	1984	module scarf
Washington Harbour	1986	bandana and napachief
Washington Hospital Center	n.d.	bandana
Washington and Lee University	1978	module scarf
Washington National Cathedral	n.d.	umbrella
Washington National Cathedral, Architectural Details	n.d.	bandana
Washington (National) Cathedral (with rose window)	n.d.	tote
Washington National Cathedral (blue and green architectural details inspired by the War Memorial Chapel)	1983	long scarf
Washington National Cathedral (Jerusalem cross with design inspired by the floor of the nave)	1983	module scarf and tote
Washington Press Club	ca. 1980	tote
Washington School for Secretaries	by 1973	module scarf
Washington Star	1979	module scarf and tote
Watergate, 1218 South (line-drawing scene with Potomac River, Kennedy Center, etc.)	n.d.	module scarf
Watergate Fitness Club	ca. 1978	tote bag and T-shirts
Watergate Hotel (script W with floral design)	ca. 1978	module scarf
Watson Ranch ("WR" with fences, for Martha Griffin)	1983	napachief and bandana
Wayne State University (WSUAA)	n.d.	module scarf
Welch House, Announcing Welch House for Sale, Ruth Guirarde and Barbara Stockton	n.d.	bandana
Welch House (line drawing of Washington, D.C., showing White House, Cathedral, etc.)	n.d.	bandana
Welch House, Charter 100	1990	napachief
West Virginia Garden Club, Inc.	1984	module scarf
Alan White and Martha Griffin wedding, Muskogee, Oklahoma	1992	napachief
White House	n.d.	bandana
White House	n.d.	necktie
Why Not? (shop in Alexandria, Va.)	n.d.	bandana and napachief
Betty Willcox, 1776–1976	1976	module scarf
Harrison "Pete" Williams	1970	long rectangle scarf

Description	Date	Type of item
James Page Williams and Peggy Glynn Welch wedding, Christ Church and Gilpin House, Alexandria, Virginia	1974	napachief
Lindsay Anne Williams	1982	napachief
Will You Be My Valentine?	n.d.	module scarf
Wintergreen Resort (Virginia)	1981	module scarf, necktie, and tote
Winthrop College	1983	module scarf
Wish Upon a Star	n.d.	bandana
Wish with Wings	n.d.	bandana
Wolf Trap Farm Park for the Performing Arts (floral design)	n.d.	module scarf
Wolf Trap Farm Park for the Performing Arts—Filene Center (abstract wolf head design)	n.d.	module scarf
Women Can Make Money in the Stock Market (with Colleen Moore signature) (for book promotion)	ca. 1969	square scarf
Women in Military Service for America Memorial	n.d.	napachief
Women of Our Hemisphere Achieving Together (NYOTA) (for Holly Coors)	1987	module scarf
Women's Auxiliary to the Texas Dental Association	1978	module scarf
Women's National Bank	ca. 1977	module scarf
Women's National Democratic Club, Woman of the Year, Rosalynn Carter	1977	module scarf
World Bank	1971	module scarf
WTOP-TV 9, a Post-Newsweek Station, a CBS affiliate	n.d.	large silk square
Douglas Yarn and Lisa Flint wedding, West Point, New York	1979	module scarf
Young Presidents' Organization (YPO) (club for individuals who become millionaires before the age of forty) (ordered by the Washington WhirlAround), Washington 78	1978	tote
Zachary and Elizabeth Fisher House	n.d.	large silk square
Zonta International (women executives' club)	ca. 1980	module scarf

Notes

The book epigraph is from Frankie Welch with Peggy Welch Williams, interview by Richard Norton Smith, September 10, 2010, Gerald R. Ford Oral History Project, Gerald R. Ford Foundation, *https://geraldrfordfoundation .org/centennial/oralhistory/frankie-welch/*.

Introduction. Let Frankie Welch Design a Scarf for You

1. Pat Lloyd, "Frankie Designs Them, Betty Buys Them," *Pensacola News Journal*, November 30, 1974; Alyce Atkinson, "A Success Story in Silk," *Greenville (S.C.) News*, November 28, 1993; Eleni Epstein, typed script for a tribute to Frankie Welch, Woman of Distinction Award at the American Showcase Theatre Company Benefit, March 29, 1990, collection of Frankie Welch, Peggy Welch Williams, and Genie Welch Leisure (hereafter Welch family collection); Dorothea Johnson, telephone conversation with author, January 23, 2020; LaDonna Harris, telephone conversation with author, February 4, 2020.
2. Peggy Welch Williams, emails to author, June 26 and July 14, 2020.
3. Genie Welch Leisure, email to author, March 30, 2020.
4. Genie Welch Leisure and Peggy Welch Williams, emails to author, March 30, 2020.
5. Lucy Rodriguez, email to Peggy Welch Williams, January 31, 2020.
6. Tricia Silva, "City's Designing Woman Returns: Frankie Welch to Lead Parade," *Rome (Ga.) News-Tribune*, October 10, 1993.
7. Frances Cawthon, "'Never in My Wildest Dreams,' Georgian's Gown Becomes Part of U.S. History," *Atlanta Journal*, June 25, 1976; Jeanne Geddes, "Frankie Welch: American Fashion at Its Best," *Alexandria (Va.) Journal*, August 4, 1983.
8. Peggy Welch Williams, email to author, April 1, 2020. For a brief history of Old Town Alexandria, see Jamila Jordan, "The Making of Old Town," *Boundary Stones*, WETA's Local History Blog, March 18, 2016, https://boundarystones .weta.org/2016/03/18/making-old-town.

9. Peggy Welch Williams, email to author, June 26, 2020; Emma Livingstone, "A Frank-ie View of Style; Scarfs Tie It All Together," *Richmond (Va.) Times-Dispatch*, February 27, 1972.

10. Raw footage for *Nation's Business Today*, an ESPN television program, Washington, D.C., for a "Making It" segment that ran on February 7, 1989, collection of the Walter J. Brown Media Archives, University of Georgia Libraries, University of Georgia (hereafter Brown Media Archives), transfer from Frankie Welch Collection, Rome Area History Center.

11. "More Fur for Bunnies," *Washington Post and Times Herald*, October 6, 1968.

12. Dorothea Johnson, telephone conversation with author, January 23, 2020.

Chapter 1. From Mary Frances Barnett of Georgia to Frankie Welch of Virginia

1. Frankie Welch, presentation, National Museum of American History, Smithsonian Institution, April 10, 1991, VHS cassette, Brown Media Archives, gift of Frankie Welch, Peggy Welch Williams, and Genie Welch Leisure (hereafter the Welch family), https://kaltura.uga.edu/media/t/0_spdju3od.

2. Ibid.; Frankie Welch, "Interview with Frankie Welch," 1984, Winthrop University, Oral History Interviews, OH 183, https://digitalcommons.winthrop.edu/oralhistoryprogram/243; Karen Peterson, "Designer Shrewd Lady," *Lima (Ohio) News*, December 1, 1974.

3. Welch, Smithsonian presentation.

4. Ibid.; list of Frankie Welch's teaching experience, ca. 1959, Welch family collection. Emphasis in original.

5. Rome High School yearbooks, 1939 and 1940; Russell McClanahan, *Legendary Locals of Rome* (Charleston, S.C.: Arcadia, 2014), 79.

6. Eleni, "Every Woman Ought to Have Some Fashion Education," Fashion Notebook, *Sunday Star* (Washington, D.C.), October 8, 1961.

7. Robin Givhan, "History, Fair and Square," *Washington Post*, June 14, 1998; Welch, Smithsonian presentation.

8. Welch, Winthrop interview. Welch also had a flower arranging scholarship, which helped her develop a lifelong love of flowers. Alice H. Johnson, "Frankie Welch Shows Furman Scarf," *Greenville (S.C.) News*, May 31, 1969.

9. "Frankie Welch: Fashion Address Planned Tuesday," *Furman Paladin*, October 7, 1966; *Bonhomie*, Furman University yearbook, 1943, 73; "Publication Officials Named at W.C.," *Furman Hornet*, April 24, 1942; "Jenness, Thomas, Barnett to Edit FU Publications," *Furman Hornet*, April 15, 1944.

10. Frankie Barnett, "For Men Only," *Furman Hornet*, March 13, 1942.

11. Frances G. Bailey, "Four WC Girls to Model in Fashion Show in City Next Friday," *Furman Hornet*, February 12, 1944; list of Frankie Welch's teaching experience. Though Greenville Woman's College and Furman University merged in the 1930s, the two campuses were still separate when Welch attended.

12. See, for example, "Students Vote on May Court Attendant," *Furman Hornet*, March 6, 1942; "Eight Selected for Beauty Section of Bonhomie in Recent Contest," *Furman Hornet*, October 30, 1943; Alice Noel, "May Day Festival Set for Saturday in Amphitheater," *Furman Hornet*, April 24, 1948.

13. Beecher Strawn, Personalities in Profile, *Furman Hornet*, January 22, 1943.

14. Just Dirty Gossip, *Furman Hornet*, April 8, 1944.

15. "Miss Barnett Weds Pfc. Calvin Welch, of U.S. Marines," *Rome (Ga.) News-Tribune*, June 4, 1944.

16. Carol Weaver, "Frankie Welch: Designer for the First Lady," *Georgia Alumni Record* 54, no. 1 (October 1974), 7.

17. Peggy Welch Williams, emails to author, April 3 and 4, 2019; list of Frankie Welch's teaching experience.

18. "Traveling Around Rome," television program hosted by Lisa Smith, Channel 4, Rome Floyd Library Channel, September 1, 1999, Brown Media Archives, gift of the Welch family, https://kaltura.uga.edu/media/t/0_4n5iz705; Elinor Lee, "Her Paris-Rome Wardrobe Cost $60," *Washington Post and Times Herald*, July 24, 1960; Carol Weaver, "Frankie Welch"; Peggy Welch Williams, email to author, April 3, 2019; list of Frankie Welch's teaching experience.

19. Emma Livingstone, "A Frank-ie View of Style; Scarfs Tie It All Together," *Richmond (Va.) Times-Dispatch*, February 27, 1972; *Bonhomie*, Furman University yearbook, 1948, 90.

20. Peggy Welch Williams, email to author, April 3, 2019.

21. Mac McConnell, Trav'lin Light, *Furman Hornet*, February 28, 1948. Welch created the green-and-white-striped "wallpaper" effect by painting green over white walls on which she had put long strips of tape that she subsequently removed. Peggy Welch Williams, emails to author, April 3 and 5, 2019.

22. Joann Harris, "Frankie Welch," *Baltimore Sun*, July 21, 1968.

23. "Roman Awarded Scholarship by New York Board," *Rome (Ga.) News Tribune*, August 6, 1950, reprinted August 6, 2000; Peggy Welch Williams, email to author, April 3, 2019; list of Frankie Welch's teaching experience.

24. List of Frankie Welch's teaching experience; "Mrs. Welch to Have Role with D.E. for Area," *Greenville (S.C.) News*, June 13, 1948; Kandy Shuman Stroud, "Eye on Washington," *Women's Wear Daily*, March 13, 1969; Leslie Ellis, "Her Scarves Are a Signature," *People Today* (Brevard County, Fla.), March 28, 1976; Manuel J. Rogers, "Easley Training Institute Opens Tomorrow," *Greenville (S.C.) News*, September 19, 1948; "In Sales Training Skit," *Easley (S.C.) Progress*, February 16, 1950.

25. "Roman Awarded Scholarship."

26. "Sew First for Fun Advises Local Expert," unidentified newspaper clipping (probably *Alexandria [Va.] Gazette*), September 1959, Frankie Welch Collection, Rome Area History Center; Lee, "Paris-Rome Wardrobe"; list of Frankie Welch's teaching experience; Ann Rundell, "President Ford Is Ex-Madisonian's Customer," *Wisconsin State Journal*, September 1, 1974. The last source also indicates that Welch audited classes at the University of Wisconsin. Edna Bryte Bishop taught in clothing programs in vocational programs for high school girls in Massachusetts and New Jersey by the late 1920s, offered courses on "commercial practices . . . for home sewing" outside of that region by 1949, and published her first book on sewing in 1951, *Teaching the Bishop Method of Clothing Construction to Beginners*. See Anna A. Kloss and Gertrude Harper, "About the Bishop Method," in Edna Bryte Bishop and Marjorie Stotler Arch, *The Bishop Method of Clothing Construction* (Philadelphia and New York: J. B. Lippincott Company, 1959); "Home

Dressmakers Are Taught Short Cuts of Garment Industry," *New York Times*, June 9, 1949.

27. Deborah Churchman, "Personal Service Draws VIPs to Chic D.C. Clothing Shop," *Christian Science Monitor*, January 26, 1982. Contrary to Welch's quoted statement, Wright did accept and encourage women as apprentices at Taliesin. See International Archive of Women in Architecture website, Virginia Tech, https://guides.lib.vt.edu/iawa/highlights; *"A Girl Is a Fellow Here": 100 Women Architects in the Studio of Frank Lloyd Wright*, a film produced by the Beverly Willis Architecture Foundation, 2009.

28. "Frankie Welch, Wrapped in Memories," *Washington Post*, June 28, 1987.

29. Churchman, "Personal Service"; Sarah Booth Conroy, "And a House That Pays as It Goes," *Washington Post*, February 10, 1980.

30. Welch, Smithsonian presentation; Welch, Winthrop interview.

31. Lee, "Paris-Rome Wardrobe"; Eleni, "Every Woman"; "William C. Welch, 54, Dies; Liaison Official with VA," *Washington Post*, April 28, 1975.

32. Raw footage for *Nation's Business Today*, an ESPN television program, Washington, D.C., for a "Making It" segment that ran on February 7, 1989, Brown Media Archives, transfer from Frankie Welch Collection, Rome Area History Center; Eleni, "Every Woman"; "Sew First."

33. List of Frankie Welch's teaching experience; "Classes for All at YWCA, Fine Points of Cooking and Dressmaking Taught," *Washington Post and Times Herald*, September 22, 1960; "Sew First"; Peggy Welch Williams, email to author, April 14, 2020.

34. Lee, "Paris-Rome Wardrobe."

35. "Frankie Welch: Fashion Address Planned Tuesday," *Furman Paladin*, October 7, 1966; Sandi Dinkins, "Teacher's Model Approach Wins Rome Trip," *Rome (Italy) Daily American*, August 6, 1960; Iris Smallwood, "She's Got That Gold Feeling," *Northern Virginia Sun*, August 25, 1960.

36. "Un beau voyage," *Paris-Jour*, July 29, 1960.

37. Lee, "Paris-Rome Wardrobe"; Anna Leesa, "Frankie Welch: Prizewinner's Goal Is Fashion Coordination," *Alexandria (Va.) Gazette*, October 20, 1960.

38. Dinkins, "Teacher's Model."

39. *Home Economics in Colleges and Universities* (Washington, D.C.: Department of Home Economics of the National Education Association, 1968), 12.

40. Leesa, "Frankie Welch."

41. Mrs. John J. Williams, "Congressional Wives Practice Egg Craft," Washington Chatter, *Wilmington (Del.) Morning News*, March 27, 1961; Eleni, "Every Woman"; Leesa, "Frankie Welch." Welch's working day by 1961 generally was from 10:00 a.m. to 3:00 p.m., so that she could be home for her children after school.

42. Helen A. Colson, "Dr. Frankie Never Welches on a Difficult Fashion Cure," *Washington Daily News*, January 30, 1963.

43. "Fashion Session Planned," *Orlando (Fla.) Sentinel*, February 13, 1963.

44. Ibid.; Colson, "Dr. Frankie Never Welches." Ten dollars in February 1963 equaled about $85 in December 2020, and fifteen equaled about $128, according to the Consumer Price Index Inflation Calculator. Later sources state that Welch had charged twenty-five dollars an hour. Livingstone, "Frank-ie View of Style."

45. "Fashion Seminar Slated for NASA Wives Club," *Orlando Sentinel*, October 19, 1961.

46. Frankie Welch, "Principles of Composition," n.d. (before fall 1963), Welch family collection.

47. Livingstone, "Frank-ie View of Style."

48. Welch, Smithsonian presentation. Betty Ford once demonstrated Welch's point system on ABC-TV. Esther Van Wagoner Tufty, "Michigan in Washington," *Holland (Mich.) Evening Sentinel*, February 18, 1967.

49. "Frankie Welch Coming Here," *Orlando (Fla.) Sentinel*, October 6, 1963.

50. "Capital Headliner," *Newsweek*, May 19, 1969, 106.

51. Frances Spatz Leighton, "And There's Protocol," *Des Moines (Iowa) Register*, January 10, 1965.

52. Kimberly Wilmot Voss and Lance Speere, "Fashion as Washington Journalism History: Eleni Epstein and Her Three Decades at the *Washington Star*," *Media History Monographs* 16, no. 3 (2013–14), 3.

53. Helen Thomas, "It's Hemline Which This Season Is Separating Women from the Girls," *Daily Northwestern* (Oshkosh, Wis.), November 18, 1970.

54. "Fashion Session Planned"; Colson, "Frankie Never Welches."

55. Colson, "Frankie Never Welches."

56. "Frankie Welch Coming Here."

57. Livingstone, "Frank-ie View of Style."

58. Jane Cahill, "Ideas and Information," Ideas and Fashions for Smaller Stores, *Women's Wear Daily*, April 26, 1965. Welch started her business with just under $25,000, which equaled approximately $213,500 in December 2020.

59. Duvall House is named after early owners William and Nancy Duvall, who sold it to the Bank of Alexandria in 1793. Anna Leesa, "Local Couple Buys 18th Century 'Old Bank Bldg.,'" *Alexandria (Va.) Gazette*, April 13, 1963.

60. Peggy Welch Williams, email to author, June 26, 2020.

61. Ruth Wagner, "At Frankie Welch's Fashions Have Art 'n' Antiques for Background," *Washington Post and Times Herald*, September 22, 1963; "Jane Glazener Hearn," *Washington Post*, August 5, 2000. Hearn worked as Welch's assistant at Frankie Welch of Virginia for many years.

62. "A Party in the Block," *Alexandria (Va.) Gazette*, September 16, 1963; Thula E. Hampton, "Frankie's Fashions Forecast," *Alexandria (Va.) Gazette*, September 13, 1963; Welch, Smithsonian presentation.

63. Raw footage for "Making It."

64. Ibid.; Frances Cawthon, "Georgia's Star Goes 'National,'" *Atlanta Journal*, October 13, 1971.

65. Wagner, "At Frankie Welch's."

66. Frankie Welch of Virginia business card, Welch family collection.

67. Ruth Wagner, "This Is the Year of the Fashion Individualist," *Washington Post and Times Herald*, September 6, 1964.

68. Rundell, "President Ford."

69. Ruth Wagner, "Trunk Full of Goodies," *Washington Post and Times Herald*, December 18, 1964.

70. Ruth Wagner, "They're Made by Hand," *Washington Post and Times Herald*, February 21, 1966; Eleni, "Fashionable Audience Views New Fashion,"

Washington Star newspaper clipping, ca. 1965, Frankie Welch Collection, Rome Area History Center. The *Washington Post and Times Herald* reported that Welch negotiated to present "a special champagne style show" in 1966 of the designs of Ann Lowe, one of the first prominent African American designers in the United States and the designer of Jacqueline Kennedy's wedding dress, but it is not clear if that happened. Maxine Cheshire, "Potpourri," Very Interesting People, *Washington Post and Times Herald*, June 16, 1966.

71. Newspaper clipping, 1966, Welch family collection; Ruth Wagner, "Fashions Swing Toe to Topknot," Here and There, *Washington Post and Times Herald*, August 14, 1966; "Frankie Welch: Fashion Address Planned Tuesday," *Furman Paladin*, October 7, 1966.

72. "Street Scene," WWDeadline, *Women's Wear Daily*, September 27, 1966; Invitation, with handwritten note "To meet Vera Maxwell," Welch family collection.

73. "An Exciting Invitation to the Indian Summer Fashion Festival," 1966, Welch family collection. Karen Kramer, curator of Native American and Oceanic Art and Culture at the Peabody Essex Museum, indicates that Welch and New were close friends and that she "collaborated with him on several pieces." Karen Kramer, *Native Fashion Now: North American Style* (Salem, Mass.: Peabody Essex Museum, 2015), 22.

74. "Street Scene"; "Exciting Invitation."

75. Frances Cawthon, "Frankie Welch Brings Down the Ceiling," *Atlanta Constitution*, October 31, 1982; Welch, Winthrop interview. When the zipper of a Frankie dress was in the front, Welch advised that the wearer could unzip it a little and fold the corners in to create a V-neck if she wanted. Peggy Welch Williams and Genie Welch Leisure, emails to author, September 25, 2019.

76. Nancy L. Ross, "'Frankie' Means Comfortable Fad," *Washington Post and Times Herald*, March 28, 1966; Eleni, "Frankie's a Find," *Washington Star*, March 22, 1964. Eleni Epstein and Welch became good friends. Peggy Welch Williams, email to author, March 24, 2020.

77. Alexandra Jacobs, "Hostesses Slip into Something a Little Practical," *New York Times*, December 23, 2011; Hostess Gown—Housecoat—Robe page of Vintage Fashion Guild website, https://vintagefashionguild.org/lingerie-guide/robe-hostess-gown-housecoat/.

78. Eleni, "Frankie's a Find."

79. Ibid.

80. Cahill, "Ideas and Information." A price range of $15–$100 in 1965 equaled approximately $124–824 in December 2020.

81. "Capital Headliner." The prices of $18 and $85 in 1969 equaled about $128 and $604 in December 2020. In 1983 Frankies sold for $45–$200, which equaled about $118–$524 in December 2020. Jean Geddes, "Frankie Welch: American Fashion at Its Best," *The Journal* (Alexandria, Va.), August 4, 1983.

82. Joann Coker Harris, "Former Roman Makes Headlines with Styles," *Rome (Ga.) News-Tribune*, October 10, 1968.

83. Cahill, "Ideas and Information." Welch was on the afternoon version of *To Tell the Truth*. Thanks to Marshall Akers for sharing information about this series. Marshall Akers, email to author, May 4, 2019; Peggy Welch Williams, email to author, May 27, 2020.

1. Frances Cawthon, "Presidents Come and Go, but Frankie Welch Is Lame-Duck Proof," *Atlanta Constitution*, January 11, 1981. One article indicates that the idea of the Cherokee Alphabet scarf took almost two years to be realized. Marni Butterfield, "A Rare Bit of Welch," *Women's Wear Daily*, July 8, 1968.

2. Frankie Welch, presentation, April 10, 1991, Carmichael Auditorium, National Museum of American History, Smithsonian Institution, VHS cassette, Brown Media Archives, gift of the Welch family, https://kaltura.uga.edu/media/t/0 _spdju30d; raw footage for *Nation's Business Today*, an ESPN television program, Washington, D.C., for a "Making It" segment that ran on February 7, 1989, Brown Media Archives, transfer from Frankie Welch Collection, Rome Area History Center.

3. Welch, Smithsonian presentation; raw footage for "Making It"; Eleanor Lambert, "Designer Scarf Is New Prestige Item," *Honolulu Advertiser*, March 10, 1966.

4. Frances Cawthon, "Her Signature Scarf Speaks Cherokee," *Atlanta Journal and Atlanta Constitution*, November 12, 1967.

5. Ted Wadley, "Sequoyah (ca. 1770–ca. 1840)," New Georgia Encyclopedia website, September 3, 2002, last edited October 5, 2018, https://www .georgiaencyclopedia.org/articles/history-archaeology/sequoyah-ca-1770-ca -1840. New Echota, which is about twenty-six miles from Rome, was a capital of the Cherokee Nation in what is now northwestern Georgia. Georgia designated New Echota as a historic site and state park in 1962.

6. Butterfield, "A Rare Bit of Welch." Though Welch's scarf received significantly more media coverage, Lloyd Kiva New previously (by 1955 or 1965) had created two printed fabrics using the Cherokee syllabary. Alex Jacobs, "Celebrating the 100th Anniversary of the Birth of Lloyd 'Kiva' New," April 18, 2016, Indian Country Today, https://newsmaven.io/indiancountrytoday/archive /celebrating-the-100th-anniversary-of-the-birth-of-lloyd-kiva-new —AuHYL862kmzdXIQEuRe-Q/; Jhane Myers, Ryan S. Flahive, Antonio R. Chavarria, Tatiana Lomahaftewa-Singer, Carmen Vendelin, Rose Marie Cutropia, and N. Scott Momaday, *Lloyd Kiva New: A New Century, The Life and Legacy of Cherokee Artist and Educator Lloyd Kiva New* (Santa Fe, N.Mex.: Art Guild Press, 2016), 38, 52.

7. "Op Art Opens Up New Design Vistas," *New York Times*, February 16, 1965; Bernadine Morris, "Fabrics Designer Returns a Salute," *New York Times*, June 23, 1966.

8. Cawthon, "Her Signature Scarf Speaks Cherokee."

9. Julian Tomchin, email to author, August 1, 2011.

10. Peggy Welch Williams, email to author, April 22, 2019; Frankie Welch brochure, folder "Ford, Betty—Fashion—Designers—Welch, Frankie," box 38, Sheila R. Weidenfeld Files, Gerald R. Ford Presidential Library, https://www .fordlibrarymuseum.gov/library/document/0126/1489758.pdf.

11. Cawthon, "Her Signature Scarf Speaks Cherokee." Possibly Welch was conflating the stories of Stand Watie, a Cherokee Confederate general, none of whose daughters were named Sabra, and Ned Christie, a Cherokee statesman and folk hero who had a granddaughter named Sabra. Thanks to Nathaniel Holly for his assistance with this story.

12. Julian Tomchin, email to author, August 1, 2011.

13. "Op Art Opens Up New Design Vistas"; "He'll Fashion Opera Scrolls," *Washington Post and Times Herald*, July 2, 1966.

14. Nina S. Hyde, "Warp, Woof and the Weave of Distinction," *Washington Post*, January 11, 1976.

15. Wauhillau La Hay, "Cherokee Alphabet Is a Big Hit," *Washington Daily News*, October 24, 1967. Barbara Cloud reported in the *Pittsburgh Press* that La Hay "likes to feel that she 'discovered' Mrs. Welch." Barbara Cloud, Fashion Focus, *Pittsburgh Press*, March 21, 1968.

16. La Hay, "Cherokee Alphabet Is a Big Hit"; Evelyn Agnor, "Unveiling of Artistic Design," Women in the News, *Alexandria (Va.) Gazette*, October 27, 1967; Thula Hampton, "Mayor's Daughter Weds Mr. Yingling," *Alexandria (Va.) Gazette*, August 18, 1970; Dorothy LeSueur, "'Frankies' Now Wrapping Around Nationally," *Washington Post and Times Herald*, October 14, 1971.

17. Cawthon, "Her Signature Scarf Speaks Cherokee"; La Hay, "Cherokee Alphabet Is a Big Hit"; Agnor, "Unveiling of Artistic Design."

18. Gay Pauley, "Designer Works for All Presidential Candidates," *Anderson (Ind.) Daily Bulletin*, July 2, 1968. In October 1967 Welch presented about $500 (which equaled more than $3,860 in December 2020) to Congressman Roy A. Taylor of North Carolina for the higher education fund of the Cherokee Indians. "Cherokee Wampum," WWDeadline, *Women's Wear Daily*, April 22, 1968.

19. Cheryl Mayfield, "Famed Designer Plots Okie Scarf Idea during Interview," *Daily Oklahoman* (Oklahoma City), June 17, 1969.

20. Cawthon, "Her Signature Scarf Speaks Cherokee."

21. Frankie Welch tribute event, VHS cassette, 1998, Brown Media Archives, gift of the Welch family, https://bmac.libs.uga.edu/pawtucket2/index.php/Detail /objects/387285.

22. When Welch, her two daughters, and her brother Horace visited with her mother's sister, her "darling Aunt Lela Austin of Alpharetta" in 1980, Lela told them about her great-grandmother Nellie being Cherokee. Cawthon, "Presidents Come and Go"; Frankie Welch, "Interview with Frankie Welch," 1984, Winthrop University, Oral History Interviews, OH 183, https:// digitalcommons.winthrop.edu/oralhistoryprogram/243; Peggy Welch Williams, email to author, April 25, 2019.

23. When researching Welch's claim to Cherokee heritage, *First American Art Magazine* learned from the Cherokee Heritage Center that she does not have any Cherokee ancestry. America Meredith, *First American Art Magazine*, email to author, July 17, 2020. Cherokee genealogist Kathy White confirmed the lack of a Cherokee connection through this line of Welch's family. Kathy White, email to author, July 21, 2020.

24. For more information about issues surrounding claims of Cherokee ancestry, see Gregory D. Smithers, "Why Do So Many Americans Think They Have Cherokee Blood?," *Slate*, October 1, 2015, https://slate.com /news-and-politics/2015/10/cherokee-blood-why-do-so-many-americans -believe-they-have-cherokee-ancestry.html; Elizabeth Poorman, "White Lies: Indigenous Scholars Respond to Elizabeth Warren's Claims to Native Ancestry," *Perspectives on History*, March 11, 2019, https://www.historians.org

/publications-and-directories/perspectives-on-history/march-2019/white-lies-indigenous-scholars-respond-to-elizabeth-warrens-claims-to-native-ancestry; Liz Goodwin, "Digging into My Family's Claims of Cherokee Ancestry," *Boston Globe*, February 22, 2018, https://www.bostonglobe.com/news/politics/2018/02/22/digging-into-family-claims-cherokee-ancestry/YsLF19KicQpC9Tw1qS5WXJ/story.html.

25. One story in particular suggests the complexities of Native American heritage and claims to Native American heritage in the region: Samuel Martin's son Jackson (Welch's great-grandfather) was praised in the *Atlanta Constitution* for his efforts to confine and remove Cherokee inhabitants in northern Georgia. S. M. Wall, "Hale and Hearty Survivor of Georgia's Indian Wars Living Near Alpharetta," *Atlanta Constitution*, April 4, 1909.

26. Frankie Welch, *Indian Jewelry: How to Wear, Buy and Treasure America's First Fashion Pieces* (McLean, Va.: EPM, 1973), 8–9.

27. Joan O'Sullivan, "Indian Jewelry Is In," *Daily Messenger* (Canandaigua, N.Y.), February 12, 1974.

28. Kandy Shuman Stroud, "Eye on Washington," *Women's Wear Daily*, March 13, 1969; Frankie Welch brochure.

29. "Scarves for Wampum," *Washington Post and Times Herald*, October 29, 1967; Cawthon, "Her Signature Scarf Speaks Cherokee."

30. Doris Hjorth, "Chic-ly Cherokee," *Oakland (Calif.) Tribune*, May 15, 1969.

31. Welch, Smithsonian presentation.

32. Mary Strasburg, "Fashion Flies in with USA Labels," *Washington Post and Times Herald*, February 29, 1968.

33. Kimberly Chrisman-Campbell, "The 1968 Fashion Show, the History Lesson Melania Missed," *Politico*, March 5, 2018, https://www.politico.com/magazine/story/2018/03/05/melania-trump-dress-fashion-1968-fashion-show-217232; Myra MacPherson, "Governors' Wives 'Discover America in Style' at White House," *New York Times*, March 1, 1968.

34. Press Release, Office of the President to Mrs. Johnson, February 28, 1968, Frankie Welch Collection, HCTC014, Historic Clothing and Textile Collection, College of Family and Consumer Sciences, University of Georgia.

35. Welch explained in 1982 that the connection between her and the White House for the Discover America event was made through Bess Abell and Liz Carpenter, Lady Bird Johnson's social and press secretaries, who were customers of her shop. Welch asked them if Johnson would like a scarf for her Discover America program, and a few days later Johnson invited Welch to the White House. According to Welch, Johnson asked her opinion on the appropriateness of hosting a fashion show at the White House, and Welch responded, "The fashion industry has been waiting 200 years for this opportunity." Deborah Churchman, "Personal Service Draws VIPs to Chic D.C. Clothing Shop," *Christian Science Monitor*, January 26, 1982. Kimberly Chrisman-Campbell, in her book *Red, White, and Blue on the Runway: The 1968 White House Fashion Show* (Kent, Ohio: Kent State University Press, 2022), notes that Lady Bird Johnson "was in the habit of giving signature scarves by American designers as diplomatic gifts," citing a letter written by Bess Abell to Barbara Kling, 5/29/68, "Lane, F-K," White House Social Files, Alpha File, Box 1336, LBJ Presidential Library. Chrisman-Campbell also

notes that Johnson gave the Discover America scarves as gifts "to the female foreign journalists who accompanied Mrs. Johnson on her April 1968 'Discover America with the First Lady' tour of Texas." Chrisman-Campbell cites Meryle Secrest, "Reflections on a Recent Texas Trip," *Washington Post and Times Herald*, April 14, 1968.

36. Frances Cawthon, "She Helps Make History," *Atlanta Journal*, March 5, 1968.

37. Welch, Smithsonian presentation.

38. Ibid.; "Welch Brings American Themes to Life on Scarves," *Journal Record* (Oklahoma City), November 25, 1992.

39. MacPherson, "Governors' Wives."

40. Press Release, February 28, 1968; Eugenia Sheppard, "'Welcome to the White House,'" Inside Fashion, *Women's Wear Daily*, March 1, 1968. Welch may have used a combination of painting, stenciling, and screen printing to produce the scarves for the fashion show; the records are unclear. The photo on page 44, though, shows her with a paintbrush in hand, confirming the use of that technique. See also photos of her assistants using paintbrushes and a small screen in Folder, "White House Fashion Show, 2/29/1968 [3 of 3]," White House Social Files, Bess Abell Files, box 23, LBJ Presidential Library, https://www.discoverlbj.org/item/whsf-ba-b23-f16.

41. Sheppard, "'Welcome to the White House.'"

42. Cawthon, "She Helps Make History."

43. Barbara Cloud in the *Pittsburgh Press* reported a different verse on the cards enclosed with the Discover America scarves:

> Columbus did it long ago
> Long before we thought of this show.
> Our order for scarves made them hit the roof
> So the one you have is just a proof.
> The hem isn't rolled and they're not color fast
> But used as a poster, they're sure to last!
> —Cloud, Fashion Focus, March 21, 1968.

44. Judith Axler, D.C. Wash, *Daily News* (New York), July 28, 1968. Some scarves were professionally screen-printed with the lighter blue as well.

45. Frankie Welch, Alexandria, Va., to Baccara, Lyon, France, January 4, 1969, Frankie Welch Papers, acc. 519, box 1, folder 2, Louise Pettus Archives and Special Collections, Dacus Library, Winthrop University (hereafter Pettus Archives). Correspondence in the LBJ Presidential Library from Welch to Lady Bird Johnson's press secretary, Liz Carpenter, indicates that Julian Tomchin (and his assistant Steve Wysocki) again worked with Welch on the design, and that Chardon Marché would produce the final scarves, though the connection was not publicized and plans may have fallen through. Tomchin denies involvement. Frankie Welch, Alexandria, Va., to Liz Carpenter, Washington, D.C., February 9, 1968, LBJ Presidential Library; Julian Tomchin, email to author, March 26, 2019. Chrisman-Campbell explains in *Red, White, and Blue on the Runway* that Tomchin and Wysocki's involvement was kept quiet so that their affiliation with the Republican Party would not embarrass the Democratic first lady. Thanks to Kimberly Chrisman-Campbell for sharing her research from the LBJ Presidential Library. See Folder, "White House Fashion Show, 2/29/1968 [1 of 3], [2 of 3,] and [3 of 3]," White House Social Files, Bess Abell Files, box 23, LBJ Presidential Library, https://www.discoverlbj

.org/item/whsf-ba-b23-f14, https://www.discoverlbj.org/item/whsf-ba-b23
-f15, https://www.discoverlbj.org/item/whsf-ba-b23-f16.

46. "Non-Partisan Fashion," Eye, *Women's Wear Daily*, May 1, 1968.

47. Ibid.

48. Butterfield, "A Rare Bit of Welch."

49. Joann Harris, "Frankie Welch," *Baltimore Sun*, July 21, 1968.

50. Butterfield, "A Rare Bit of Welch."

51. Jean Sprain Wilson, "Women Have Become Walking Political Billboards," *Press* (Binghamton, N.Y.), June 27, 1968.

52. Ibid.; Selwa Roosevelt, "Toni Peabody Opens an HHH Pharmacy," *Washington Post and Times Herald*, July 4, 1968. One hundred dollars in 1968 equaled about $746 in December 2020. For the opening of the Pharmacy, Welch designed pharmacist coats in blue with green trim and called the design "The Hubert." Jane Day, "Buy Partisan: Politics Steps Out in Fashion," *National Observer*, August 5, 1968.

53. Wilson, "Walking Political Billboards"; Day, "Buy Partisan"; Marian McBride, "Campaign Couture," *Milwaukee Sentinel*, July 4, 1968; "Campaign Baubles, Bangles, Beads," *Windsor (Ont.) Star*, August 8, 1968.

54. Axler, D.C. Wash.

55. Ibid.; "Boutique Apparel Proclaims Feminine Political Backers," *Holland (Mich.) Evening News*, July 9, 1968. Welch's RNC fabric was inspired by a floral print Julian Tomchin designed for a party honoring Norman Norell in 1967. Peggy Welch Williams, text message to author, April 29, 2021; Enid Nemy, "Culture, Couture and Conviviality: 7th Avenue Salutes All Three," *New York Times*, October 24, 1967.

56. Eugenia Sheppard, "Equal Time for the GOP," Inside Fashion, *Women's Wear Daily*, April 22, 1968.

57. Diane L. Fagan Affleck, introduction to Diane L. Fagan Affleck and Paul Hudson, *Celebration and Remembrance: Commemorative Textiles in America, 1790–1990* (North Andover, Mass.: Museum of American Textile History, 1990), 21–23.

58. Sheppard, "Equal Time for the GOP"; Eleni, "So Everything GOP Is Coming Up Daisies," *Evening Star* (Washington, D.C.), May 2, 1968; Joan Nielsen McHale, "Styled by Frankie Welch: Republicans Have Own Design," *Miami (Fla.) News*, June 19, 1968.

59. Mary Strasburg, "GOP Elephant Has Rival in Daisies," *Washington Post and Times Herald*, May 2, 1968; photo of Frankie Welch with caption, *Kingston (N.Y.) Daily Freeman*, May 7, 1968.

60. "Non-Partisan Fashion."

61. Dorothy McCardle, "For Number 218, Some Numbers Lowered Sum," *Washington Post and Times Herald*, June 19, 1968. Betty Ford also bought yardage of the RNC fabric to make a bedspread and curtains for her daughter's room. Axler, D.C. Wash.

62. Day, "Buy Partisan."

63. Myra MacPherson, "If You Think a Political Button Isn't Enough . . . ," *New York Times*, June 20, 1968; Wilson, "Walking Political Billboards." Twenty-eight dollars in June 1968 equaled approximately $210 in December 2020.

64. Cawthon, "Presidents Come and Go."

65. Axler, D.C. Wash; "Non-Partisan Fashion." Toni Peabody reported that when the Democratic National Committee asked her to design a Humphrey

dress, she said that she could not, but she got Welch to do it. Gloria Negri, "'Pharmacy' Set Up by Toni Peabody," *Boston Globe*, August 23, 1968.

66. Axler, D.C. Wash.

67. MacPherson, "If You Think." Twelve dollars in June 1968 equaled approximately ninety dollars in December 2020. The first dresses, for Humphrey's announcement luncheon, featured lace trim rather than rickrack.

68. "HHH Women Don H-Liner," *Daily Chronicle* (Centralia, Wash.), May 23, 1968.

69. Betty Beale, "Johnson Barely Misses Indorsing [*sic*] Humphrey," *Indianapolis Star*, May 5, 1968; Joann Harris, "Frankie Welch."

70. MacPherson, "If You Think."

71. Peggy Welch Williams, email to Anne Howard-Tristani (Hubert H. Humphrey's niece), May 8, 2020.

72. "The H Dress," WWDeadline, *Women's Wear Daily*, September 13, 1968.

73. Ibid.; Joann Coker Harris, "Former Roman Makes Headlines with Styles," *Rome (Ga.) News-Tribune*, October 10, 1968.

74. MacPherson, "If You Think"; Maxine Cheshire, "Mrs. Ford Was Dressing for the Wrong Party," Very Interesting People, *Washington Post and Times Herald*, June 20, 1968. Ford even mentioned this event in her autobiography: "Once [Frankie] came into her shop, caught me parading around in a dress I thought was really pretty, and hooted. 'Take that off. You don't want that, Betty; it was designed for Hubert Humphrey's campaign workers.' Sure enough, the decorative stripes down the sides, and the white band across the waist, formed a very nice capital H." Betty Ford with Chris Chase, *The Times of My Life* (New York: Harper & Row, 1978), 107–8.

75. Axler, D.C. Wash.

76. Harris, "Former Roman"; Harris, "Frankie Welch"; "Popular Pocketbucket," WWDeadline, *Women's Wear Daily*, June 24, 1968.

77. "HHH Scarf," *Women's Wear Daily*, June 25, 1968; "Triple Exposure," *Women's Wear Daily*, June 26, 1968. On the Humphrey scarves, Welch's name is included discreetly on the small label sewn to the back with the fabric content. Welch designed a related scarf for Senator Warren Magnuson, a Democrat from Minnesota, in 1968, in red, white, and blue with Ms (that read as Ws from the opposite direction) in a checkerboard and a signature block in one corner, and possibly a campaign dress as well. Marie M. Peden, "Frankie Welch, Furman Graduate, Designs Inaugural Ball Scarves," *Greenville (S.C.) Piedmont*, January 20, 1969; Herbert Ridgeway Collins, *Threads of History: Americana Recorded on Cloth, 1775 to the Present* (Washington, D.C.: Smithsonian Institution Press, 1979), 524.

78. Day, "Buy Partisan." For more Humphrey campaign garments, see the Minnesota Historical Society Online Collections, http://collections.mnhs.org /cms/.

79. Georgia Young of Erlebacher's made Guest's dress. "Campaign Baubles"; Wauhillau La Hay, "Wives Wearing Campaign Styles," *Pittsburgh Press*, June 18, 1968. Two hundred dollars in August 1968 equaled about $1,488 in December 2020.

80. Welch, Smithsonian presentation; undated note from Frankie Welch about the Hubert Humphrey scarf, Welch family collection.

81. Welch, Smithsonian presentation.

82. Day, "Buy Partisan"; Mary Wiegers, "The New Majority Rocks into Pop Politics," *Washington Post and Times Herald*, July 17, 1968; Axler, D.C. Wash.

83. Axler, D.C. Wash.

84. Day, "Buy Partisan."

85. Strasburg, "GOP Elephant"; MacPherson, "If You Think."

86. Pauley, "Designer Works for All Presidential Candidates."

87. Cindy Creasy, "Shop Started to Meet House Payments Is Style Center," *Richmond (Va.) Times-Dispatch*, September 11, 1983.

88. Butterfield, "A Rare Bit of Welch."

89. Axler, D.C. Wash.

90. Henry J. Wolfinger, compiler, *Preliminary Inventory of the Records of the 1969 Inaugural Committee: Record Group 274* (Washington, D.C.: National Archives and Records Service, General Services Administration, 1974), 18; "Youth for Nixon Campaign Aims to Win Under-30 Vote," *Cincinnati Enquirer*, March 19, 1972.

91. Welch, Smithsonian presentation. At least one article credits Leslie C. Arends, cochair of the 1969 inaugural ball, as helping with the scarf's design. Patricia Shelton, "What's for the Inaugural?," *Christian Science Monitor*, January 15, 1969.

92. "Inaugural Guests to Get Scarves, Cuff Links, Bracelets," *New York Times*, January 10, 1969; Shelton, "What's for the Inaugural?"; "Don't Stand Pat," *Women's Wear Daily*, January 10, 1969; Welch, Winthrop interview.

93. "Inaugural Guests"; Welch, Smithsonian presentation; Shelton, "What's for the Inaugural?"

94. Mildred Mikkanen, "Pat Nixon Chuckles at Preview," *Niagara Falls (N.Y.) Gazette*, January 11, 1969.

95. Mary Wiegers, "Battle Scarves," *Washington Post and Times Herald*, June 9, 1969.

96. "Neck-ing," Eye, *Women's Wear Daily*, March 6, 1969.

Chapter 3. Frankie Welch Signature Scarves

1. Nicky Albrechtsen and Fola Solanke, *Scarves* (New York: Thames & Hudson, 2011), 92.

2. Susan Seid with Jen Renzi, *Vera: The Art and Life of an Icon* (New York: Abrams, 2010), 35.

3. Ibid., 30; Eugenia Sheppard, "Signature Scarf Wraps Up Fashion Designers," *Washington Post and Times Herald*, December 26, 1966; Eleanor Lambert, "Designer Scarf Is New Prestige Item," *Honolulu Advertiser*, March 10, 1966.

4. Sheppard, "Signature Scarf"; Peg Zwecker, "Scarves Sign In," *Washington Post and Times Herald*, June 19, 1968; Dee Dee Bower, "Fashion Picture Is All Tied-Up in Smart Knots," *Shreveport (La.) Times*, February 12, 1969.

5. Lambert, "Designer Scarf."

6. Rubye Graham, "Scarves' New Uses," *Philadelphia Inquirer*, March 1, 1968; Zwecker, "Scarves Sign In"; Jean Sprain Wilson, "Scarf Blouse May Become Dress," *Troy (N.Y.) Record*, October 13, 1966.

7. Seid and Renzi, *Vera*, 35; Wilson, "Scarf Blouse." These price ranges of $2–$10 and $20–$50 from 1966 equaled about $16–80 and $159–$398 in December 2020, respectively.

8. Frankie Welch of Virginia brochure, box 38, folder "Ford, Betty—Fashion—Designers—Welch, Frankie," Sheila R. Weidenfeld Files, Gerald R. Ford Presidential Library, https://www.fordlibrarymuseum.gov/library/document/0126/1489758.pdf. The prices of $9 and $22 in 1969 equaled about $63 and $155 in December 2020, respectively.

9. Enid Nemy, "New Status Symbol: Scarf Floating Airily in the Breeze," *New York Times*, October 16, 1967; Zwecker, "Scarves Sign In."

10. Zwecker, "Scarves Sign In"; "The Scarf Very Big This Year," *Kansas City Times*, June 14, 1968; Albrechtsen and Solanke, *Scarves*, 13.

11. Nemy, "New Status Symbol"; Enid Nemy, "The Signature Market: For Designers, the Sky's the Limit," *New York Times*, July 2, 1969; Cheryl Mayfield, "Famed Designer Plots Okie Scarf During Interview," *Daily Oklahoman* (Oklahoma City), June 17, 1969; Frankie Welch of Virginia brochure; Eleni, "Jewels, Frankie and Indian Idiom," *Washington Star-News*, November 4, 1973. A price of $45 in 1967 equaled about $351 in December 2020, while $22 in 1969 equaled about $156 in December 2020.

12. Evelyn Livingstone, "Year of the Scarf," *Chicago Tribune*, May 24, 1969.

13. Albrechtsen and Solanke, *Scarves*, 13.

14. Nemy, "Signature Market."

15. "Neck-ing," Eye, *Women's Wear Daily*, March 6, 1969.

16. Frankie Welch of Virginia brochure.

17. "Capital Headliner," *Newsweek*, May 19, 1969, 104.

18. Nancy Ball, "Cherokee Scarf Leads to Success in the Fashion World," *Binghamton (N.Y.) Press*, June 20, 1969.

19. "Capital Headliner."

20. Marian Christy, Eyeful, *Boston Globe*, August 22, 1977. Initially Welch's minimum custom order was for eighty of the 32-inch silk square scarves at $12.50 apiece ($1,000 total), or three hundred of the 22-inch silk or cotton squares. Rubye Graham, "Custom Scarves Personalized," *Philadelphia Inquirer*, April 16, 1969.

21. Frankie Welch with Peggy Welch Williams, email to author, July 15, 2011. The introduction of the name Frankie Welch of America happened by 1975.

22. "Frankie Welch Scarf Fashions to Be Feature of Furman Alumni Event," *Greenville (S.C.) News*, May 11, 1969; "Three Furman Alumni to Be Honored," *Greenville (S.C.) News*, May 28, 1969; Alice H. Johnson, "Frankie Welch Shows Furman Scarf," *Greenville (S.C.) News*, May 31, 1969; "Scarves Arrive, Now on Sale," *Furman Magazine* 17, no. 3 (August 1969), 35.

23. The See Georgia First scarf was "adopted as part of the official uniform for the state's hostesses of welcome centers." Frances Cawthon, "Hometown Fetes Designer," *Atlanta Constitution*, September 28, 1969.

24. Genie Welch Leisure, email to author, July 10, 2020.

25. Eleni, "It All Began with Cherokee Alphabet," *Washington Star*, June 7, 1970; Deborah Churchman, "Personal Service Draws VIPs to Chic D.C. Clothing Shop," *Christian Science Monitor*, January 26, 1982. Welch stated, "I design in the module, like Frank Lloyd Wright." Into the mid-1970s, Welch generally had a minimum order of three hundred scarves, ranging in price from about $3.50 to $5.50 apiece depending on fabric and quantity. A wholesale price sheet from the mid-1970s lists the following: for Qiana scarves, 32" squares: 1,000

at $22.50, 500 at $23.50, 300 at $24.50; 8" x 36" scarves: 1,000 at $5.00, 500 at $5.25, 300 at $5.50; napas on cotton: 4,000 at $1.00, 1,200 at $1.10. Frankie Welch, Wholesale Prices sheet, Betty Ford folder, Frankie Welch Collection, Rome Area History Center. In a letter to a client in 1974, Welch listed these figures for 8" x 36" scarves: Qiana: 400 @ $5.00, 1,000 @ $4.50, 2,000 @ $4.25, 3,000 @ $4.00; and cotton: 500 @ $4.00, 1,000 @ $3.75, 3,000 @ $3.50. Frankie Welch to Martha U. Pritchard, Administrative Assistant, Commonwealth of Virginia, Office of the Governor, Richmond, Virginia, April 9, 1974, Frankie Welch Collection, Rome Area History Center. Later in the 1970s and early 1980s, she charged about $4.75 to $6.00 per scarf, and $150 per screen for printing. *Women's Wear Daily* in 1979 reported that 50 percent of her business volume was scarf designs. "Inside Out," Eye, *Women's Wear Daily*, March 15, 1979.

26. Virginia Shields, "Frankie Welch's First Edition Library Scarf to Be Introduced at GLA Conference on Jekyll," *Brunswick (Ga.) News*, October 27, 1971; Pat Gaines, "Frankie Welch Designs New Scarf for Libraries," *Rome (Ga.) News-Tribune*, July 11, 1971; "Welch Scarf Created for Book Lovers," *Atlanta Constitution*, October 28, 1971.

27. Frankie Welch Napa-Chief flyer, Frankie Welch Textile Collection, MS 2003, Hargrett Rare Book and Manuscript Library, University of Georgia Libraries (hereafter Hargrett Library).

28. Raymonde Alexander, "They're Much More Than an Accessory," *Atlanta Constitution*, May 24, 1978.

29. Esther Smith, "Frankie Welch on Designing the Corporate Image," *Business Review of Washington*, October 19, 1979.

30. See, for example, Mayfield, "Famed Designer."

31. Peggy Welch Williams, email to author, May 27, 2020.

32. Alyce Atkinson, "A Success Story in Silk," *Greenville (S.C.) News*, November 28, 1993.

33. Susan W. Thompson, letter to Frankie Welch, April 9, 2020.

34. "This Is Their South," *Southern Living*, February 1970, 52.

35. Store Policy, Frankie Welch of Virginia, Frankie Welch Collection, Rome Area History Center.

36. Esther Smith, "Frankie Welch."

37. Frankie Welch, "Interview with Frankie Welch," 1984, Winthrop University, Oral History Interviews, OH 183, https://digitalcommons.winthrop.edu /oralhistoryprogram/243. Though the unusual Lear Fan 2100 plane with its rear propeller never went into production, the scarves and totes did. Later, when Welch learned that a friend's son-in-law, musician Steven Tyler, owned a Learjet, she sent him a Lear Fan scarf, which he displayed in his plane. Dorothea Johnson, telephone conversation with author, January 23, 2020.

38. Wanda Lesley, "Success All Tied Up," *Greenville (S.C.) News*, September 11, 1975; Atkinson, "Success Story in Silk."

39. Frankie Welch with Peggy Welch Williams, email to author, July 15, 2011.

40. Leslie Ellis, "Her Scarves Are a Signature," *People Today* (Brevard County, Fla.), March 28, 1976.

41. Handwritten note in Burke & Herbert file, Frankie Welch Textile Collection, MS 2003, box 1:31, Hargrett Library; "The History of Burke & Herbert Bank,"

Burke and Herbert Bank website, https://www.burkeandherbertbank.com /aboutthebank/history.aspx.

42. Eleni, "Cherokee Alphabet."

43. Frankie Welch to Linda Royall, Alexandria, Virginia, January 21, 1985, Welch family collection.

44. Frankie Welch of America, Inc., booklet of guidelines for office operating procedures, Welch family collection.

45. McDonald's Design, card 50, Frankie Welch Textile Collection, MS 2003, box 9:1, Library Index Cards folder, Hargrett Library; Margo Kline, "The Corporate Scarf," *On the Town* (Alexandria, Va.), February 20, 1980; *Frankie Welch Designs* brochure for exhibition at the University of Georgia Libraries, 1982. Welch's friend Al Neher recalled them visiting the McDonald's headquarters in Illinois and meeting Ray Kroc, the founder. Welch joined Kroc in Paris for an opening of the restaurant there, and she designed a second scarf to celebrate the opening of the 4,000th McDonald's location, in Montreal. Al Neher, email to Peggy Welch Williams, July 24, 2011.

46. Mayfield, "Famed Designer"; Lesley, "Success All Tied Up."

47. Peggy Welch Williams, email to author, May 27, 2020.

48. Frankie Welch and Baccara records, Frankie Welch Papers, acc. 519, Pettus Archives. Some of the scarves Baccara printed include Cherokee Alphabet, Discover America, Genie, and Iberian Imports.

49. Frankie Welch and Bellotti records, Frankie Welch Papers, acc. 519, Pettus Archives; Frankie Welch and Maxwell Industries records, Frankie Welch Papers, acc. 519, box 7, folder 25, Pettus Archives. The scarves Chardon Marché printed include Cherokee Alphabet, Greek Alphabet, Industrial College of the Armed Forces, the Frankie Welch signature, Congress, and an early design for Rome, Georgia.

50. Frankie Welch and Onondaga records, Frankie Welch Papers, acc. 519, Pettus Archives; Monica D. Murgia, "Onondaga Textiles via the Design Center," August 9, 2013, https://blog.monicadmurgia.com/tag/onondaga-silk-company/ (website discontinued); Frankie Welch and Fisher & Gentile Ltd. records, Frankie Welch Papers, acc. 519, Pettus Archives.

51. Frankie Welch and Sabana Grande Embroidery records, Frankie Welch Papers, acc. 519, box 8, folder 33, Pettus Archives.

52. Mary Tuthill, "Potomac Jottings," *Ironwood (Mich.) Daily Globe*, April 26, 1977; Sarah Booth Conroy, "An Apartment with Walls to Go," *Washington Post*, February 10, 1980; Peggy Welch Williams, email to author, February 11, 2020.

53. Frankie Welch of America booklet of guidelines.

54. Ibid., 2–3.

55. Ibid., 2.

56. Carolyn Bengston, "Secret Out: DuPont's Newest Fiber, Qiana, Unveiled in New York Thursday," *Austin (Tex.) American-Statesman*, June 29, 1968; "Silky Nylon Developed by DuPont," *News Journal* (Wilmington, Del.), June 27, 1968.

57. Frankie Welch to Bruce G. Sundlun, Executive Jet Aviation, Columbus, Ohio, July 6, 1973, Frankie Welch Textile Collection, MS 2003, box 3:2, Executive Jet Aviation folder, Hargrett Library.

58. Frankie Welch to Morty Bloom, New York, February 4, 1977, Frankie Welch Papers, acc. 519, box 1, folder 3, Pettus Archives.

59. S. Diane Barnard, "Qiana Nylon: DuPont Chemical Company Attempt to Offer a Replacement for High Cost Silk," International Textile and Apparel Association (ITAA) Annual Conference Proceedings, 2013, https://lib.dr.iastate .edu/cgi/viewcontent.cgi?article=2798&context=itaa_proceedings. The peak year for Qiana's popularity is based on a survey of newspaper advertisements by author.

60. McCormick Spice Design, card 51, Frankie Welch Textile Collection, MS 2003, box 9:1, Library Index Cards folder, Hargrett Library.

61. Dorothea Johnson, telephone conversation with author, January 23, 2020.

62. John T. Molloy, *The Woman's Dress for Success Book* (Chicago: Follett, 1977), 38, 77–79. Molloy decried signature scarves, though.

63. Peggy Welch Williams, email to author, April 20, 2020.

64. Invoices, 1976, Frankie Welch Papers, acc. 519, box 2, folders 5 and 6, Pettus Archives.

65. Seid and Renzi, *Vera*, 35.

66. Albrechtsen and Solanke, *Scarves*, 9, 12, 70.

67. Mary C. Mathews, University of Alabama, to Frankie Welch, Alexandria, Va., Frankie Welch Collection, Rome Area History Center.

68. Brooks Jackson, "Rep. Bella Abzug . . . Congresswoman Battles for Action, Not Respect," *News-Journal* (Mansfield, Ohio), December 5, 1971.

69. "NPR Opens Up 'Forum for the World,'" *Sioux City (Iowa) Journal*, June 30, 1973.

70. "New Presentation," *Daily News-Journal* (Murfreesboro, Tenn.), June 14, 1973.

71. Welch, never missing an opportunity, also produced a necktie for the National Press Club. Fisher & Gentile Ltd. invoice to Frankie Welch of Virginia, February 16, 1973, Frankie Welch Papers, acc. 519, box 6, folder 21, Pettus Archives.

Chapter 4. Americana Scarves and Garments

1. Doris Hjorth, "Chic-ly Cherokee," *Oakland (Calif.) Tribune*, May 15, 1969.

2. Raymonde Alexander, "Fashionata Has Individual Approach to Fashionable Dressing for the Fall," *Atlanta Constitution*, September 8, 1966; Raymonde Alexander, "Cling Is the Thing: Hemline Issue Is Dead," *Atlanta Constitution*, November 30, 1970.

3. Myra MacPherson, "New China Service for White House Is Pure Americana," *New York Times*, May 10, 1968; Jean Gilmore, "Designer May Have Everyone Dressed Alike," *Daily Oklahoman* (Oklahoma City), April 15, 1972; Fifty State Flowers Design, card 142, Frankie Welch Textile Collection, MS 2003, box 9:1, Library Index Cards folder, Hargrett Library; Draft description of Fifty State Flowers Scarf, August 14, 1975, Frankie Welch Papers, acc. 519, box 7, folder 29, Pettus Archives.

4. "Frankie Is Supimly Good," *Oakland (Calif.) Tribune*, May 21, 1970.

5. Frances Cawthon, "Former Georgia Designer Has a Bloomin' Good Idea," *Atlanta Journal*, May 15, 1970.

6. "State Scarf," Eye, *Women's Wear Daily*, April 30, 1970; Eleni, "It All Began with Cherokee Alphabet," *Sunday Star* (Washington, D.C.), June 7, 1970.

7. See also Ashley Callahan, "Scarf and Dress Designs by Frankie Welch: Highlighting Georgia through Her Americana," *Proceedings from the Seventh*

Henry D. Green Symposium of the Decorative Arts (Athens: Georgia Museum of Art, 2016), 91–106.

8. Emma Livingstone, "A Frank-ie View of Style; Scarfs Tie It All Together," *Richmond (Va.) Times-Dispatch*, February 27, 1972.

9. Joann Coker Harris, "Former Roman Makes Headlines with Styles," *Rome (Ga.) News-Tribune*, October 10, 1968.

10. Frances Cawthon, "Frankie Welch Brings Down the Ceiling," *Atlanta Constitution*, October 31, 1982. Cawthon also reported that a Parisian government official wore a long Cherokee Alphabet scarf when she attended an opera opening as part of a group including President Georges Pompidou in 1969. Frances Cawthon, "Hometown Fetes Designer," *Atlanta Constitution*, September 28, 1969.

11. Advertisement, Frankie Welch of Virginia, *Washington Post and Times Herald*, June 20, 1970. Lord and Taylor carried the dress in silk. Sarah C. Casey, "Fashion Turns to the Indian," *Philadelphia Inquirer*, April 20, 1970.

12. Helen Thomas, "It's Hemline Which This Season Is Separating Women from the Girls," *Daily Northwestern* (Oshkosh, Wis.), November 18, 1970.

13. The caption below the image reads, "The gleam of Bénédictine's copper stills, the bright white of woven polyester with the feel of silk and the hand-screened markings of the Cherokee alphabet in Bénédictine brown. Now that's a combination to drink a toast to!" Advertisement, Bénédictine, *Vogue*, November 1, 1970, 31. A related Bénédictine advertisement in *Vogue* featured a floral print dress and scarf by Welch. Advertisement, Bénédictine and Peck & Peck, *Vogue*, November 1, 1970, 30.

14. "Guess What She's Doing in Town?," *Beach Sun* (Miami Beach, Fla.), May 14, 1971; "Indian Theme Emphasized by Chieftains Band Leader," *Rome (Ga.) News-Tribune*, September 15, 1974.

15. "Cherokee Alphabet," *Washington Post and Times Herald*, March 1, 1970; Cawthon, "Former Georgia Designer."

16. "Cherokee Alphabet," *Washington Post and Times Herald*; Eleni, "Cherokee Alphabet."

17. LaDonna Harris, telephone conversation with author, February 4, 2020.

18. Maxine Cheshire, "Democrats Have Problems? They R.S.V.P.'d Ann Landers," Very Interesting People, *Washington Post and Times Herald*, August 27, 1968; newspaper clipping with photograph of Mrs. Fred Harris, Muriel Humphrey, and Mrs. Walter Mondale, possibly *Washington Post and Times Herald*, ca. August 1968, Frankie Welch Collection, Rome Area History Center. LaDonna Harris also donned Humphrey scarves and a long H-Line dress. Wauhillau La Hay, "Wives Wearing Campaign Styles," *Pittsburgh Press*, June 18, 1989; Jessica R. Metcalfe, "Frankie Welch, Politics, and That Cherokee Scarf," Beyond Buckskin, March 22, 2012, http://www.beyondbuckskin.com/2012/03/frankie-welch-politics-and-that.html.

19. Charlotte Curtis, "Indians Whoop It Up," *Corpus Christi (Tex.) Caller-Times*, August 8, 1970.

20. The Harrises were on the July 13, 1970, episode of *The Dick Cavett Show* along with Sly Stone.

21. LaDonna Harris, telephone conversation with author, February 4, 2020.

22. "Over 7,000 Attend Cherokee Nat'l Holiday, Many Events Held," *Cherokee Nation News*, September 11, 1973.

23. Gloria Steinem, "Wilma Mankiller," *Time*, December 27, 2010, 124. Mankiller also wore the long Cherokee Alphabet scarf when she gave a press conference at Ball State University in 1994: https://www.youtube.com/watch?v=e-84VjijK7k.

24. Frances Cawthon, "Georgia's Star Goes 'National,'" *Atlanta Journal*, October 13, 1971; Turtle Scarf, card 150, Frankie Welch Textile Collection, MS 2003, box 9:1, Library Index Cards folder, Hargrett Library.

25. Cawthon, "Georgia's Star."

26. Susan Seid with Jen Renzi, *Vera: The Art and Life of an Icon* (New York: Abrams, 2010), 37.

27. Cawthon, "Georgia's Star." The turtle quote often is credited to Harvard president and chemist James B. Conant, though he attributed it to unnamed atomic scientists, possibly with the Manhattan Project. "Behold the Turtle," Quote Investigator website, https://quoteinvestigator.com/2019/09/13/turtle/. Thanks to Nathaniel Holly at the University of Georgia Press for his assistance interpreting Welch's use of the turtle motif.

28. Dorothy LeSueur, "'Frankies' Now Wrapping Around Nationally," *Washington Post and Times Herald*, October 14, 1971; "Strike It Rich," Eye, *Women's Wear Daily*, October 14, 1971; Cawthon, "Georgia's Star."

29. LeSueur, "'Frankies' Now Wrapping"; Advertisement, Rich's Regency Shop, *Atlanta Constitution*, October 17, 1971.

30. Thula Hampton, "Alexandria Designer Makes National Scene," *Alexandria (Va.) Gazette*, October 14, 1971.

31. Frankie Welch, "Fashion Notes from Frankie Welch," *Southern Living*, November 1971, 77.

32. Welch was fashion editor at *Southern Living* from October 1971 through March 1972, a position likely ended by a restructuring at the magazine. She contributed a page titled "Fashion Notes from Frankie Welch" with sketches and practical fashion tips.

33. Mildred Whitaker, "'Frankie' Goes to Fiesta," *San Antonio (Tex.) News*, April 19, 1972; "Boutique Fashions in Traditional Show," *San Antonio (Tex.) Express/News*, April 16, 1972.

34. Press Release, Frankie Welch of Virginia, March 31, 1973, and "Biographical Background of Frankie Welch" sheet, both in Welch family collection.

35. Jinny O'Leary, "Indian Lore Inspiration for Designs," *Alexandria (Va.) Gazette*, April 26, 1973.

36. Advertisement, Goldwater's, *Arizona Republic* (Phoenix), April 15, 1973; Nina S. Hyde, "A Salute to American Indians," *Washington Post and Times Herald*, April 12, 1973; Press Release, Frankie Welch of Virginia, April 5, 1973, Welch family collection; Eleni, "Tension in the Air," *Evening Star and Daily News* (Washington, D.C.), April 12, 1973.

37. Hyde, "Salute"; Eleni, "Tension in the Air."

38. Advertisement, Goldwater's, *Arizona Republic* (Phoenix), April 15, 1973.

39. Ellie Schultz, "Fashion Folio: Indian Designer Arrives," *Arizona Republic* (Phoenix), April 16, 1973.

40. Jinny O'Leary, "Frankie's New Book Was the Toast of the Town: Others Seek Out Celebrities," *Alexandria (Va.) Gazette*, November 7, 1973; Ellie Schultz, "Designer's Novel Ideas Make Simple Patterns Unique," *Arizona Republic* (Phoenix), May 13, 1973.

41. Advertisement, Hightower, *Daily Oklahoman* (Oklahoma City), April 13, 1973.

42. Ibid.; O'Leary, "Frankie's New Book"; press releases, April 5, 1973, March 31, 1973.

43. Schultz, "Designer's Novel Ideas."

44. Philip Joseph Deloria, *Playing Indian* (New Haven, Conn.: Yale University Press, 1999), 137.

45. Joan O'Sullivan, "Indian Jewelry Is In," *Daily Messenger* (Canandaigua, N.Y.), February 12, 1974.

46. Lucia Johnson Leith, "Indians Striving to Preserve Culture," *Daily Press* (Newport News, Va.), June 10, 1973; Carol Weaver, "Frankie Welch: Designer for the First Lady," *Georgia Alumni Record*, October 1974, 7; "Women of the Year 1973," *Ladies' Home Journal*, June 1973, 67–69.

47. Welch, *Indian Jewelry*, 10.

48. Cory Arnet, "Book Notes," *Wassaja* (San Francisco), February 1974.

49. Vicki Ostrolenk, "Frankie's New Book Was the Toast of the Town: Some Talk about 'That Other Thing,'" *Alexandria (Va.) Gazette*, November 7, 1973; O'Leary, "Frankie's New Book."

50. "McComb Attends Book Party," *Cherokee Nation News*, March 5, 1974.

51. Ostrolenk, "Frankie's New Book"; O'Leary, "Frankie's New Book"; Betty Beale, "The Book Arrived with Dearest Love," *Washington Star-News*, November 11, 1973.

52. "Welch Brings American Themes to Life on Scarves," *Journal Record* (Oklahoma City), November 25, 1992.

53. Ibid. When the Oklahoma Hall of Fame inducted Griffin as a member in 1992, Welch had the honor of introducing her. "Hall of Fame Presenters Named," *Oklahoman* (Oklahoma City), August 23, 1992.

54. For an example of the current debate about fashion and cultural appropriation, see Vanessa Friedman, "Homage or Theft? Carolina Herrera Called Out by Mexican Minister," *New York Times*, June 13, 2019, https://www.nytimes.com/2019/06/13/fashion/carolina-herrera-mexico-appropriation.html.

55. Lauren D. Whitley, *Hippie Chic* (Boston: MFA Publications, Museum of Fine Arts, Boston, 2013), 113–17.

56. "Hand-dyed Fabric Growing in Popularity," *Cherokee Advocate*, October 1979.

57. Karen Peterson, "Designer Shrewd Lady," *Lima (Ohio) News*, December 1, 1974; Wanda Lesley, "Success All Tied Up," *Greenville (S.C.) News*, September 11, 1975.

58. Lesley, "Success All Tied Up."

59. The George Washington centennial kerchief is reproduced in Herbert Ridgeway Collins, *Threads of History: Americana Recorded on Cloth, 1775 to the Present* (Washington, D.C.: Smithsonian Institution Press, 1979), 283.

60. For the John Adams bandana, see ibid., 76.

61. Abraham Lincoln Design, card 24, Frankie Welch Textile Collection, MS 2003, box 9:1, Library Index Cards folder, Hargrett Library. The New-York Historical Society owns one of the campaign kerchiefs from 1864 that inspired Welch: object 1944.146, https://www.nyhistory.org/exhibit/campaign-kerchief-2.

62. Examples of the original Roosevelt bandana have appeared at Lori Ferber Presidential Collectibles (https://www.loriferber.com/teddy-roosevelt -bandana-collectible-scarf.html) and Treadway Gallery (https://www .treadwaygallery.com/lotInfo.php?i=6744). See also Collins, *Threads of History*, 371.

63. Jean Geddes, "Frankie Welch: American Fashion at Its Best," *Alexandria (Va.) Journal*, August 4, 1983.

64. Leslie Ellis, "Her Scarves Are a Signature," *People Today* (Brevard County, Fla.), March 28, 1976.

65. Frankie Welch to Sportland Gift, Logansport, Indiana, October 9, 1975, Frankie Welch Papers, acc. 519, box 4, folder 16, Pettus Archives.

66. Al Neher, email to Peggy Welch Williams, July 24, 2011. See also Army and Air Force Exchange Service records, Frankie Welch Papers, acc. 519, box 5, Pettus Archives.

67. Larry Wines, "The Story of the 1975–1976 American Freedom Train," https:// www.freedomtrain.org/american-freedom-train-home.htm; Advertisement, Frankie Welch of Virginia, *Washington Post*, August 25, 1974.

Chapter 5. First Ladies and Fashion

1. Frankie Welch with Peggy Welch Williams, interview by Richard Norton Smith, September 10, 2010, Gerald R. Ford Oral History Project, Gerald R. Ford Foundation, https://geraldrfordfoundation.org/centennial/oralhistory /frankie-welch/. The Welches later attended St. Paul's Episcopal Church and Christ Church. Peggy Welch Williams and Genie Welch Leisure, emails to author, March 14, 2020.

2. Frankie Welch to Betty Ford, n.d. (around the time of *Indian Jewelry*), "Ford, Betty—Fashion—Betty Ford Scarf" folder, Sheila Weidenfeld Files, Gerald R. Ford Presidential Library, https://www.fordlibrarymuseum.gov /library/document/0126/1489754.pdf.

3. "Non-partisan Fashion," Eye, *Women's Wear Daily*, May 1, 1968.

4. Betty Beale, "The Book Arrived with Dearest Love," *Washington Star-News*, November 11, 1973. Elaine Tait reported in 1974 that Betty Ford bought 99 percent of her wardrobe from Frankie Welch during the previous dozen years. Elaine Tait, "If One Is Good, Two Are Better," *Philadelphia Inquirer*, August 18, 1974.

5. "China See," Eye, *Women's Wear Daily*, June 23, 1972; Elaine Tait, "Vendeuse Is a Designer of Scarves and 8-Way Dress," *Philadelphia Inquirer*, August 18, 1974; Frankie Welch, "Interview with Frankie Welch," 1984, Winthrop University, Oral History Interviews, OH 183, https://digitalcommons.winthrop .edu/oralhistoryprogram/243.

6. Susan Bluttman, "Frankie Welch's Boutique—Where Mrs. Ford Shops," *People* (September 16, 1974).

7. Ibid.; Eleni, "New First Lady Likes American Designers," *Daytona Beach (Fla.) Morning Journal*, August 14, 1974; "Frankie Welch—First 'Fashion Advisor,'" *Rome (Ga.) News-Tribune*, September 1, 1974. Ford also wore the Fifty State Flowers scarf, just visible inside her collar, in a photograph on the cover of *Newsweek* on October 7, 1974, for a feature article about her experience with

breast cancer. First Lady Dr. Jill Biden adopted the same patriotic and unifying theme of the state flowers for the embroidered dress and coat by Gabriele Hearst that she wore on the evening of her husband's inauguration in 2021.

8. "Mrs. Ford Sees Dress Designer Instead of Her Doctor," *New York Times*, August 9, 1974; John Robert Greene, *Betty Ford: Candor and Courage in the White House* (Lawrence: University of Kansas Press, 2004), 35.

9. "The Fords' First Day as First Family," *New York Times*, August 10, 1974.

10. Elaine Tait, "First Lady Wears Blue Jacket Dress at Inaugural," *Philadelphia Inquirer*, August 11, 1974.

11. "Frankie Welch—First 'Fashion Advisor.'" Betty Ford attended one of Peggy's engagement parties earlier in the year. Tait, "If One Is Good."

12. Pat Lloyd, "Frankie Designs Them, Betty Buys Them," *Pensacola (Fla.) News Journal*, November 30, 1974.

13. "Frankie Welch—First 'Fashion Advisor.'"

14. Anne Behrens, "The Fashion for First Ladies," *Washington Post Magazine*, February 2, 1986.

15. Welch, Smith interview; Marian Christy, "Betty Ford's Style: Modest but Chic," *Boston Globe*, December 17, 1974.

16. Gay Pauley (UPI Women's Editor), "New First Lady Prefers Basically Simple Clothes," *Monitor* (McAllen, N.Y.), August 28, 1974.

17. Eleni, "New First Lady." Welch also helped First Daughter Susan Ford prepare to be photographed for a feature article on her in *Seventeen* magazine in 1975. Welch, Smith interview.

18. Pauley, "New First Lady"; Kandy Stroud, "The 1974 Model Fords," Newsmaker, *Women's Wear Daily*, December 10, 1973.

19. Elaine Tait, "Mrs. Ford Knows What She Likes in Fashion," *San Francisco Examiner*, August 9, 1974.

20. Kristin Skinner, "First Lady Betty Ford's Casual Elegance: The Style of an Ordinary Woman in Extraordinary Times," *White House History Quarterly* 52 (2019), 60.

21. *Women's Wear Daily*, November 15, 1974, and others, cited in "Ford, Betty—Fashion—Philosophy" folder, Sheila Weidenfeld Files, Gerald R. Ford Presidential Library, https://www.fordlibrarymuseum.gov/library/document/0126/1489761.pdf.

22. Christy, "Betty Ford's Style."

23. "Frankie Welch—First 'Fashion Advisor.'"

24. Skinner, "First Lady Betty Ford's Casual Elegance," 60.

25. Welch, Smith interview.

26. Ibid.; Frankie Welch, journal page, January 1976, Welch family collection. (Unfortunately, there is not a full journal.)

27. Welch, Winthrop interview; Welch, Smith interview.

28. Welch, Smith interview. See also "William C. Welch, 54, Dies; Liaison Official with VA," *Washington Post*, April 28, 1975.

29. "Guests at Last Night's White House Dinner for Australia's Prime Minister," *Washington Post*, July 28, 1976; Peggy Welch Williams, email to author, June 25, 2020.

30. Margaret Hodges to Betty Ford, August 25, 1975, "Ford, Betty—Fashion—Betty Ford Scarf" folder, Sheila Weidenfeld Files.

31. Betty Ford Design, card 30, Frankie Welch Textile Collection, MS 2003, box 9:1, Library Index Cards folder, Hargrett Library. Welch had designed a previous scarf for Betty Ford to use as gifts for her first Christmas at the White House, a painterly image of strawflowers. Ford sent the first one to Second Lady Happy Rockefeller, who framed it for her bedroom. Welch then printed the scarf in a couple of other colorways and sold them through her shop. Frankie Welch, presentation, National Museum of American History, Smithsonian Institution, April 10, 1991, VHS cassette, Brown Media Archives, gift of the Welch family, https://kaltura.uga.edu/media/t/0_spdju30d.

32. Welch, Smithsonian presentation.

33. "102: Toast at a Dinner Honoring the Nation's Governors, February 20, 1975," *Public Papers of the Presidents of the United States: Gerald R. Ford, Book 1, January 1–July 17, 1975* (Washington, D.C.: U.S. Government Printing Office, 1977), 267.

34. Diana McLellan, "Stella Hackel Is Being Bronzed," Ear on Washington (from the *Washington Star*), *Fort Lauderdale News*, March 21, 1979.

35. "Betty's Mail Is 3–1 against Rights Stand," *New York Daily News*, February 21, 1975.

36. Frankie Welch to Betty Ford, August 5, 1975, "Ford, Betty—Fashion—Betty Ford Scarf" folder, Sheila Weidenfeld Files.

37. The Frankie made from the Betty Ford scarf design and a note card recording where Betty Ford wore it appeared on eBay in 2018 but did not sell.

38. Advertisement, "Betty Ford Bi-Centennial Scarf at Miller Brothers," *Baltimore Sun*, March 2, 1976; Speed Letter to Fisher & Gentile from Frankie Welch of America, November 18, 1975, Frankie Welch Papers, acc. 519, box 6, folder 21, Pettus Archives.

39. Ernestine West, "Historic Day for Designer Frankie Welch," *Rome (Ga.) News-Tribune*, June 24, 1976.

40. Welch, Smithsonian presentation.

41. Frances Cawthon, "'Never in My Wildest Dreams,' Georgian's Gown Becomes Part of U.S. History," *Atlanta Journal*, June 25, 1976.

42. Penny Girard in *Women's Wear Daily* reported in 1976 that the dress cost $300, though Welch later, in 1990, stated that Ford paid $2,500. In a 1984 interview, Welch said that the fabric cost eighty dollars a yard, and the dress cost $1,200 to make, counting labor and material. Penny Girard, "The Non-Inaugural Gown," Eye, *Women's Wear Daily*, June 28, 1976; Donnie Radcliffe, "Reader Leaders: The Literacy Honors," *Washington Post*, February 13, 1990; Welch, Winthrop interview.

43. "Security Was Tighter than Ever," Eye, *Women's Wear Daily*, December 12, 1974; Welch, Winthrop interview; Eleni, "Just a Shop Owner," *Washington Star-News*, August 11, 1974; Joel C. Carrier, "First Lady of Fashion Show," *Grand Rapids (Mich.) Press*, April 26, 2001. Welch made another series of dresses, with Empire waistlines, for Ford as well. Sandra McElwaine, "As American as Betty Ford," *Vogue*, September 1974, 299.

44. Eleni, "New First Lady"; Skinner, "First Lady Betty Ford's Casual Elegance," 63; Peggy Welch Williams and Genie Welch Leisure, email to author, January 23, 2020. Welch noted in a letter to Ford that Marshall made the duplicate of the Smithsonian dress. Frankie Welch, Alexandria, Va., to Betty Ford,

Washington, D.C., July 7, 1975, "Ford, Betty—Fashion—Betty Ford Scarf" folder, Sheila Weidenfeld Files.

45. Dorothy Marks, "Friends Asking: 'Is There a New Betty Ford?,'" *Rocky Mount (N.C.) Telegram*, May 14, 1974. Jeanette M. Black, Mariko Marshall's daughter, recalls that her mother included an invisible zipper in the front of the dress, as Ford requested, but that Marshall was distressed by the choice and had wanted to use frog fasteners, which were more closely associated with Asian fashion. Jeanette M. Black, email to author, May 22, 2020.

46. West, "Historic Day."

47. Elaine Tait, "1st Lady's Gown by Frankie Displayed at Smithsonian," *Philadelphia Inquirer*, June 25, 1976; "Mrs. Ford Selects Virginia-made Gown for Smithsonian Display," *Frederick (Md.) News-Post*, July 12, 1976.

48. Membership in the Friends of First Ladies group was $10,000 for those over thirty-five years of age and $5,000 for those under. Nancy Scott Anderson, "Gown 'Friends' Visit First Lady," *San Diego Tribune*, April 4, 1990; Janis Johnson, "Potomac Periscope," *Akron (Ohio) Beacon Journal*, November 14, 1990. The itinerary for one of the group's gatherings included tea with Barbara Bush at the White House, cocktails at Duvall/Welch House, breakfast at the Octagon House, and lunch at the Congressional Club. Sarah Booth Conroy, "First Ladies' Gown Gang: The Friends, Saving the Smithsonian Dress Collection," *Washington Post*, April 29, 1990. For another Friends of First Ladies event, Welch hosted a lunch at Duvall/Welch House with Chrys Fisher, president of Hermès USA. Sarah Booth Conroy, "The Global Gourmets; On the Social Circuit, Going International," *Washington Post*, October 7, 1990; Janis Johnson, "Fashion Fling," Washington Peopletalk, *Philadelphia Inquirer*, November 8, 1990; Johnson, "Potomac Periscope."

49. Welch, Winthrop interview.

50. Pat Shellenbarger, "A Celebration of Candor," *Grand Rapids (Mich.) Press*, April 7, 1998.

51. "Happy Anniversary Frankie" invitation, hosted at Duvall/Welch House by Helen Thomas, Judith Terra, and Holly Coors, June 16, 1998, Welch family collection.

52. Joan Nielsen McHale, "How Frankie Welch Became the Fashion Guru of Washington, D.C. (Her Story)," The Good News Writes Again: Journalism and Reporting the Tools of the Trade, November 13, 2012, https://goodnewswritesagain.blogspot.com/2012/11/how-frankie-welch-became-fashion-guru.html.

53. Nina S. Hyde, "Fashion Notes," *Washington Post*, December 12, 1976.

54. Nina S. Hyde, "Fashion Notes," *Washington Post*, January 16, 1977.

55. Mary Deese, "Rome's 'Designing Woman,'" *Rome (Ga.) News-Tribune*, September 12, 1999; "Welch Brings American Themes to Life on Scarves," *Journal Record* (Oklahoma City), November 25, 1992.

56. According to newspaper reports, Rosalynn Carter ordered scarves about the same time as Katherine Godwin, wife of the Virginia governor, Mills E. Godwin, and they both requested quilt designs. Since Godwin ordered first, she got the quilt design. Welch's preliminary drawings for Godwin, interestingly, present several combinations of quilt elements and peanuts; the final design features a quilt pattern with apples and

peanuts. Frankie Welch Collection, Rome Area History Center; Christy, "Betty Ford's Style."

57. "Nutty but Nice," *Atlanta Constitution*, June 25, 1973.

58. Frankie Welch to Mrs. James Carter, Office of the Governor, Atlanta, Georgia, May 29, 1974 (copy of a letter), Frankie Welch Textile Collection, MS 2003, box 2:1, Jimmy Carter folder, Hargrett Library. See also Callahan, "Scarf and Dress Designs by Frankie Welch," 91–106.

59. Frances Cawthon, "Presidents Come and Go, but Frankie Welch Is Lame-Duck Proof," *Atlanta Constitution*, January 11, 1981.

60. Along with the peanut scarf, Welch sold a gold-tone choker with a peanut dangle and a gold-tone bracelet with a peanut at the clasp. Frankie Welch of Virginia, Advertisement, *Washington Post*, January 31, 1977.

61. David S. Broder, "Unity Talks Begun: Carter Sweeps to Victory in Georgia, Indiana Races Summary," *Washington Post*, May 5, 1976; David Alpern with Anthony Marro and Evert Clark, "Where Carter Comes From," *Newsweek*, May 3, 1976, 19; UPI photo caption of First Lady and President Carter, August 26, 1980, image U2017257, Getty Images.

62. Mental Health Association Scarf, card 44, Frankie Welch Textile Collection, MS 2003, box 9:1, Library Index Cards folder, Hargrett Library.

63. Mary Tuthill, "Potomac Jottings," *Ironwood (Mich.) Daily Globe*, April 26, 1977; Donnie Radcliffe, "A Low-Key Debut Appearance by the First Lady," *Washington Post*, April 6, 1977.

64. "Whirling through the Third World," *Time*, April 10, 1978, 14; photograph by Wally McNamee, Corbis, March 30, 1979, https://www.gettyimages.fi/detail /news-photo/amy-carter-stands-in-front-of-her-mother-first-lady-news -photo/577838114?adppopup=true.

65. "Rosalynn Boosts Book by Georgians," *Atlanta Constitution*, September 10, 1980; Nina S. Hyde, "Fashion Notes," *Washington Post*, September 14, 1980.

66. Keith B. Richburg, "Does Anybody Want to Buy an Inaugural License Plate?" *Washington Post*, December 20, 1980; "Former Roman Frankie Welch Creates Inaugural Designs," *Rome (Ga.) News-Tribune*, January 11, 1981; Jacquelyn Smith, "Alexandria Designer Puts Wrap on Presidential Neck," *Alexandria (Va.) Gazette*, January 18, 1985. For the 1981 inaugural, Welch also designed Boxcar tote bags that held lunches for special guests traveling on buses between venues as well as totes featuring her Washington, D.C., design for guests at the Watergate Hotel. Smith, "Alexandria Designer." The Clinton bandanas were used as gifts at the Arkansas Blue Jean Ball. "Etc.," *Atlanta Constitution*, January 17, 1993; Maura Corrigan, "Famous Alumna Gives Clinton Scarf," *Red and Black* (University of Georgia student newspaper), January 21, 1993.

67. "Campus Briefs," *Furman Paladin*, November 17, 1995.

Chapter 6. Frankie Welch beyond the Scarf

1. Emma Livingstone, "A Frank-ie View of Style; Scarfs Tie It All Together," *Richmond (Va.) Times-Dispatch*, February 27, 1972.

2. Peggy Welch Williams and Genie Welch Leisure, emails to author, March 24, 2020. Welch's daughter Genie describes Bozek as her mother's personal or

executive assistant and her responsibilities as handling "the administrative details of the scarf design business," Welch's business and social calendar, travel arrangements, and bills. Genie Welch Leisure, email to author, October 12, 2020. Opal Beverly moved to the Washington area in 1967 and began working for Welch soon after. She continued working for her until around 1980. Jamie Waldrop (Beverly's daughter), telephone conversation with author, October 21, 2020.

3. Peggy Saunders, "She Wears Three Hats . . . Not to Mention Scarves, Dresses," *Boston Herald American*, October 22, 1975.

4. LaDonna Harris, telephone conversation with author, February 4, 2020.

5. Jamie Waldrop, telephone conversation with author, October 21, 2020.

6. Deborah Churchman, "Personal Service Draws VIPS to Chic D.C. Clothing Shop," *Christian Science Monitor*, January 26, 1982. Though Welch tried to prevent women from showing up to events in matching dresses, which the card system helped, in 1966 a particular dress, "a textured silk Balenciaga copy," proved so popular that its repeated appearances at social events made headlines. Libby Cater, wife of presidential assistant Douglas Cater, wore it in bright green to a White House dinner; Betty Ford, whose husband, Gerald, was Republican minority leader of the house at the time, wore it in shocking pink, as did Shirley Boone, wife of actor Pat Boone. Newspapers listed many other women who wore the dress, and though a few made purchases in other places, the majority were from Welch's shop. Ford stated that it was still her favorite, despite its popularity, and that she would order "another for Fall in flowered velvet." Maxine Cheshire, "Dress Creates Hall of Mirrors," Very Interesting People, *Washington Post and Times Herald*, June 19, 1966; Maxine Cheshire, "Balenciaga Copy Meets Itself in Washington," *Boston Globe*, July 12, 1966.

7. Livingstone, "Frank-ie View of Style."

8. "Frankie Welch of Virginia—Southern Designer," Frankie Welch of Virginia Press Release, June 24, 1976, Welch family collection.

9. Frances Cawthon, "Georgia's Star Goes 'National,'" *Atlanta Journal*, October 13, 1971; Marian McBride, "Campaign Couture," *Milwaukee Sentinel*, July 4, 1968.

10. Carol Weaver, "Frankie Welch: Designer for the First Lady," *Georgia Alumni Record*, October 1974, 7; Nina S. Hyde, "Fashion Notes," *Washington Post*, February 13, 1977.

11. Joan Gilmore, "Designer May Have Everyone Dressed Alike," *Daily Oklahoman* (Oklahoma City), April 15, 1972.

12. Helen Kirby records, Frankie Welch Papers, acc. 519, box 6, folder 24, Pettus Archives.

13. Frankie Welch of America, Inc., booklet of guidelines for office operating procedures, Welch family collection.

14. Frankie Welch, "Fashion Notes from Frankie Welch," *Southern Living*, November 1971, 77; Cawthon, "Georgia's Star."

15. On the Go with AAUW, #34 Frankie Welch, November 1993, VHS cassette, Brown Media Archives, gift of the Welch family.

16. Peggy Welch Williams, email to author, April 11, 2019; Esther Smith, "Frankie Welch on Designing the Corporate Image," *Business Review of Washington*, October 19, 1979; Sarah Booth Conroy, "And a House That Pays as It Goes," *Washington Post*, February 10, 1980.

17. Helene DeGroodt, "She Leaves Imprint on Fashion World," *Brevard (Fla.) Sentinel Star*, April 7, 1976; Frances Cawthon, "Newest Frankie Welch Creation—Her Boutique," *Atlanta Journal*, September 22, 1976.

18. "A Grand Opening," *Alexandria (Va.) Gazette Packet*, September 2, 1988.

19. Frankie Welch with Peggy Welch Williams, email to author, July 15, 2011.

20. Peggy Welch Williams, email to author, April 11, 2019.

21. Livingstone, "Frank-ie View of Style"; Peggy Welch Williams, email to author, March 2, 2020.

22. Helen Pundt, "A Famous Clothing Designer," *Journal of Home Economics* 67, no. 1 (January 1975), 14.

23. Frankie Welch with Peggy Welch Williams, email to author, July 18, 2011.

24. See, for example, "The Sheraton-Carlton Presents Today's Fashions by Frankie Welch," April 28, 1971, program, Frankie Welch Collection, Rome Area History Center.

25. Jamie Waldrop, telephone conversation with author, October 21, 2020.

26. Virginia Mansfield, "Alexandria Shop Ends a Fashionable Era," *Washington Post*, February 22, 1990.

27. "Football Buffet Needs Preplanning," *Central New Jersey Home News* (New Brunswick), September 20, 1972; "After the Game Is Over," *Fond Du Lac (Wis.) Commonwealth Reporter*, September 19, 1972; "Informal Frankie: Easy-Do Supper Matches New Easy-Do Hostess Gown," *Van Nuys (Calif.) Valley News*, September 21, 1972.

28. "After the Game" booklet, Welch family collection; "Frankie Welch, An American Designer Is Designing in Cotton," *Cotton U.S.A.* 1, no. 3 (June 1972), 2, Frankie Welch Collection, Rome Area History Center; Peggy Welch Williams, email to author, April 11, 2019.

29. Thalhimers, Frankie Welch advertisement, *Richmond (Va.) Times-Dispatch*, November 4, 1973.

30. Marian Christy, "Betty Ford's Style: Modest but Chic," *Boston Globe*, December 17, 1974; Maxine Cheshire, "Mileage from a Nixon Deal: A Zip in Time VIP Polpourri," *Washington Post*, September 30, 1975.

31. Frances Cawthon, "Frankie Comes Home: Georgian Brings Her Scarves to Atlanta," *Atlanta Journal*, November 9, 1977.

32. Frankie Welch Ultrasuede brochure, Frankie Welch Collection, Rome Area History Center.

33. Pat Lloyd, "Frankie Designs Them, Betty Buys Them," *Pensacola (Fla.) News Journal*, November 30, 1974; "Going South with Frankie," Eye, *Women's Wear Daily*, September 4, 1974; Mary Beth Newell, Southern History Department, Birmingham Public Library, email to author, June 26, 2020.

34. Marian Christy, Eyeful, *Boston Globe*, August 22, 1977; "Frankie Welch to Address Women of the Year" sheet, Frankie Welch Textile Collection, MS 2003, box 9:3, Hargrett Library; Cawthon, "Frankie Comes Home"; "Peanut Power," Eye, *Women's Wear Daily*, July 14, 1978.

35. Marcie Auton, "Fashion Designer Returns to Her Native Georgia," *Marietta (Ga.) Journal*, November 13, 1977.

36. Diana McLellan, The Ear . . . on Washington, *Baltimore Evening Sun*, April 19, 1978; Advertisement, "Frankie Welch, A New Fashion Dimension Downtown," *Washington Post*, September 19, 1978.

37. "Peanut Power."

38. Frankie Welch and Peggy Welch Williams, email to author, July 11, 2011.

39. Mansfield, "Alexandria Shop Ends"; Donnie Radcliffe, "Reader Leaders: The Literacy Honors," *Washington Post*, February 13, 1990; "Making It" segment on *Nation's Business Today*, an ESPN television program, Washington, D.C., February 7, 1989, Brown Media Archives, transfer from Frankie Welch Collection, Rome Area History Center.

40. "Inside Out," Eye, *Women's Wear Daily*, March 15, 1979.

41. Eleni, "Every Woman Ought to Have Some Fashion Education," Fashion Notebook, *Sunday Star* (Washington, D.C.), October 8, 1961.

42. Peggy Welch Williams, email to author, February 2, 2020.

43. Jura Koncius, Personalities, *Washington Post*, June 27, 1978.

44. "Inside Out"; Diana McLellan, "Stella Hackel Is Being Bronzed," Ear on Washington, *Fort Lauderdale (Fla.) News*, March 21, 1979; Margo Kline, "The Corporate Scarf," *On the Town* (Alexandria, Va.), February 20, 1980; Sarah Booth Conroy, "An Apartment with Walls to Go," *Washington Post*, February 10, 1980.

45. Constance Stapleton, "Grand Illusion," *Washington Home and Garden/ Regardie's*, January 1991, 35; Peggy Welch Williams, email to author, February 1, 2020.

46. Conroy, "Apartment with Walls"; Conroy, "And a House."

47. Conroy, "Apartment with Walls"; Jura Koncius, "Trading Winter Warmth for Cool Summer Tones," *Washington Post*, July 16, 1987; Esther Smith, "Frankie Welch."

48. Conroy, "Apartment with Walls."

49. Joan Sayers Brown, "Inside Decorating: Functional Design for a Small Apartment," *Southern Accents*, Fall 1981, 112, 114.

50. Ibid., 112; Mickey Palmer, "Watergate: A Washington Nest for High-Flyers," *Washington Dossier*, February 1982, 15.

51. Pauline Innis, *The Secret Gardens of Watergate: Hints for Balcony, Rooftop and Patio Gardeners Gleaned from Washington's High-Level Horticulture* (McLean, Va.: EPM, 1986), 68.

52. Stapleton, "Grand Illusion"; Palmer, "Watergate."

53. Smith, "Frankie Welch on Designing." Welch charged $1,000 per day for her consulting, and slightly less if the corporation was in town. That amount in 1979 equaled approximately $3,560 in December 2020.

54. Cindy Creasy, "Shop Started to Meet House Payments Is Style Center," *Richmond (Va.) Times-Dispatch*, September 11, 1983.

55. Ibid.; Frances Cawthon, "Frankie Welch Brings Down the Ceiling," *Atlanta Constitution*, October 31, 1982; Kathleen Sterritt, "Fashion Notes," *Washington Post*, June 12, 1983. Welch designed a second bag for Taylor for the Broadway run of *Private Lives*.

56. Creasy, "Shop Started."

57. "Annabelle's File," *Washington Dossier*, September 1980, 7; "Keeping Fitfully Fit in Washington," *Washington Dossier*, April 1975, 10; "A Designer's Brunch," *Washington Dossier*, April 1981, 54; "Along Party Lines," *Washington Dossier*, March 1977, 52; "Around Town," *Washington Dossier*, April 1982, 33. See *Washington Dossier* website by David Adler, http://www.washingtondossier.com.

58. "Noon to Five—Color and Verve," *Washington Dossier*, February 1981, 28.

59. Diana McLellan, "Defense and Tapley the Teddy Bear," *Baltimore Sun*, June 16, 1983; Diana McLellan, "Where Are They Now," Ear on Washington, *Baltimore Evening Sun*, April 19, 1978. McLellan was a longtime gossip columnist for the *Washington Star* and the *Washington Post*.

60. "Uncharacteristic Models," *Washington Post*, April 26, 1987.

61. Frances Cawthon, "'Never in My Wildest Dreams,' Georgian's Gown Becomes Part of U.S. History," *Atlanta Journal*, June 25, 1976.

62. Designer Scarf Donation records, Frankie Welch Papers, acc. 519, box 4, folder 13, Pettus Archives.

63. "Designer's Brunch."

64. Pat Lloyd, "Art Guild Salutes Members, Volunteers," Around the Town, *Pensacola (Fla.) News Journal*, April 18, 1977; Peggy Welch Williams, email to author, June 24, 2020.

65. Susan Bluttman, "Frankie Welch's Boutique—Where Mrs. Ford Shops," *People*, September 16, 1974, 60; Weaver, "Frankie Welch," 7.

66. "Why Some People Entertain Casually . . . and Some Don't," *Washington Star*, September 19, 1976.

67. Lloyd, "Art Guild Salutes Members."

68. Radcliffe, "Reader Leaders"; Mansfield, "Alexandria Shop Ends."

69. Maura Corrigan, "Famous Alumna Gives Clinton Scarf," *Red and Black* (University of Georgia student newspaper), January 21, 1993; Peggy Welch Williams, email to author, January 8, 2020.

70. Peggy Welch Williams, emails to author, May 21 and November 5, 2020; Anni Irish, "A History of the Humble Tote Bag," Racked, May 5, 2017, https://www.racked.com/2017/5/5/15409374/tote-bag-history.

71. Frankie Welch, presentation, National Museum of American History, Smithsonian Institution, April 10, 1991, VHS cassette, Brown Media Archives, gift of the Welch family, https://kaltura.uga.edu/media/t/0_spdju3od.

72. Alyce Atkinson, "A Success Story in Silk," *Greenville (S.C.) News*, November 28, 1993.

73. Marcia Feldman, "Seven Super Designers," *Washingtonian*, April 1973, 134.

74. Ginger Howard, telephone conversation with author, October 27, 2020.

75. Chris Tucker Haggerty, telephone conversation with author, November 6, 2020.

76. Lora Mackie, "Target of Ads Changing with Role of Women," *Richmond (Va.) Times-Dispatch*, April 18, 1975.

77. Frankie Welch, "Interview with Frankie Welch," 1984, Winthrop University, Oral History Interviews, OH 183, https://digitalcommons.winthrop.edu/oralhistoryprogram/243.

78. Peggy Welch Williams, emails to author, May 27, 2020.

79. Welch, Smithsonian presentation. Welch's daughter Peggy notes that many of the tassel scarves likely were manufactured by a small company in England. Peggy Welch Williams, email to author, February 11, 2020.

80. Atkinson, "Success Story in Silk." A card presented with the Republican Senatorial Trust scarf describes Welch as a lifelong Republican. Frankie Welch Collection, Rome Area History Center.

81. Welch, Smithsonian presentation.

82. Mildred Whitaker, "'Frankie' Goes to Fiesta," *San Antonio (Tex.) News*, April 19, 1972; Bluttman, "Frankie Welch's Boutique"; Conroy, "And a House."

83. "Former Roman and 'Designing Woman' Frankie Welch Coming to Rome," *Rome (Ga.) News-Tribune*, October 16, 2010; Peggy Welch Williams, email to author, February 11, 2020.

Conclusion. Frankie Welch's Legacy

1. Peggy Welch Williams, email to author, February 11, 2020.

2. Sydney Van Lear, "Original Designs a Hit," *Alexandria (Va.) Gazette*, November 13–19, 1980.

3. Ibid.; Eleni, "Handing Out Mementos for a Rainy Day," *Washington Star*, October 5, 1980; Textile Museum Shop Catalogue, 1980–81, Frankie Welch Textile Collection, MS 2003, box 9:7, Hargrett Library; Sumru Belger Krody, Senior Curator, George Washington University Museum and the Textile Museum, email to author, January 31, 2020.

4. "Frankie Welch Scarves to Be on Display Here," *Columns* (University of Georgia), October 25, 1982.

5. Frances Cawthon, "Frankie Welch Brings Down the Ceiling," *Atlanta Constitution*, October 31, 1982; H. Perk Robins, Vice President for Development and University Relations, University of Georgia, to Frankie Welch, Alexandria, Virginia, June 25, 1976, Frankie Welch Textile Collection, MS 2003, box 9:3, Hargrett Library.

6. "Interview with Frankie Welch," 1984, Winthrop University, Oral History Interviews, OH 183, https://digitalcommons.winthrop.edu/oralhistoryprogram /243.

7. Calendar, *Austin (Tex.) American-Statesman*, February 5, 1984; "Alexandria the Great," *Washington Dossier*, September 1987, 78; Press release, "Former First Lady Betty Ford . . . ," June 17, 1987, Frankie Welch Collection, Rome Area History Center.

8. Alyce Atkinson, "A Success Story in Silk," *Greenville (S.C.) News*, November 28, 1993; On the Go with AAUW, #34 Frankie Welch, November 1993, VHS cassette, Brown Media Archives, gift of the Welch family; Pamela V. Ulrich, Under Armour Professor and Head, Department of Consumer and Design Science, College of Human Sciences, Auburn University, email to author, April 18, 2020.

9. "Frankie Welch Textile Exhibit," *The Window: News & Views from the Rome Area History Museum*, September 1999; "Textile Exhibit Features International Designer," *Cedartown (Ga.) Standard*, August 19, 1999; "Former Roman and 'Designing Woman' Frankie Welch Coming to Rome," *Rome (Ga.) News-Tribune*, October 16, 2010; Severo Avila, "Style with Substance: The Designs of Frankie Welch," *Northwest Georgia News*, January 19, 2020. Welch donated a large collection of archival materials to the Rome Area History Museum around 2000.

10. Karen Kramer, *Native Fashion Now: North American Indian Style* (Salem, Mass.: Peabody Essex Museum, 2015), 40–41, 48–49.

11. Photograph of Mrs. Lyndon Johnson and Frankie Welch with caption, *Alexandria (Va.) Gazette*, May 29, 1968.

12. "Frankie Welch of Virginia—Southern Designer," press release, Frankie Welch of Virginia, June 24, 1976, Welch family collection.

13. Jean Nowak, "Scarf Maven," *Georgetown and Country*, July 1998.

14. Northwood University, 1997 Distinguished Women Awards entry for Frankie Welch, https://www.northwood.edu/dw/archives/678_A.

15. "Frankie Welch Does It All," AASCU Foundation (American Association of State Colleges and Universities), newsletter clipping, undated, Frankie Welch Collection, Rome Area History Center; "Ceremony Draws Distinguished Individuals," *Journal Record* (Oklahoma City), August 18, 1992.

16. Nowak, "Scarf Maven."

17. "Textile Exhibit Features International Designer"; Frankie Welch Designs for Colleges and Universities brochure, Frankie Welch Collection, Rome Area History Center; "Frankie Welch Does It All."

18. Anne Scarborough Philbin, "Daughters of Distinction: Frankie Welch, Designer," *Daughters of the American Revolution Magazine*, February 1999, 75; Nowak, "Scarf Maven"; Frankie Welch, presentation, National Museum of American History, Smithsonian Institution, April 10, 1991, VHS cassette, Brown Media Archives, gift of the Welch family, https://kaltura.uga.edu/media/t/0_spdju3od.

19. Frankie Welch tribute event, VHS cassette, 1998, Brown Media Archives, gift of the Welch family, https://bmac.libs.uga.edu/pawtucket2/index.php/Detail/objects/387285.

20. "Tribute to Frankie Welch," *Congressional Record—Senate* 144, no. 75 (June 11, 1998), S6259.

21. "Frankie Welch Introduces New Scarf for Berry College," *Rome (Ga.) News-Tribune*, October 6, 1983; Calendar, *Austin (Tex.) American-Statesman*, February 5, 1984; "Designer Donates Special Collection," *Prospectus* 2, no. 3 (1987), Department of Clothing and Textiles, College of Home Economics, University of Missouri-Columbia, newsletter. Lists in the Frankie Welch Collection at the Rome Area History Center also indicate that she gave scarves to Virginia Commonwealth University and Syracuse University, though the current location of those materials is unclear.

22. Winthrop University, Manuscript Collection, Frankie Welch Papers—acc. 519 description, https://digitalcommons.winthrop.edu/manuscriptcollection_findingaids/1128/; "Designer to Give Lectures," *Johnsonian* (Winthrop College newspaper), December 6, 1982; Kay Arrowood, "WC Rededication Events Scheduled," *Johnsonian* (Winthrop College newspaper), October 29, 1984.

23. Eleni, typed script for tribute to Frankie Welch, Woman of Distinction Award at the American Showcase Theatre Company Benefit, March 29, 1990, Welch family collection.

Selected Bibliography

Selected Archival Collections

Frankie Welch Collection, Rome Area History Center, Rome, Georgia (extensive uncatalogued collection comprising approximately 70 cardboard boxes of clippings and photographs, dresses, scarves, and notebooks of scarf designs)

Frankie Welch Papers, Louise Pettus Archives and Special Collections, Winthrop University, accession 519 (4,500 pieces, 2.25 linear feet, primarily business records)

Frankie Welch Textile Collection, Hargrett Rare Book and Manuscript Library, University of Georgia Libraries, MS 2003 (12.8 linear feet: 8 document boxes, 1 half box, 3 oversized boxes, 1 carton, 2 oversized folders, 15 framed items, with several more boxes housed at the Hargrett in the Frankie Welch Collection in the College of Family and Consumer Sciences' Historic Clothing and Textile Collection HCTC014)

Selected Articles and Publications

Affleck, Diane L. Fagan, and Paul Hudson. *Celebration and Remembrance: Commemorative Textiles in America, 1790–1990*. North Andover, Mass.: Museum of American Textile History, 1990.

Agnor, Evelyn. "Unveiling of Artistic Design Takes Place at Local Museum." *Alexandria (Va.) Gazette*, October 27, 1967.

Albrechtsen, Nicky, and Fola Solanke. *Scarves*. London: Thames & Hudson, 2011.

Alexander, Raymonde. "Scarves: They're Much More Than an Accessory." *Atlanta Constitution*, May 24, 1978.

Anthony, Carl Sferrazza. *The Way They Wore It: The Politics and Pop Culture of First Ladies' Fashion*. Yorba Linda, Calif.: Richard Nixon Foundation/Library/Museum, 2018.

Atkinson, Alyce. "A Success Story in Silk." *Greenville (S.C.) News*, November 28, 1993.

Auton, Marcie. "Fashion Designer Returns to Her Native Georgia." *Marietta (Ga.) Journal*, November 13, 1977.

Axler, Judith. D.C. Wash. *Daily News* (New York), July 28, 1968.

Ball, Nancy. "Cherokee Scarf Leads to Success in the Fashion World." *Press and Sun-Bulletin* (Binghamton, N.Y.), June 20, 1969.

Baseman, Andrew, ed. *The Scarf*. New York: Stewart, Tabori & Chang, 1989.

Beale, Betty. "Johnson Barely Misses Indorsing [*sic*] Humphrey." *Indianapolis Star*, May 5, 1968.

Bluttman, Susan. "Frankie Welch's Boutique—Where Mrs. Ford Shops." *People*, September 16, 1974.

Brown, Joan Sayers. "Inside Decorating: Functional Design for a Small Apartment." *Southern Accents*, Fall 1981, 112–14.

Butterfield, Marni. "A Rare Bit of Welch." *Women's Wear Daily*, July 8, 1968.

Cahill, Jane. "Ideas and Information." Ideas and Fashions for Smaller Stores. *Women's Wear Daily*, April 26, 1965.

Callahan, Ashley. "Frankie Welch, Americana Fashion Specialist." *Ornament* 35, no. 1 (2011), 26–31.

———. "Scarf and Dress Designs by Frankie Welch: Highlighting Georgia through Her Americana." In *Proceedings from the Seventh Henry D. Green Symposium of the Decorative Arts*, 91–106. Athens: Georgia Museum of Art, 2016.

"Capital Headliner." *Newsweek*, May 19, 1969.

Cawthon, Frances. "Former Georgia Designer Has a Bloomin' Good Idea." *Atlanta Journal*, May 15, 1970.

———. "Frankie Comes Home: Georgian Brings Her Scarves to Atlanta." *Atlanta Journal*, November 9, 1977.

———. "Frankie Welch Brings Down the Ceiling." *Atlanta Constitution*, October 31, 1982.

———. "Georgia's Star Goes 'National.'" *Atlanta Journal*, October 13, 1971.

———. "Her Signature Scarf Speaks Cherokee." *Atlanta Journal and Atlanta Constitution*, November 12, 1967.

———. "Hometown Fetes Designer." *Atlanta Constitution*, September 28, 1969.

———. "'Never in My Wildest Dreams,' Georgian's Gown Becomes Part of U.S. History." *Atlanta Journal*, June 25, 1976.

———. "Newest Frankie Welch Creation—Her Boutique." *Atlanta Journal*, September 22, 1976.

———. "Presidents Come and Go, but Frankie Welch Is Lame-Duck Proof." *Atlanta Constitution*, January 11, 1981.

———. "She Helps Make History." *Atlanta Journal*, March 5, 1968.

Chrisman-Campbell, Kimberly. "The 1968 Fashion Show, the History Lesson Melania Missed." *Politico*, March 5, 2018, https://www.politico.com/magazine/story/2018/03/05/melania-trump-dress-fashion-1968-fashion-show-217232.

———. *Red, White, and Blue on the Runway: The 1968 White House Fashion Show*. Kent, Ohio: Kent State University Press, 2022.

Christy, Marian. "Betty Ford's Style: Modest but Chic." *Boston Globe*, December 17, 1974.

Churchman, Deborah. "Personal Service Draws VIPs to Chic D.C. Clothing Shop." *Christian Science Monitor*, January 26, 1982.

Collins, Herbert Ridgeway. *Threads of History: Americana Recorded on Cloth, 1775 to the Present*. Washington, D.C.: Smithsonian Institution Press, 1979.

Colson, Helen A. "Dr. Frankie Never Welches on a Difficult Fashion Cure." *Washington Daily News*, January 30, 1963.

Conroy, Sarah Booth. "An Apartment with Walls to Go." *Washington Post*,
   February 10, 1980.
——— . "And a House That Pays as It Goes." *Washington Post*, February 10, 1980.
Creasy, Cindy. "Shop Started to Meet House Payments Is Style Center." *Richmond
   (Va.) Times-Dispatch*, September 11, 1983.
Day, Jane. "Buy Partisan: Politics Steps Out in Fashion." *National Observer*,
   August 5, 1968.
Deese, Mary. "History Museum Welcomes Home One of Rome's Own." *Rome (Ga.)
   News-Tribune*, August 27, 1999.
——— . "Rome's 'Designing Woman.'" *Rome (Ga.) News-Tribune*, September 12,
   1999.
DeGroodt, Helene. "She Leaves Imprint on Fashion World." *Brevard (Fla.)
   Sentinel Star*, April 7, 1976.
Eleni. "Every Woman Ought to Have Some Fashion Education." Fashion Notebook.
   Sunday Star (Washington, D.C.), October 8, 1961.
——— . "Frankie's a Find." *Washington Star*, March 22, 1964.
——— . "Handing Out Mementos for a Rainy Day." *Washington Star*, October 5, 1980.
——— . "It All Began with Cherokee Alphabet." *Washington Star*, June 7, 1970.
——— . "Jewels, Frankie and Indian Idiom." *Washington Star-News*, November 4, 1973.
——— . "Just a Shop Owner." *Washington Star-News*, August 11, 1974.
——— . "So Everything GOP Is Coming Up Daisies." *Evening Star* (Washington,
   D.C.), May 2, 1968.
Ellis, Leslie. "Her Scarves Are a Signature." *People Today* (Brevard County, Fla.),
   March 28, 1976.
"A Famous Clothing Designer." *Journal of Home Economics* 67, no. 1 (January
   1975), 12–14.
"Fashion Designer Alum Gives 'Life's' Work to the University." *Columns* (University
   of Georgia newsletter), November 1, 1982.
Feldman, Marcia. "Seven Super Designers." *Washingtonian*, April 1973, 131–34.
"Former Roman Frankie Welch Creates Inaugural Designs." *Rome (Ga.) News-
   Tribune*, January 11, 1981.
"Frankie Welch, an American Designer Is Designing in Cotton." *Cotton U.S.A.* 1,
   no. 3 (June 1972), 2.
"Frankie Welch—First 'Fashion Advisor.'" *Rome (Ga.) News-Tribune*, September 1,
   1974.
"Frankie Welch, Wrapped in Memories." *Washington Post*, June 28, 1987.
Geddes, Jean. "Frankie Welch: American Fashion at Its Best." *Alexandria (Va.)
   Journal*, August 4, 1983.
Gilmore, Jean. "Designer May Have Everyone Dressed Alike." *Daily Oklahoman*
   (Oklahoma City), April 15, 1972.
Givhan, Robin. "History, Fair and Square." *Washington Post*, June 14, 1998.
Graham, Rubye. "Custom Scarves Personalized." *Philadelphia Inquirer*, April 16,
   1969.
Gregory, Linda. "Mrs. Ford Selects Virginia-Made Gown for Smithsonian Display."
   Frederick (Md.) News-Post, July 12, 1976.
Gunn, Tim, with Ada Calhoun. "Ties and Scarves: Color Me Beautiful, Hermès,
   and Other Cults." Chap. 9 in *Tim Gunn's Fashion Bible: The Fascinating History
   of Everything in Your Closet*. New York: Gallery Books, 2012.

Hampton, Thula E. "Alexandria Designer Makes National Scene." *Alexandria (Va.) Gazette*, October 14, 1971.

———. "Frankie's Fashions Forecast." *Alexandria (Va.) Gazette*, September 13, 1963.

Harris, Joann. "Former Roman Makes Headlines with Styles." *Rome (Ga.) News-Tribune*, October 10, 1968.

———. "Frankie Welch." *Baltimore Sun*, July 21, 1968.

Hjorth, Doris. "Chic-ly Cherokee." *Oakland (Calif.) Tribune*, May 15, 1969.

Kramer, Karen. *Native Fashion Now: North American Indian Style*. Salem, Mass.: Peabody Essex Museum, 2015.

La Hay, Wauhillau. "Cherokee Alphabet Is a Big Hit." *Washington Daily News*, October 24, 1967.

———. "Wives Wearing Campaign Styles." *Pittsburgh Press*, June 18, 1968.

Lee, Elinor. "Her Paris-Rome Wardrobe Cost $60." *Washington Post and Times Herald*, July 24, 1960.

Leesa, Anna. "Local Couple Buys 18th Century 'Old Bank Bldg.'" *Alexandria (Va.) Gazette*, April 13, 1963.

Lesley, Wanda. "Success All Tied Up." *Greenville (S.C.) News*, September 11, 1975.

LeSueur, Dorothy. "'Frankies' Now Wrapping Around Nationally." *Washington Post and Times Herald*, October 14, 1971.

Livingstone, Emma. "A Frank-ie View of Style; Scarfs Tie It All Together." *Richmond (Va.) Times-Dispatch*, February 27, 1972.

Lloyd, Pat. "Designer Doesn't Work for Peanuts Anymore." *Pensacola News Journal*, January 20, 1981.

———. "Frankie Designs Them, Betty Buys Them." *Pensacola News Journal*, November 30, 1974.

MacPherson, Myra. "Governors' Wives 'Discover America in Style' at White House." *New York Times*, March 1, 1968.

———. "If You Think a Political Button Isn't Enough." *New York Times*, June 20, 1968.

Mansfield, Virginia. "Alexandria Shop Ends a Fashionable Era." *Washington Post*, February 22, 1990.

Mayfield, Cheryl. "Famed Designer Plots Okie Scarf Idea during Interview." *Daily Oklahoman* (Oklahoma City), June 17, 1969.

McBride, Marian. "Campaign Couture." *Milwaukee Sentinel*, July 4, 1968.

McHale, Joan Nielsen. "Styles by Frankie Welch: Republicans Have Own Design." *Miami News*, June 19, 1968.

"Mrs. Ford Sees Dress Designer Instead of Her Doctor." *New York Times*, August 9, 1974.

"Neck-ing." Eye. *Women's Wear Daily*, March 6, 1969.

"Non-Partisan Fashion." Eye. *Women's Wear Daily*, May 1, 1968.

Nowak, Jean. "Scarf Maven." *Georgetown and Country*, July 1998.

O'Leary, Jinny. "Frankie's New Book Was the Toast of the Town: Others Seek Out Celebrities." *Alexandria (Va.) Gazette*, November 7, 1973.

———. "Indian Lore Inspiration for Designs." *Alexandria (Va.) Gazette*, April 26, 1973.

Ostrolenk, Vicki. "Frankie's New Book Was the Toast of the Town: Some Talk about 'That Other Thing.'" *Alexandria (Va.) Gazette*, November 7, 1973.

O'Sullivan, Joan. "Indian Jewelry Is In." *Daily Messenger* (Canandaigua, N.Y.),
  February 12, 1974.

——— . "Tie One On." *Post-Register* (Idaho Falls, Idaho), February 8, 1971.

Pauley, Gay. "Designer Works for All Presidential Candidates." *Anderson (Ind.)
  Daily Bulletin*, July 2, 1968.

——— . "Test Your Fashion IQ." *San Francisco Examiner*, May 10, 1966.

Peterson, Karen. "Designer Shrewd Lady." *Lima (Ohio) News*, December 1, 1974.

Philben, Anne Scarborough. "Daughters of Distinction: Frankie Welch, Designer."
  Daughters of the American Revolution Magazine 133, no. 2 (February 1999), 75.

"Romans Greet Frankie Welch at Atlanta Opening." *Rome (Ga.) News-Tribune*,
  November 13, 1977.

Ross, Nancy L. "'Frankie' Means Comfortable Fad." *Washington Post and Times
  Herald*, March 28, 1966.

Rundell, Ann. "President Ford Is Ex-Madisonian's Customer." *Wisconsin State
  Journal* (Madison), September 1, 1974.

Saunders, Peggy. "She Wears Three Hats . . . Not to Mention Scarves, Dresses."
  Boston Herald American, October 22, 1975.

Schultz, Ellie. "Designer's Novel Ideas Make Simple Patterns Unique." *Arizona
  Republic* (Phoenix), May 13, 1973.

——— . "Fashion Folio: Indian Designer Arrives." *Arizona Republic* (Phoenix),
  April 16, 1973.

Seid, Susan, with Jen Renzi. *Vera: The Art and Life of an Icon*. New York: Harry N.
  Abrams, 2010.

Sheppard, Eugenia. "Equal Time for the GOP." *Women's Wear Daily*, April 22, 1968.

——— . Inside Fashion. *Women's Wear Daily*, April 22, 1968.

——— . "Signature Scarf Wraps Up Fashion Designers." *Washington Post and
  Times Herald*, December 26, 1966.

Shields, Virginia. "Frankie Welch's First Edition Library Scarf to Be Introduced at
  GLA Conference on Jekyll." *Brunswick (Ga.) News*, October 27, 1971.

Sinick, Heidi. "Women Go Forward Together in Fashion." *Washington Post and
  Times Herald*, March 7, 1969.

Skinner, Kristen. "First Lady Betty Ford's Casual Elegance: The Style of an
  Ordinary Woman in Extraordinary Times." *White House History Quarterly* 52
  (2019), 56–77.

Smith, Esther. "Frankie Welch on Designing the Corporate Image." *Business
  Review of Washington*, October 19, 1979.

Smith, Jacquelyn. "Alexandria Designer Puts Wrap on Presidential Neck."
  Alexandria (Va.) Gazette, January 18, 1985.

Stapleton, Constance. "GOP Elephant Has Rival in Daisies." *Washington Post and
  Times Herald*, May 2, 1968.

——— . "Grand Illusion." *Washington Home and Garden/Regardie's* (January/
  Winter 1991), 33–35, 42–43.

Stroud, Kandy Shuman. "Eye on Washington." *Women's Wear Daily*, March 13, 1969.

Tait, Elaine. "1st Lady's Gown by Frankie Displayed at Smithsonian." *Philadelphia
  Inquirer*, June 25, 1976.

——— . "If One Is Good, Two Are Better." *Philadelphia Inquirer*, August 18, 1974.

——— . "Vendeuse Is a Designer of Scarves and 8-Way Dress." *Philadelphia
  Inquirer*, August 18, 1974.

"This Is Their South." *Southern Living*, February 1970.

Thomas, Helen. "Virginia Designer's Shop Mecca for Washingtonians." *Redlands (Calif.) Daily Facts*, November 23, 1970.

Van Lear, Sydney. "Original Designs a Hit." *Alexandria (Va.) Gazette*, November 13–19, 1980.

Wagner, Ruth. "At Frankie Welch's Fashions Have Art 'n' Antiques Background." *Washington Post and Times Herald*, September 22, 1963.

——— . "They're Made by Hand." *Washington Post and Times Herald*, February 21, 1966.

Weaver, Carol. "Frankie Welch: Designer for the First Lady." *Georgia Alumni Record* 54, no. 1 (October 1974), 4–7, 39.

"Welch Brings American Themes to Life on Scarves." *Journal Record* (Oklahoma City, Okla.), November 25, 1992.

Welch, Frankie. "Frankie Welch, President, Frankie Welch Textile Designs, Alexandria, Virginia." In *America's New Women Entrepreneurs: Tips, Tactics, and Techniques from Women Achievers in Business*, ed. Patricia Harrison, 214–19. Washington, D.C.: Acropolis, 1986.

——— . *Indian Jewelry: How to Wear, Buy and Treasure America's First Fashion Pieces*. McLean, Va.: EPM, 1973.

——— . Presentation, National Museum of American History, Smithsonian Institution, Washington, D.C., April 10, 1991, VHS cassette, Walter J. Brown Media Archives, University of Georgia Libraries, University of Georgia, gift of Frankie Welch, Peggy Welch Williams, and Genie Welch Leisure, https://kaltura.uga.edu/media/t/0_spdju30d.

West, Ernestine. "Historic Day for Designer Frankie Welch." *Rome (Ga.) News-Tribune*, June 24, 1976.

Whitaker, Mildred. "'Frankie' Goes to Fiesta." *San Antonio News*, April 19, 1972.

"Why Some People Entertain Casually . . . and Some Don't." *Washington Star*, September 19, 1976.

Wilson, Jean Sprain. "Women Have Become Walking Political Billboards." *Press (Binghamton, N.Y.)*, June 27, 1968.

Index

scarves *(continued)*

173, *170–73*, 286n56; Princeton Club, *6*, 69, 71; RCA ("Go"), *6*; Red Cross, *90*, 91; Rome, *70*, 113, 278n49; Rotary International, *219*; Kitty Rotruck, 78, *108*; See Georgia First, *64*, 69, *70*; Senatorial Trust, 212, *215*, 291n80; Smithsonian Institution National Air and Space Museum scarf, *72*, *105*; Society of American Military Engineers, *114*; St. Luke's Episcopal Church, *114*; Tandem Computers, *115*; tennis, *82*; Textile Museum, *73*, *115*, 229; Time Life, *82*, 229; Tobacco Institute, *112*; United States Naval Academy, *216*; United States Senate, *76*; United Virginia Bank, *112*; University of Alabama, 91, *111*; University of Georgia, *96*, 234; University of Virginia, *109*; Veterans Administration, *160*; Virginia Home Economics Association, *99*; Virginia Women's Meeting, 92; Washington and Lee University, *110*; Washington, D.C., *72*, 91, *93*; *Washington Star*, 113, *232*; West Point Class of '46, *115*; Peggy Welch Williams wedding, 92, *93*; Woman's National Democratic Club (Rosalynn Carter), 170, *174*; Women's Auxiliary to the Texas Dental Association, *73*, 92, *112*; Women's National Bank, *108*; World Bank, *100*; Zonta International, 92, *94. See also* Bicentennial scarf designs; Discover America scarf; Ford, Betty: scarves designed for; Humphrey, Hubert H.: campaign scarf; inaugural designs; Native American–inspired scarf and fabric designs; Welch, Genie: scarf design

Schlumberger, São and Pierre, 53

Severance, Richard W., 85

Simmel, Harriet, *38*, *41*

Skinner Fabrics, 196

Smith, Helen, 182

Smithsonian Institution: Cooper Hewitt, 239; First Ladies Collection, 5, 164, *165*, 166, 248, 286n48; National Air and Space Museum scarf, *72*, *105*, 252; National Museum of History and Technology / National Museum of American History, 7, 121, 148, 211, 212, 239, 248, 252

Southern Living, 74, 129, 281n32

Spriggs, Elissa, 2

Steiger, Janet Dempsey, *57*

Steinem, Gloria, 92

Sundlun, Bruce, 88

Supima cotton, *v*, 123, 257

Taylor, Elizabeth, *116*, 207, 257, 290n55

Tejera París, Josefina, *28*, 37

Terra, Judith, 236

Textiles and Clothing Board, Department of Defense, 235

Thomas, Helen, 37, 123, 236

Tomchin, Julian, 31–32, *32–33*, 40, 272n45, 273n55

tote bags, *67*, 78, 123, *125*, 173, 207, 211, *232*, 237, 277n37, 287n66, 290n55

Udall, Ermalee, 25

Ultrasuede, 196, *197–98*

umbrellas, *8–9*, 40, *41*, 47, *57*, *61*, 173, 211, 229, *233*

University of Georgia: donations, 5, 7, 234, 237; education, 15, 234; exhibitions, 234, *234–35*; scarves, 92, *96*, 234, 245, 259

Vera Neumann, 65, 91, 129

Veterans Administration, 17–18, 91, *160*, 202, 259

Watergate: real estate complex, 202, *204–6*, 205, 207, *208–10*, 229, 254, 260, 287n66; scandal, 146, 148

Welch, Genie: childhood, 2, *16–17*, 18, 23, *43*; describing mother, 4, 5; Frankie Welch of Virginia and, *175*, 181, *182*, *198*, 199, *201*, 211; modeling scarves and garments, *75*, *82*, 89, *125*, 182, 189, *198*, *201*; photographs of, *4*, *16–17*, *43*, *230*, *231*; scarf design, 69, 129, *131*, *134*, *136–38*, 248, 254, 278n48

Welch, Peggy: childhood, 2, *16–17*, 23, 53; describing mother, 2, 5, 23, 74, 91, 161; modeling scarves and garments, *82*, 89, *125*, 189; photographs of, *4*, *16–17*, *175*, *230*, *231*; tote design, 248, 253; wedding, 1, 92, *93*, 261, 284n11

Welch, William Calvin "Bill," 1–2, *3*, 4, *14–17*, 15–17, 23, 156, 161, 198, 202, 211, 236

White House fashion show, 5, 39–40, *41–46*, 51, 246, 271n35, 272n40, 272n43

Williams, Peggy Welch. *See* Welch, Peggy

Wilson, Jerry, 147

Wilson, General Louis H., Jr., *92*

Wright, Frank Lloyd, 17, 25, 69, 266n27, 276n25

Yeates, Margaret H., 196

Ziegler, Nancy, *126*, 146